Ben

Ben

Missing since 1991.
His mother's heartbreaking story
of endurance and hope.

KERRY NEEDHAM

EBURY
PRESS

1 3 5 7 9 10 8 6 4 2

This edition published 2014

First published in 2013 by Ebury Press, an imprint of Ebury Publishing

A Random House Group company

Copyright © Kerry Needham and Jeff Hudson 2013

Kerry Needham and Jeff Hudson have asserted their right to be identified as the
authors of this Work in accordance with the Copyright, Designs and Patents Act 1988

The Random House Group Limited Reg. No. 954009
Addresses for companies within
The Penguin Random House Group can be found at:
global.penguinrandomhouse.com

A CIP catalogue record for this book is available from the British Library

Penguin Random House is committed to a sustainable future for
our business, our readers and our planet. This book is made from
Forest Stewardship Council® certified paper.

Designed and set by seagulls.net

Printed and bound in Great Britain by Clays Ltd, Elcograf S.p.A.

ISBN 9780091950880

For Ben and Leighanna:
my children and my life...

CONTENTS

PROLOGUE

IT'S BEN

'Kerry! Kerry! Come! Come!'

I couldn't help rolling my eyes as Jorgas, the night porter at the Palm Beach Hotel where I worked as a waitress, came fussing out to find me. It was 10.30 p.m. and I was about to enjoy my customary bottle of lager at the pool bar after a long day of cooking and serving. I'd just finished preparing the restaurant for the following morning's breakfast shift. As far as I was concerned, there wasn't so much as a fork out of place. Not for the first time, Jorgas clearly thought otherwise.

What is it now? I wondered as he led me back inside the main building. *A smudge on one of the serving spoons? A tea towel on the wrong rack?*

It was only when Jorgas walked straight past the restaurant that I entertained the idea that it wasn't about my work. Even so, it never occurred to me that it had anything to do with the commotion coming from the reception area. It was the end of July 1991, peak season on the idyllic holiday isle of Kos. Holidaymakers there weren't the most reserved of people at the best of times. The fact that a lot of people were already in bed didn't enter into it.

I still didn't put two and two together when I spotted the pair of waiting policemen illuminated under the harsh entrance lights.

All I could think about was the uncontrollable howling coming from just outside the door. The voice sounded familiar but it couldn't be…

'Mum?'

I found my mother huddled on the stone steps, her sobbing face tucked between folded bare arms. Her skin felt cold to cuddle, and not because of the thin shorts and sun top she was wearing. I'd never seen her like this. I'd never seen *anyone* like this.

For a few moments the world stopped. All I could think about was holding her close, just as she'd comforted me and my younger brothers so many times over the years. I don't know how many seconds passed before I noticed we weren't alone out there. But it wasn't Jorgas standing next to us now. It was the two policemen from inside.

That's when I realised they'd all arrived together. That's when I realised I felt sick to the stomach with fear.

'What is it, Mum?' I tried to keep the rising panic from my voice. 'What's happened?'

She was crying too hard to speak. I squeezed her tightly and felt her relax. She cleared her throat, looked up at the policemen, then back into my expectant eyes and broke down again.

'Is it Dad? Has something happened to him?'

Mum shook her head.

'Is it Stephen? Or Danny?' If anything had happened to my kid brothers I would not have been able to cope.

But Mum shook her head again, took a deep breath and, holding my gaze this time, said, 'It's Ben.'

'What about him?'

'He's gone. I've lost him.'

CHAPTER ONE

EVERYONE'S GOING

That day, 24 July 1991, wasn't just the day my son disappeared. In a way, it was also when I faded away as well. For twenty-two years now I've been known as 'Ben Needham's mum'. Journalists call me that. Strangers in the street ask if that's who I am.

I'm always proud to answer 'yes'. I couldn't carry on putting myself through the daily hurt if I weren't.

But before I was Ben Needham's mum, I was Edwin and Christine Needham's little girl. In their eyes I still am. Dad was working on the fairgrounds when they met, travelling the country and sleeping in a caravan. It's fair to say that at nineteen years old he was already a bit of a jack-the-lad. About 5'6", stocky, dark haired and brown eyed, like a lot of the guys on the fairgrounds, his arms were covered in tattoos. There's an old girlfriend's name on there somewhere, although that's nowhere near as embarrassing these days as the 'Love' and 'Hate' etched on his fingers. They all had that then. It was fashion more than anything.

Dad obviously had a way with words and my mum, not yet sixteen then, fell for him. She couldn't have been more different physically. Tiny, size 8, slim, blonde haired and blue eyed. The closest she ever came to a tattoo was holding Dad's hand.

But they were in love.

Suddenly, travelling around with the fairground and his Irish Gypsy friends didn't seem to Dad like such an exciting job because it took him away from Mum too much. She couldn't leave her factory job so he bit the bullet and began learning a trade as a builder. Then, eight years after they'd met, Eddie and Christine finally married, on 30 January 1971. They got a little terraced house in Masbrough, near Rotherham and, thinking ahead, they found one with two bedrooms. It was just as well. I was born ten months later, on 23 November.

Apart from the fact it backed onto the railway line, I don't remember anything about that house in Midland Road because we moved when I was two. I did know why we moved, though. It was because we needed an extra bedroom.

Our new home was in a cul-de-sac in the old Rotherham mining town of Thorpe Hesley. It was a council house but it had three bedrooms. Mum and Dad were at the front and I was at the back with my new brother, Stephen. My room was slightly smaller than his, even though I was older, but it was lovely. Pierrot clowns were all the rage in the 1970s so I had lots of little dolls scattered along the windowsill, masks pinned to the purple walls, and pillowcases and wallpaper to match. I loved it.

Downstairs also had three main rooms – until Dad got hold of them. He loved knocking walls down and making things as open-plan as possible, so what was once a lounge, dining room and kitchen became one large space with an archway in between. That became his trademark in later houses. That, and installing an open fireplace. You're not supposed to renovate council properties, but he always did a good job so no one complained.

Dad was a great builder but maybe he should have been a farmer. The house had a massive back garden and he filled it with all sorts of animals. We had geese, chickens, ferrets and – once Dad had dug the pond – fish of all different colours. He also built all the pens and hutches for the animals. One of my earliest memories is trotting out to the chicken coop and collecting the warm eggs every morning. I stayed clear of the ferrets, though. Their sharp teeth scared me.

I didn't have a problem with the geese – although they seemed to have a problem with Stephen. They used to chase him all over the garden, hissing and squawking. Maybe it was his red-and-black lumberjack coat that attracted them. I remember him wearing it when he was helping Dad dig the pond. Even though he had a large shovel in his hand, the geese kept coming for him!

Dad and Stephen were always very close, but Dad always wanted to get Stephen doing more physical things. I don't recall him playing with Stephen's train set or Scalextric, and he certainly never would have suggested sitting down to do anything like that. Once Stephen was old enough, Dad strung up a punchbag in the garden and took him out there most nights and weekends for some sparring. He loved the open air. That was the Travellers' way. He wasn't a gypsy but it was certainly a lifestyle he had enjoyed. If it wasn't in his blood, it was in his dreams.

I was a very girly girl. I liked pushchairs and dolls, make-up, dressing-up clothes and things like that. One Christmas I got a Tiny Tears doll – the one that 'cries real tears' on the adverts. They didn't say it poos and wees as well! Sindy was the popular doll then, as well. More so than Barbie. I had a lot of her things. I liked pretending to be her mum. I'm sure even then I couldn't wait to be a real one.

As I got older, Mum would let me play out at the front of the house. Because it was in a cul-de-sac there was no danger from traffic. There were four other little girls I used to play with: if one was out or having her tea, there was always someone else. I never lacked a playmate.

Rotherham is only half a dozen miles from Sheffield, where a lot of Mum and Dad's family lived. Sometimes my aunties used to come and visit but more frequently Mum, Stephen and I would jump on a bus and go and visit her mum and dad.

When I turned eight, I remember asking Mum one day if we could visit Grandma and Granddad but she said, 'Sorry, love, I've got too much to do here.'

'Can I go on my own then?' I asked.

I didn't know where those words came from. I hadn't planned to say it. But Mum thought about it for a few moments, then said, 'Let me give your gran a call.'

An hour later, Mum was seeing me off at the bus stop. I felt like a queen when I handed my two pence over to the driver. Independence at last! But as soon as the doors closed and I saw Stephen and Mum waving outside I felt like the loneliest person in the world. I'd done the trip dozens of times with them but everything looked strange on my own. Still, I knew it was ten stops, and I was standing by the door from the ninth one. I'd never been happier to see anyone than I was when Grandma swooped me down from the bus.

After that success, I began nagging Mum to let me do it on my own again at every opportunity. I loved having my own little bit of freedom. Best of all, I loved staying with Grandma and Granddad. Sometimes, Gran would take me shopping or we'd all go to the local working men's club. There was a kids' room set up there so I was never short of new friends to play with. I never grew tired of seeing Grandma Edna's face as the bus pulled up.

'I'll always be here for you, Kerry.'

And she would be, long after I stopped catching buses.

I didn't know any different at the time but, looking back, we were not a well-off family, by any means. Dad worked all hours but he didn't bring home much more than what was needed to cover the basics: roof, clothes, food. We never went without any of those.

The only thing Dad couldn't always provide us with, I learnt much later, was time. He came from a 'work hard, play hard' background and nowhere was that lifestyle better exemplified than on a building site. Most of his workmates thought nothing of putting in a ten-hour shift of hard labour then drowning the stresses of the day in a pub at night. Mum didn't mind Dad doing it occasionally, but only ever with warning. On the times he'd just not come home until we were all in bed – and his dinner was in the bin – Mum told me there were harsh words spoken. It's testament to them as parents that us kids knew nothing about those rows, even though Mum now admits she came close to calling it a day more than once.

It didn't help that the construction business was going through one of its downturns and Dad was forever chasing work. I remember him having contracts for Tarmac and Murphys, which were local. Sometimes the only jobs around were too far away to commute to every day, so Dad just moved out for a few weeks or months. We knew he was only doing it for our benefit but it was hard. We missed him, especially Stephen.

Mum had the rawer deal. Holding down a job herself while looking after two kids and struggling to make ends meet couldn't have been easy for her, although at least she didn't have the nightly dread that he'd come home drunk. I remember her counting down the days to the weekend, when Dad's money would come through. We ate well on Sundays, then it was watching the pennies again for the rest of the week.

What my parents lacked in funds they made up for in imagination. Summer holidays were out of the question most years but occasionally, whenever there was a bit of spare cash, we would jump in the car and take a weekend break in a caravan in Skegness or nearby Chapel St Leonards, in Lincolnshire. The beaches there were wonderful. Once, when times were really hard – so hard that we no longer had a car to get to the seaside – Mum and Dad came up with an alternative:

Hitch-hiking.

Stephen and I had shoulder bags and Mum and Dad had rucksacks, sleeping bags and a tent and we just walked to the main road and stuck our thumbs out! We weren't there long when an articulated lorry the size of a house pulled over.

The driver called down to Dad, 'Where are you going?'

'Anywhere you're going,' Dad replied. 'Especially if it's near the seaside.'

'I can drop you in Whitby?'

'Perfect.'

So Whitby it was.

We all climbed into the cab but instead of staying there, Mum, Stephen and I went behind the seats to the driver's little cabin area. He had a bed in there for us to sit on and there was plenty of room for our luggage. Best of all, he said, 'Help yourself to a Lion Bar from the box.'

You can't get a better start to a holiday than that.

I can't believe we did it now – and Mum and Dad are horrified when Stephen and I remind them. In fact, they've apologised for being so stupid but I don't think it was stupid at all. They couldn't afford trains and hotels so they did what they could. It was what it was: a great adventure. And Stephen and I have never forgotten it.

If money was tight before then, it was even more so following the arrival of a new little baby brother in 1979. I couldn't have been happier when Mum brought little Danny home from hospital. I think I thought he was a doll I could play with. For practical reasons, when Dad's next work opportunity came up – once again, miles away – he and Mum decided it wasn't fair on her if he stayed away from home.

The first I knew about it was coming home from school and discovering Mum loading some of my clothes into a suitcase.

'What are you doing with my things, Mum?'

'I'm packing them up, love. We're moving.'

'Where to?'

'Chapel St Leonards.'

I couldn't believe it.

'Wow, our new house is going to be at the seaside!'

I was so desperate to tell Stephen that I didn't realise that Mum had only smiled at that. She hadn't said yes, she hadn't said no.

On the weekend after the school summer term ended, Dad piled everything into his Mini and we all squeezed in where we could.

'Next stop, Chapel St Leonards,' he said.

I couldn't wait to get going. We'd only been to Chapel for weekends before, and now we were going to stay for ever. If we got there at all…

Even though Mum and Dad had sold all our furniture and bulkier belongings, the Mini was still packed to the brim. We could barely see each other in the back for all the bin bags and boxes around us, and the boot didn't have an inch of space left. All of which must have made the little Mini very heavy because an hour after we'd set off, I suddenly heard Dad start to swear, moments before we ground to a halt. I looked out of the front window and realised we were on a hill – and there was no way the poor Mini was going to get up it.

Half an hour later, Mum, us kids, and half the contents of the car were on the side of the road. Even then the gradient was too steep. Eventually, Dad squeezed us in again and set off back down the hill to find an alternative route. He managed to laugh about it later, but for a while the air was blue.

I think I must have nodded off after that because the next thing I knew the Mini was going slowly again. Dad seemed to be taking a short cut between two rows of white static caravans.

'When will we be there?' I asked.

'Right about… Now,' Dad said, and swung the Mini to a halt next to one of the caravans. 'Welcome to our new home.'

The caravan was nice. There was a permanent double bedroom at one end, a toilet, a kitchen and a dining and lounge area. Giving up my own room full of my beloved Pierrot masks to sleep on the lounge seat-cushions with my two brothers was not exactly the trade-up of the century, but I didn't think twice about that because we'd always had so much fun in caravans on our weekend breaks. Stephen and I loved converting the table and seat into beds. We didn't feel hard done by at all. Like so many of the things we did with Mum and Dad, it was an adventure. Who wouldn't want to live so near the beach and amusement arcades for the whole summer holidays?

It was no coincidence that we ended up in the caravan. Dad's new job was renovating and decorating a chalet park across the road. There were about fifty that needed their brickwork repointing and paintwork doing up. Part of the deal was that we got full use of a caravan while he worked. The second part of the deal was that we could then move into a chalet as soon as one was ready. On top of that, I think Dad still missed his old Traveller days. This was his compromise.

As much as we tried to pretend it was a holiday, by the time September came around, Stephen and I had to join our new primary school. I think children today would be a lot quicker to take the mickey out of us for living in a caravan. In fact, most of the kids I met thought it was cool. And in any case, our 'foreign' accents were much easier targets for ribbing than where we lived. I guess our Yorkshire tones did make us stand out in Lincolnshire, but I couldn't work out why anyone was laughing at us. They were the ones who sounded like farmers. Maybe I shouldn't have told them that...

We moved into one of the Kingsfield Park chalets in time for winter. I think we were the only people on the whole site. Seasides empty when the seasons turn, and coming back after school was like entering a ghost town.

The following spring I took – and failed – my 11-plus and in May I joined Lumley Comprehensive. Not long after, the school merged with another local comp and became the Earl of Scarbrough High School. I didn't notice much difference except the uniform changed from burgundy to black and white.

Dad's work on the chalets finished in time for the new season and so, suddenly, he was looking for work again – and we were looking for a new home. We didn't have to look far. Mum got a job at the chip shop in the Kings Oak caravan park to help out financially and, as part of the package, we were allowed to move into one of the vans. Dad bought an old blue Transit flat-bed truck and started going out collecting scrap metal. It went well. For once we had a bit of money coming in, but there was a price. With two parents out, who was getting our tea ready? Who was cleaning the house? Who was picking up ten-year-old Stephen and five-year-old Danny after school?

I didn't mind doing any of it, not at first. What sister doesn't enjoy bossing around her kid brothers? It wasn't so different from playing the parent with my dolls, especially when Danny was young. For as long as I could remember, I'd always known I wanted to be a mum, and my little brother was the perfect guinea pig. He drew the line at letting me dress him up but I think we all had fun in those early years, when the age difference wasn't such an issue. In any case, what was the alternative? If you see your mum and dad working every hour God sends, then that rubs off. Stephen had his chores and I had mine. That's just the way it was.

But then one day my eyes were opened. I'd started getting the bus home and my friend Tina said, 'Are you coming into the village?'

'What for?'

Tina looked at me like I was an alien. 'To hang about. Everyone's going.'

I said I couldn't. I had to pick up Stephen and Danny, get them home and start on my jobs.

'Tomorrow, then?' Tina said.

I shook my head. 'I have to do it every day.'

'Oh. Poor you.'

That was the first time I realised there was a world going on outside my family. And I couldn't take part in it. I didn't mind helping out around the house – it seemed only fair. But why couldn't I play with my friends as well?

Mum did her best to make it up to me. For my thirteenth birthday I was thrown a surprise party at the local pub. They hired the back room and all my friends and family were there, waiting to spring out when I arrived. I remember getting a lovely jewellery box. Mum said it was because I was growing up, now I was entering my teens.

We were all growing up, in a way. Mum got a job at Wilkinson's Home and Garden Store and before long we left our caravan for a bungalow on Wilton Avenue. It was only rented, but after a year or two in holiday lets, it felt like a real home. The only downside was having further to walk to look after my brothers after school. Then Mum was promoted to supervisor and, what with Dad's scrap business doing well, we moved again. To another bungalow.

That we owned.

Sandy Lodge was a three-bedroom bungalow on Sandy Lane, a leafy road that ran parallel with the beach. The only things separating us from the sea was a bank of trees, then sand dunes and the occasional beach hut. I'd always liked everywhere we lived but this place, with its beautiful green gardens in front of the vast wash of golden sand, looked different. It felt different, too. Everyone just seemed happier, Mum and Dad included. I could sense it. Especially when Dad started his usual thing of knocking down walls and putting in fireplaces. This time he went even further and converted the loft to give Stephen his own room up there. It really was a great time.

I was starting to have fun outside the house as well. For some reason I took up karate lessons once a week. Mum and Dad were friends with the teacher, a giant guy called Mick Baxendale, so I guess that's how I fell into it. I didn't go for long and, in fact, when I next saw Mick again it would be under very different circumstances.

Weekends were my real chance to see my friends. None of us had much money so there was a lot of time spent hanging around the village square or going down to the beach and chatting in the shelters there. At fourteen and fifteen, I noticed I naturally gravitated towards the boys' groups. It wasn't a flirty thing – not at first – because we were all just pals. The girls just seemed a bit too bitchy; most of the talk was about who was going to be seen with the best-looking boy. For a while, that boy was Darren Seabrook. It seemed that everyone who wasn't going out with him seemed to be bitching about whoever was. Which is how I knew, one day, that they were bitching about me.

Darren was my first boyfriend but we both knew he wasn't what anyone would call 'a keeper': his eye was always on someone else. I suppose that's how I'd caught him in the first place. What's more, as soon as we were all in a group he'd blank whatever girl he was with to speak to the other lads. Still, when you're that age you don't know any better. And he was, after all, considered the most handsome boy in the group.

But boys were definitely on the agenda and there was no better place than Chapel St Leonards to meet them. Like every seaside town, it had a constant flow of new blood. As soon as the weather improved, they arrived – and went – like the tide, as hotels and B&Bs welcomed that week's holidaymakers. And where did they all hang out? At the pleasure beach and the arcades – in other words, the same places we already were.

I don't think I was a bad girl by any means. Not compared to some of my friends, and definitely not considering I was only allowed out at weekends and, as I got older, for an hour or two after dinner. But it was nice to have attention from fresh faces. More than that, it was just refreshing to see different people, hear different voices and get more of a flavour of what was going on outside Chapel.

Looks were becoming more important for me. Most of my friends dressed like every other Lincolnshire teenager. A lot of the holiday crowd were variations on the same theme. My style came direct from *Top of the Pops*.

I suppose I was fifteen when I first fell in love with Boy George. The problem was, I was already infatuated with Madonna. So, one day I'd have ribbons in my crimped hair and very loud make-up like a Culture Club tribute act; the next I'd be wearing a polka-dot ra-ra skirt, day-glo legwarmers and matching boob tube with the flimsiest netting covering my stomach. To complete the Madonna look, I'd backcomb my hair. For Boy George, I even bought a hat like the one he wore in the 'Karma Chameleon' video. I once won a fancy-dress competition because people liked my Boy George costume so much. What the judges didn't know was that that was how I dressed all the time.

After three years of being Danny and Stephen Needham's babysitter, I was finally getting my own personality. Unfortunately, I didn't have many opportunities to show it. I was still only allowed out till eight in the evening, and it was beginning to hurt. Dad had strict ground rules on how long a girl should be out on her own, and that was about the limit. Of course, all my friends were out later. Even Stephen was allowed to come home at nine. That, I suppose, grated the most. He was two years younger than I was, and it was because of him and Danny I wasn't able to go out with friends after school. For the first time in my life I found myself saying, 'It's not fair.'

But there was no getting out of it, however often I begged.

'We're a team,' Dad would say. 'We all have responsibilities. Yours is to look after your brothers until we get home.'

I couldn't argue, as much as I wanted to. But I felt trapped. In the daytimes it was school, in the afternoons it was doing chores and at night it was bed. Then one day I thought, *If I can't get out of my chores, I'll have to get out of something else.*

That only left school and bed.

With a village full of that week's new faces, wasting every day at the Earl of Scarbrough comp was the last thing I wanted to do. So I stopped going. It began innocently. A boy called Craig whom I'd met that Saturday said, 'Fancy meeting up tomorrow lunchtime?'

I thought about how long it would take to get the bus back to the village square and decided.

'Yes. All right. I'll meet you at 12.15 by the clock tower.'

That would give me half an hour with him, then fifteen minutes to get back for afternoon classes. It was doable. But when the moment came to get back on the bus, I didn't take it.

I'd never bunked off school before and for an hour or two I couldn't relax. Even though Craig and I had run down to the beach, I still expected to see teachers come crawling out of the dunes hunting for me. But they didn't come. And the next day at morning registration, nobody mentioned anything. As far as my form tutor was concerned, I'd been there all day.

The second I had that lightbulb moment I thought, *Well, they won't miss me this afternoon either!*

At first I did it a couple of times a week, always waiting nervously for the hand-on-the-shoulder moment. Then it became more and more frequent and, eventually, I was almost brazen about it. I wasn't getting up to anything naughty with these lads and I still got back in time to collect seven-year-old Danny and get him home and the dinner on. What was I doing wrong?

Lots, obviously. Eventually, the teachers worked out my little ruse and told my parents. Dad, as expected, hit the roof. Mum waited till he'd calmed down and then told me the same things in calmer tones. They were disappointed in me. What was I playing at? How could I deceive them both like that?

And of course she kept asking me why I'd done it. But the truth was I couldn't tell her. I couldn't say, 'You've kept me indoors looking after my brothers for so long, cooking dinners, ironing and cleaning, when I should have been out there with my friends. I'm just trying to have the childhood you never let me have!'

If I'd said half of that it would have broken her heart. So I took the tears, took the punishment of being grounded for a week, and let Dad drive me to school the next day. And then I caught the bus into the village at lunchtime as usual, and didn't go back.

Again, it was a week before the school twigged. Dad was called in with me to see the head, which didn't please him because it meant time off work. The head told him that I'd been absent again, and made the mistake of asking what he was going to do about it.

'What am *I* going to do about it? I drove her to school every day. I marched her through the doors. It's your bloody job to keep her here!' With that he gave me a look and said, 'I'll see you later.'

I couldn't have been more nervous waiting for Mum and Dad to come home that night. I made more of an effort than usual getting dinner read: I really pulled out all the stops, as though that would stop me getting punished for skipping school and, even worse, showing Dad up in front of the head.

I'll be honest, I was expecting the slipper. Instead, Mum said, 'We've spoken to the school. They're recommending sending you to a psychiatrist.'

I hadn't seen that coming. I don't think anyone had. Mum looked sad as she said it. But they were at their wits' end. The school said I had psychological problems. I wasn't a normal child. I needed specialist help.

Living in a caravan had never bothered me. But having my friends discover I was seeing a 'shrink' was too humiliating to imagine. I tried everything to get out of going, to no avail. Mum drove me to the therapist's office, then sat in the waiting room until my hour was up. Then she was called in without me and it was my turn to wait.

When the door opened again, the psychiatrist was smiling and Mum was in tears.

I'd poured my heart out to that stranger and, by the looks of it, she'd repeated every word back to Mum. How I'd felt denied a childhood. How I felt robbed of the chance of making friends, of fitting in, each time they'd moved us. How I hadn't felt valued as anything other than as a glorified babysitter. How I'd played mummy to a seven-year-old and a thirteen-year-old when I should have been trying on lipsticks in Boots with my friends.

I suppose I had been rebelling, but not intentionally. I'd never meant to hurt anyone, it was just how I felt. And I think Mum understood. The psychiatrist made sure of that. Mum couldn't wait to apologise. Dad did too, in his own way. Stephen was old enough to look after Danny now, and do more around the house. I think he realised that maybe I should have more time to call my own.

Best of all, the psychiatrist told them I wasn't mad. 'Kerry won't need to come again unless she wants to. She's just a girl who wants a childhood she feels she never had.'

I wasn't a wayward teenager. I was just a normal one.

After that, family life was sweet. For a while. Quite a short while, actually. Mum and Dad did cut me some slack and I tried to stay at school as often as I could bear.

But then I met Simon.

CHAPTER TWO

YOU CAN ALWAYS
COME BACK

Being allowed to go out straight from school made a huge difference to my life. Still, though, Mum insisted I go home first to change. My friends weren't made to do this but I didn't mind. It meant by the time I got back to the beach or the square or wherever we were meeting, I'd stand out in my Madonna number among a sea of kids all bedecked in the same black and white blazers and tops.

If anything, the boys looked more identical than the girls: there wasn't much they could do to personalise school trousers and shirts. But even on weekends or when they'd changed, they all seemed to appear wearing the same casual 'uniform'. It was as if they didn't dare stand out. Which was probably why us girls found it so easy to drift from one lad to another: they looked the same, they acted the same, they may as well have been the same. I was dating a nice boy called Mark Williams at the time. We were just kids fooling around. He'd rather have been with his mates and me with mine, but going out was what we were expected to do. It would only be a matter of time before he swapped me for one of my friends or I him for one of his.

And then one day a stranger arrived.

I noticed him because he looked different. Not wild or over the top like I could be, just not like the rest. He wore dark Farah trousers and a Fred Perry top, while all the others were in unmarked 'man at C&A' gear bought by their mums. He was tall, about six foot, and skinny, so whatever he wore would have looked good. And didn't he know it. I could tell he was cocky without speaking to him. The problem was I really wanted to, because he also had something else the others didn't.

A Yorkshire accent!

His name was Simon Ward. He was a year above me, in the fifth year, and his parents had just retired to Chapel St Leonards from Sheffield. And I was right: with all his designer labels and big-city experiences, he thought he was the bees' knees. I couldn't stand him for it. I'd spent enough of my life hanging out with little kids; I didn't need to spend my free time with teenagers who acted like it.

Fortunately, there were many other distractions. Beer was the latest one. And dancing. The clubs on the caravan sites had discos every night so those of us who looked old enough started sneaking into those. My favourite was the one in the Kings Oak caravan park. The bouncer on the door was a friend of my dad's so when he let us in he said, 'I'll keep an eye out for you.' I knew then that no harm could come my way: if any boy or bloke tried it on, he was only a few yards away.

Unfortunately, there were things Dad's pal couldn't control. Like, for example, the amount I drank. Normally I preferred dancing to drinking, but, on one occasion, I was sitting at the bar chatting to someone, letting them buy me a lager or wine, and by the time it came to leave I'd forgotten how to walk. That was when I needed my own friends: they were the ones who called the cab and poured me into it. But even as I got in, I knew Dad's mate was feet away. I was safe. Daft, but safe.

I just wish Mum and Dad saw it that way. Waking them up as you try to get your key into the lock is no way to prove you're okay. It was only the fact Stephen and Danny were still asleep that stopped Dad shouting the place down. But even quietly, and in the state I was in, I heard the words.

'You're grounded.'

I argued, of course. Probably only made matters worse. And the next morning I felt terrible. But from the booze, not the punishment, because I had a plan…

It was a couple of days later, at breakfast, when I asked if I could go out that night. Mum shook her head. Dad jabbed his fork in my direction.

'Have you forgotten our agreement, young lady?'

I shrugged.

'You're grounded until further notice.'

I didn't push it. I went to school, stayed for the whole day, came home, prepared tea, ate with my family, then retired to my room in a sulk. Or so it appeared. I just wanted an excuse to leave the table. An hour later, I was in my best make-up and dressed to the nines listening at the door. One by one, I heard my brothers, my father and then my mother head off to bed. They all called out 'goodnight' to me, but no one came in when I didn't answer. They must have assumed I was asleep. In fact, I was already by the window, throwing my handbag out onto the grass and beginning to climb out after it. The advantage of living in a bungalow!

And so life went on. Sometimes I stayed at school and some-times I didn't. Sometimes I stayed in at night and other times I just pretended to. I didn't think I was doing any harm. I certainly wasn't getting into trouble with boys. We were all too young to be serious. I, particularly, wasn't in the mood to be pinned down. I'd always dreamed of a family of my own but there would be plenty of time for that. Right then, after years of being a surrogate mum, I just wanted to stretch my wings for a while and be as carefree as I could for as long as possible. But, as each day passed, that became harder and harder. The reason was about six foot tall and had beautiful blue eyes.

Just being part of our crowd meant Simon and I came into contact and, over the months, I realised his bravado was just a front. When you actually listened to him, he spoke a lot more sense than a lot of the guys I'd known for years. And so, when he asked me out one day, I said yes.

We didn't last long together but no one's relationships at that time had any staying power. We all drifted around: no hard feelings, no hearts broken. That's how everyone was. That's how I had always been. Yet, going to bed over the next few weeks I found myself thinking more frequently about the boy so skinny his eyes seemed to bulge: I didn't mind the others calling him 'frog eyes', and I didn't care about his bad teeth. I even ignored the fact that he was so obsessed about wearing the latest fashion labels. There was something about this Simon that I couldn't get enough of. And so one day I told him.

I'd been Eddie Needham's little girl, Stephen Needham's babysitter and now I was Simon Ward's girlfriend. It was official.

Being in love – or at least infatuated – at fifteen, even if you don't realise it yourself, is a powerful thing.

I suppose it sort of crept up on me. Darren Seabrook had been the most popular guy when I went out with him, as was Mark Williams when we dated. And by the time Simon and I got together, a year or more after he'd arrived, he was the cool one to be around. But he was nice, too. He didn't brush me aside when he was with his mates. He included me, made me feel part of everything. And he seemed more mature as well. He looked a jack-the-lad but he'd been brought up with strong family values and morals. Just like me.

Simon had joined the Earl of Scarbrough just in time for exams, then left. By the time my final term came around I spoke to my teachers, then had the same conversation at home. I'd been missing from school more than I'd attended. I had no chance of passing any CSEs or O-levels. There really was no point in me even turning up.

As much as they tried to argue, I think everyone agreed I was right. Very quietly, I dropped out of school without a qualification to my name. I only got away with it because I'd said I had offers of work. That wasn't strictly true at the time, but I'd had a weekend job for a while. One conversation with the bosses later, and within a fortnight of taking off my school uniform for good, I was in full-time employment.

'Working on the land', they called it. Basically, I was part of a team that worked for the Etchers Brothers – Pete, Mick and Roy – who had contracts with farmers all over the east of the country. If a farm in Boston needed carrots picking, half a dozen of us would be driven out and that's what we would do. Or if a place in Spalding had cabbages needing cutting or daffodils planting, we'd ride out there. It was back-breaking stuff and you were only paid for what you did. But on an average week I could take home £200 – £250 if I pulled out all the stops. It was serious money for a sixteen-year-old. Serious money for anyone, as it turned out, because I hadn't been doing it long before Mum gave up her post at Wilkinson's to join me!

I loved having free time and money to spend on myself. The giant East Gate Market on a Saturday was a must-visit place for me. I soon had a hundred shoes and clothes galore. We went out at weekends to pubs and clubs. Even after paying my parents twenty quid board money, I still had plenty left for going out with Simon.

We hadn't been going out for long when Simon first said, 'When I'm eighteen, I'm getting out of here.'

'Oh. Where will you go?'

'Sheffield. My brothers and sister are there. They've all got good jobs. I can go and work with them.'

He kept saying things like that, even once we were an item. I never thought too much about it: boys were always boasting they were going to do things. I never thought any of them would. Then we were at the shelter across the dunes from Sandy Lodge one night and Simon said it again, this time adding, 'Will you come too?'

I was blown away. We were having fun, that's all, I thought. No one had said anything about packing up and moving out.

'Go to Sheffield?' I said. 'What would I do down there?'

Simon didn't have an answer to that. I think it was just his dream to go there. He hadn't thought it through any further. He didn't even plan to tell his parents.

'But you can't just run away,' I said.

He shrugged. Obviously he thought he could.

'Come on,' he said. 'It will be an adventure.'

I think he saw it as romantic. Us two, packing our bags and making a new life together. He had three brothers and one sister and they'd all made a go of it in Sheffield. They all had partners and houses and, apart from his housewife sister, Jane, decent jobs. He was young, he was seventeen and he just wanted to follow in their footsteps. His parents had brought him up to value hard work and a settled family life. That was his dream, and he wanted me to be part of it – just not here. On top of that, he thought he was missing out on real life by living in a village.

I laughed it off and the subject didn't come up again for a while. I was sixteen, still trying to have fun. Why would I tie myself down so young?

As winter came, another birthday passed, the land work became harder and I got a part-time job waiting tables; then another working in a bar on one of the caravan sites. I enjoyed seeing other people out and about, even if I was only serving them. In the bar, strangers would talk to me and I liked that. Some gave me tips or bought me a drink as a result, but I wasn't working there for the money. I still felt like I'd been denied fun earlier in my life. Mingling with drinkers, even when I was sober, was just a nice thing for a seventeen-year-old to do.

And then one day Simon mentioned Sheffield again, and I knew I'd made up my mind. I hadn't even been aware I was thinking about it. But as soon as he said his eighteenth birthday was in a couple of weeks, I just knew I'd be going with him.

I was terrified of telling my parents. But I did, and their response was exactly as I'd feared:

Devastation.

I told Mum first. She begged and begged me not to go. 'Don't,

Kerry. It will be the biggest mistake of your life. Don't rush into anything.'

She was crying and holding on to me like I was going to disappear that minute.

'What if it doesn't work out? It's such a long way!'

In other words, *'What if you split up with Simon?'*

I didn't think we would but, honestly, that didn't matter. Even more than being with him, I wanted to be in Sheffield. Chapel St Leonards was a ghost town in winter. There was nothing for me there apart from my family. And in Sheffield I had plenty of family and a city full of opportunities. My grandma and granddad and aunts and uncles and cousins were all in Sheffield or thereabouts. I knew Ecclesfield and Chapeltown as well as I knew Skegness. What's more, Simon's family was there as well. If anything, I'd know more people in Sheffield than I did at home. On top of that, I was growing up; I needed independence. As lovely as my parents were, the idea of not having them looking over my shoulder all the time was something I relished.

I didn't say this to Mum – or Dad, when he came in later. But when he'd come down from the ceiling and Mum had wiped her eyes, they both said the same thing.

'Well, if that's what you want to do, Kerry.'

'It is.'

'Okay. But if anything happens, anything at all, you know you can always come back, don't you?'

I wish I'd listened...

They still kept trying to talk me out of it. Even now, my dad would have us all live under the same roof if he could. He missed out on a lot of our childhoods while he was working, and he still wants to make up for that. I was their little girl in their eyes. They didn't want me to go. On the other hand, Dad had worked on the fairgrounds. He had that wanderlust and he saw the same in me. As much as he wanted to, he couldn't stand in my way.

Eventually, that day in January 1989 came. Simon's brother, Steve, had been up to visit their parents and he was going to drive us south in his silver Scirocco. Neither of us had anything other than clothes – no kitchen appliances, white goods or electronics – so we travelled pretty light. I could almost smell the freedom as I kissed Mum and Dad and the boys goodbye. I was so focused on my independence that it didn't even occur to me to wonder where we were going to live. Simon had said he'd sorted it, and that had been fine.

In fact, he'd arranged for us to stay with his sister Jane, her husband Shaun, and their daughter. I didn't care for Shaun much, but Jane was nice and I'd always liked her visits. The main thing, though, was being in Sheffield. With Simon.

All the way down the A1, following the coast, Simon and I couldn't stop chatting about our new life. We were buzzing. And Steve added to it. He promised Simon that there was a job working for him as a builder for as long as we wanted it. It really seemed like a dream come true.

And then we pulled up outside Jane's maisonette, and it turned into a nightmare.

I'm not a snob. I've lived in bungalows, chalets and caravans. I was born into a council house. I've got nothing against any of them. But I had never seen anything like this street or the whole surrounding estate. Grey, dark, dirty and oppressive, it was like something out of the bleakest science fiction film. And the noise! There were kids of all ages, from two to sixteen, running and shouting and swearing, with mums hanging over the balconies or out of front doors swearing back, even louder. It was terrifying.

I sat in the back of the Scirocco and stared, open-mouthed. My family was poor, we were working class, but we were clean. This lot looked like they hadn't seen soap in months.

I couldn't help thinking, *I've left a lovely, quiet, beach-front bungalow with beautiful gardens to come and live in this, a concrete jungle. I must be mad!*

I honestly wanted to turn back there and then.

I think Steve picked up on my mood, but one look at Simon's beaming face told me he couldn't see anything wrong.

'That's us,' he said, grinning from ear to ear. I couldn't spoil it. Whatever I thought, it was Simon's dream come true.

The weather didn't help. It had been pretty grim all the way down and we got soaked carrying our bags in. But at least the locals got a wash, even if they didn't shut up.

Inside wasn't much better. It was clean enough, although whatever money Shaun earned wasn't spent on the décor. But then Jane showed us to our room, we closed the door and for a few minutes all my worries faded away.

'We've done it,' Simon said. 'We're on our own.'

It wasn't how I'd imagined it but he was right. We'd left home, we had our independence and we were together. We were seventeen and eighteen years old. What else did we need?

To my dismay, rather than join Steve, Simon was persuaded by Shaun to work with him selling domestic goods door-to-door. Pegs, dishcloths, washing agents, that sort of thing. Despite initial reservations, we settled into a rhythm. He was pulling in a wage and I was helping Jane with the household chores and looking after their daughter. Everything was great. But then I'd step outside the front door to go to the shops and I'd know I was kidding myself.

We'd moved in at the weekend, but even midweek there were just as many kids running around, and just as many mums yelling, 'Get in here, you bleeder!' from their verandas. I hated it. Hated being there and even began to hate Simon for bringing me there.

On our third night I said to him, 'I can't do it. I can't live here.'

He just smiled. 'It's only for a little while. Till I get a proper job and we find a place of our own. Don't worry, we won't be staying.'

Then he kissed me and everything was all right. He was such a romantic and so positive and when we were together it rubbed off on me. I believed him. I believed in him. But when I was on my own, the fears would come again.

I didn't like the flat, but I hated being outside more. Despite this, I found myself a job waiting on tables at a local restaurant called Sharavale. It wasn't ideal but I had experience, and it got me out of the concrete jungle for a few hours. At the end of every shift, though, I'd have the same sense of dread as I pictured the walk home.

After a month of this, it didn't matter if Simon was in or not when I arrived home. I didn't want to be there. After three months I was completely stressed. I was off coffee, tea. I could barely eat anything.

The worst thing was not being able to confide in Jane. I could hardly tell her that her house and her area were making me ill. We were together for so long during the day and I was obviously suffering, so I would have to say something. But what?

In the end, it was actually Jane who approached me. I couldn't believe what she said.

'Kerry, I think you're pregnant.'

CHAPTER THREE

THERE'S ANOTHER OPTION

The idea of popping into Superdrug for an off-the-shelf pregnancy test kit never occurred to me. I don't think I even knew they existed. As far as I was concerned, if you wanted to know if you were pregnant you had to go to the doctor's. So, more for Jane's sake than mine, I made an appointment. Off I went thinking, *What a waste of time.*

I knew I couldn't be pregnant because I was on the pill. I hadn't been sick, in the morning or any other time. I hadn't skipped a period and I certainly didn't have any sign of a bump.

It took twenty minutes to walk to the surgery – and only half that time to get home, because I skipped all the way. I couldn't help it: I was on cloud nine. I was seventeen and the doctor had been adamant. The test was positive.

I *was* pregnant.

It was the happiest day of my life and for a couple of hours it was my secret. How would everyone else react? Jane was great, very supportive. But I dreaded telling my parents. I was too young. I was just a child myself. What did I know about being a mum? I knew what they would say before I even picked up the phone.

And then there was Simon. I knew he had dreams of a family life, but not yet. We weren't ready. We didn't have our own home. We could barely support ourselves. How on earth would we cope with a baby?

Obviously Simon had to be told first. I worked out exactly how I was going to do it. I would make his dinner, set the table, create the right mood. And pray he didn't say, 'Get rid of it.'

By the time I was halfway through chopping carrots I was trembling so much the knife was missing as many pieces as it hit. I'd never been more nervous about anything. I looked at the clock. Half an hour till he arrived home. There was nothing else to do but wait. Wait and wait.

The plan was, let Simon settle down to his meal, ask him about this day, and build up to it. This wasn't the sort of news he should have to deal with as soon as he stepped through the door.

Part one went to plan. I heard the key in the front door and let Simon get all the way into the kitchen before I said, 'Simon, I've got something to tell you.' Even before he'd realised I hadn't simply said, 'Hello', I added, 'I'm pregnant!'

I couldn't help it. I just blurted the words out. 'I'm going to have a baby. *We're* going to have a baby.'

And then I waited. Poor Simon was shell-shocked. He hadn't even got his boots off yet. He pulled out a chair from the kitchen table and fell into it. I tried reading his face. It was blank. Illegible. I wished he'd respond, one way or other. The suspense was criminal.

I watched as Simon ran his hand through his hair. He sighed, loud and meaningfully, then, at last, he spoke.

'Are you sure?'

'I went to the doctor's.'

'I thought you were on the pill.'

'I am.'

'Why didn't you tell me before?'

'I wanted to be sure.'

He sighed again, louder and longer this time, like all the air was being blown out of him. My heart sank. He wasn't happy. He was going to say I'd conned him by getting pregnant. He was going to say we had to abort it. I realised I was holding my breath.

'Well,' he said, finally. 'I suppose we need to find somewhere to live then.'

For the second time in a day, I was the happiest person in the world.

My smile almost vanished a few days later when my blood test came back from the lab. For a moment I thought the doctor had said I was already four and a half months gone. That was impossible. I would have noticed.

He smiled. 'There's no doubt about it, Kerry. You'll be a mum before Christmas.'

For the first time I had a real sense of panic. We no longer had most of a year to find a decent home for our new baby, like we'd thought. We had a month or two. Could we find anywhere in that time and get it ready for a baby? And then there was my waitressing job. I'd have to think about giving that up sooner rather than later, but I needed the money. We didn't have a thing for a baby. No home, no cot; not even a bottle.

There were a few stressful days at Jane's after that. I couldn't help telling Simon he would have to pull his finger out, even though I knew he was doing his best. I admit I was beginning to get frightened – we both were, I realised later – and I suppose we took it out on each other. It didn't help that his work was taking him further and further from Sheffield. Sometimes he'd have to stop over in Birmingham or Wales, and I wouldn't see him for two or three nights. When we did, our money worries and home problems just caused more rows. And then one day, we just stopped arguing.

It was at the hospital. I'd gone for my scan. Most women have one at twelve weeks but I was way beyond that. Simon came with me and held my hand as the nurse lifted my top back and rubbed the cold gel on my tummy. Then we both looked at each other open-mouthed as she started probing the gel with what looked like a TV remote control and images began to flicker on the screen next to her.

For a few seconds the nurse didn't say anything. She just stared at the monitor as she jabbed the remote control this way and that on my belly. I couldn't make out what she was looking at. To me, it looked like television interference. Then she stopped moving her hand and said, 'Found you!'

That's when I realised she wasn't talking to me or Simon. She was talking to our baby.

'There's the heart, can you see it?'

I thought she was having me on. I honestly did. I could only see a snowstorm on the screen. I looked at Simon. He was obviously seeing the same swirling mess as I was. I started to get anxious. What was I doing wrong?

And then for some reason my eyes just focused and I saw him. A tiny little shape: little hands, little feet, little head; folded over and bobbing around. And there was the heart. Pulsing and throbbing.

It was my baby.

There were all these questions I wanted to ask but my mouth was just hanging open. I was watching my little baby in my tummy and I already knew I loved him. And I loved Simon too. Watching him, watching our baby, all the arguments of the last few days disappeared. Look what we'd made together! That was the only thing that mattered in the world. He wasn't even born yet, but our baby had the power to bring us together.

Simon was obviously motivated by the experience because a couple of days later he announced we had a new home. It took me under an hour to pack. Thirty minutes after that, we were standing outside a block of flats.

We were only a short walk from Jane's place in Pitsmoor so I knew it was never going to be a palace. But when we walked in the front door, I burst into tears. It was disgusting. The carpets felt like they'd been soaked in superglue, sticky with God-knows-what. There were tea or beer stains splashed head-height up the walls and the furniture stank. Of what, I couldn't bear to imagine.

'I can't bring my baby to live here!'

Simon was as horrified as I was. He denied it, but I don't think he had actually visited before agreeing to move in. Still, it was all we could afford. 'We can make this work, Kerry,' he promised. 'Trust me.'

Still wiping back the tears, I listened to Simon's plans. He was going to strip the walls, hang wallpaper, paint the doors. There were decorating grants you could get if you were on a low income. 'And look at the size of the rooms,' he said. 'You said you wanted somewhere bigger.'

In the end it wasn't anything Simon said that persuaded me to put my bags down; it was the realisation that however bad the flat was, it was our own. It was somewhere we could bring our little baby, close the door and be a family. That was all that mattered.

All mums-to-be get that 'nesting' instinct, and that took over. We spent the whole day scrubbing and cleaning and washing the kitchen and bathroom, and then I did it all over again the following day. Then we moved on to the rest of the place. The previous tenants hadn't cleaned a day in their life. I was on my hands and knees pregnant, with my little bump finally showing.

By the end of the weekend, Simon had even started painting so it really began to feel and smell more like a home. Now I could do something I'd been putting off for weeks – for months, in fact. I could tell my mum and dad.

I don't know why I hadn't already. I suppose I didn't want them to be disappointed in me and I knew they would have been if they'd seen where I lived before. They'd have demanded I return home with them and I would have gone, and that would have been the end of my independence. But now we'd made our little flat okay, I could do it. I could honestly say I was all right. I missed them like crazy but I was standing on my own two feet – just – and I was happy.

I forced myself to go for a walk and I found a phone box. It was the height of summer so just getting out of the house was gruelling. I had a bag of ten-pence pieces and I knew Mum's number. All I had to do was pick up the phone. It was one of the hardest things I've ever done. That phone felt so heavy. I fished a coin from the bag and held it over the slot. Then I dialled the number I knew off by heart, and prayed no one would answer.

'Hello?'

On those old phones you had a few seconds after making a connection to insert your money. I nearly chickened out. Five minutes later, I realised I'd been worrying over nothing. Once Mum had got over the shock of being told she was going to be a grandparent in a couple of months, she switched into practical mode.

'Move back in with us. We'll help you. You can't be on your own at seventeen and raise a baby.'

I really, really wanted to say yes. Right then, in that phone box on that estate in Pitsmoor, I couldn't think of anything better. For me, or my baby.

'Kerry, are you there?'

I realised I was staring at the phone. If I waited long enough the pips would sound and Mum would be cut off. I was tempted to let that happen, I really was. Then I wouldn't have to decide.

But I owed it to Mum to talk. So I said, 'I can't move back with you, Mum. I'm with Simon now. I've made my life. I'll be all right.'

Going back to Chapel St Leonard would have been embarrassing, but there was no problem seeking help from the family already in Sheffield. I began to spend more and more time visiting my grandma. Jane, too, even though she was technically Simon's family, was always good to see – although at my place, not hers. It was she who gave me the most bits and bobs for the baby. They were all hand-me-downs but beggars can't be choosers. It was also Jane who asked the question no one else had dared mention:

'Are you sure you want to keep it?'

My hand flew instantly to my bump. 'It's too late for an abortion, Jane. I'm seven months.'

'There's another option. Have you thought about adoption?'

37

'I haven't and I won't, Jane.'

'There's no shame in it, you know. No one will judge you.'

She explained how hard it would be for me as a teenage mum with no money. She knew, as she'd been in exactly the same position.

'I know what it's like living hand-to-mouth, not knowing if you can afford the next packet of nappies.'

I know she wasn't being malicious. A baby for such a young couple can cause all sorts of problems. She knew that. She was just trying to protect me and Simon.

'Jane, I've thought about this. I'm young, I know nothing about the world but I know I can be a good mum. It's all I've ever wanted to be.'

Even so, her doubts resonated around the empty flat over the next few weeks as Simon worked longer and longer hours away from home. When he did return for a night or two, he was too tired to do any decorating. I was getting too big to do much either. It seemed unfair to nag him when we saw less and less of each other, but I needed him. I needed things from him for the baby. I knew now how Mum had felt waiting for Dad's money to be sent home when he was working away.

One Friday, Simon came home from work after three nights away up north and seemed even quieter than usual. Still, we had a nice meal together, but he was still too tired to do any decorating.

Then, about six o'clock in the evening on the Sunday, Simon pulled his coat on and said, 'I'm going out.' He grabbed his travel bag, gave me a hug and walked out of the door.

And I knew he wasn't coming back.

CHAPTER FOUR

IT'S A BOY

Alone. Abandoned. Afraid.

I'd been conning myself. Without looking forward to Simon coming home and being part of our own little family, I could see our flat once more for what it was: horrible. I hated the days and nights I spent there alone.

I thought about phoning my parents but I was too proud. I still thought I could make it work. Do it on my own.

Wednesday came and went with no sign of Simon, just as I had feared. Thursday, Friday, the following Wednesday all had the same story. Each night I cried. Not out of loneliness. I was scared. Scared to be seventeen, scared to be pregnant and scared to be alone.

Simon's money ran out very, very quickly. Even if he didn't want to be with me, he still had a duty to his unborn child, so I called Jane to see if she knew where he was. She didn't. Nor, she said, did his brothers or his parents. I believed her. She asked if I needed any help. I said no, but I burst out crying as I did and hung up as quickly as possible.

The next day there was a knock at my door. It was Grandma. Jane had called her, asked her to check on me and here she was.

I felt the tears coming again. Hers was the first friendly face I'd seen in weeks.

I told Grandma everything was okay, and that the cot and the pushchair and Moses basket were coming in a few days.

She let me finish then said, 'Let me call your mum and dad, Kerry. They'll help you out.'

'No, Grandma, I'm fine. I have to do this on my own.'

'You don't, you know.'

'I do.'

That's how we left it. Grandma went home, I made myself dinner and sobbed myself to sleep again, terrified at the mess I'd allowed myself to get into. I don't know if it was hormones or desperation or actual love, but I never gave up hoping that Simon would walk back through that front door. Every sound in the corridor got me listening for his voice. Sometimes I went for days without hearing anyone, but the hope remained.

Then one day there was a knock. It took me a while to prise myself out of my chair and waddle to the door, allowing me time to think who it could be. Simon had a key, but perhaps he was too embarrassed to use it. I chided myself for being silly. It was probably a cold-caller. One of the other tenants must have let them into the block. I opened the door...

... and burst into tears again.

'Kerry, love, we've come to take you home.'

I'd never been happier to see anyone. Annoyed as I was at Grandma for telling my parents that I was in trouble, I was more annoyed at myself for not making it work on my own. At least now I didn't have to pretend. Mum and Dad were rescuing me, taking me home to look after me and my baby.

They loaded all my things into a van and we drove back. Mum did most of the talking, telling me their plans for me and their grandchild. I sat back and listened, smiling all the way to Chapel St Leonards.

Neither of them once said, 'I told you so.' I knew they never would.

I thought they'd been wonderful enough already, but then Mum took me shopping and bought me a cot, a pushchair, Moses basket and all the nappies and clothes we would need for the first few weeks. She and Dad were so generous. I put everything in my room and did the only thing left to do. Wait.

I'd been given 15 October as a due date and so obviously the night before I was very nervous. My bump felt like it was full of butterflies. But the 15th came and went with no change. In fact, a week passed, then another. I'm sure I'd doubled in size. I was like a balloon, but with these silly skinny arms and legs sticking out. I thought, *If the baby doesn't come soon, I'll burst!*

The anticipation was crippling. I realised I'd set my heart on meeting my baby on the due date. I was really sad after that. The longer it dragged on, the more anxious I got. What sort of a mum would I be? Would I be good enough? I was seventeen and single. How would I cope emotionally? How would I know what to do? I had bottles and steamers and nappies and creams and powders and leaflets on everything from breastfeeding to sleeping, eating and winding – you name it. But what if I didn't bond with my baby? What if I got it wrong?

The fears got worse every day that the baby didn't come. Then, on 28 October, everything changed. It was a Saturday night. Mum and Dad had gone out to a party. It was eleven o'clock and I'd spent the night trying to get comfortable in front of the television when things began to happen. I was going into labour.

I ran to the phone and called Mum at her friend's house. Twenty minutes later we were all in the car heading towards Boston's Pilgrim Hospital, about an hour away but still the closest maternity unit. Mum sat in the back with me, holding my hand, telling me not to worry, assuring me I was doing fine, that everything was all right. I wanted to believe her but the pain was incredible. No one warned me having a baby would hurt! By the time we arrived I was doubled up in agony and dreading it getting worse with the birth. I'd gone from wanting the baby out as quickly as possible to now not wanting it to come at all!

The midwives at Boston were brilliant. They got me into a bed and put me on gas and air. When that didn't work I was given a shot of pethidine in my leg. Then, to speed things up, they broke my waters. I felt like a spectator in my own show.

Mum stayed at my side the whole time, comforting and encouraging me. I was sweating and scared, but she was calm and looked at me with such love in her eyes. Even when I was screaming in agony she was a rock. The only time she looked away was at six o'clock the following morning as her grandchild made an appearance.

'It's a boy!'

A boy! Those two words were the greatest painkiller of all and I couldn't wait to hold him. I watched patiently as the nurse did her checks then saw her wrap him in a towel and pass him to Mum. Mum couldn't resist giving him a cuddle and a kiss, then she lowered the little pink bundle down onto my chest and we both cried. It was wonderful, and I just kept repeating the same thing: 'It's like a miracle. A little miracle.' Because it was. I couldn't get over how this tiny little person had grown and grown in my tummy. I'd made him. This little bundle with his shock of black hair, little button nose, really cute lips and lovely blue eyes had come from me. It was so much to take in.

I couldn't take my eyes off him. He weighed 6lb 6oz, which wasn't large considering how overdue he'd been, and his skin was as smooth as silk. The nurse had said late babies usually came out wrinkly. I think she was trying to prepare me for the shock in case I thought I'd given birth to an alien, but there wasn't a line on him. I remember thinking how soft he felt, how warm. Even a couple of little birthmarks – a strawberry one on the nape of his neck and a darker patch above the right knee – just made him seem all the more perfect.

It was only once I had cuddled him that I realised how tired I was. By that time I'd been up for twenty-four hours, the last third of those in unimaginable discomfort. But it had been worth it. I'd done it. I had my baby boy. Now I could relax – and sleep.

First, though, I had to ask Mum something.

'What do you think of "Ben", then?'

'Ben? Is that what you're calling him?'

'Yes. Not Benjamin or Benny – just Ben. Ben Stephen Needham.'

'I think that's lovely.'

I don't know where the name had come from. I hadn't planned any in advance because I didn't even know what sex I was expecting. But he was definitely a Ben, and 'Stephen' had a decent ring to it. It wasn't intended as a tribute to my brother but I knew he would never believe that!

All I wanted to do was close my eyes but the nurses had other ideas: 'You can sleep when Ben does.'

I spent a lot of that day being shown how to breastfeed, but I panicked in case I did it wrong and the more I flustered, the more impossible it seemed. I think my fears passed down to Ben because he wouldn't take to it, which only got me more and more worked up. Eventually, a nurse showed me how to mix formula instead. Even getting Ben to suck on a bottle was traumatic but we did it. Watching his little mouth draw the milk from the teat was magical. So tiny, so young and he was feeding himself.

By contrast, learning how to wind him seemed a bizarre ritual, almost barbaric. Like everything else, once you get the hang of it and understand why it's so important, it becomes second nature. At first, though, even raising a finger to my precious little bean seemed so wrong.

There seemed so much to take in, it was like being back in school. There were lessons in nappies, bathing, sleeping – you name it.

'Don't worry,' Mum said, 'I'll always be there to help.'

I honestly don't know what I would have done without her there. Mum was only thirty-six and we both felt that Ben had come into the world blessed with two mothers. Just entertaining that idea, however, brought its own cloud. Yes, Ben was lucky to have so many people who loved him from his first breath; Dad, Danny, Stephen, Grandma and Granddad all visited as soon as they were allowed. But the one person who should have been there was missing.

Then, on my second day in hospital – the second day of Ben's life – a nurse came to say there was a phone call for me. I gave Ben to Mum and went out to the ward's public phone. Just walking took its toll. I remember thinking, *This had better be important.*

I picked up the receiver and said, 'Hello?'

'Hello, Kerry.'

'Simon? Is that you?'

'Yes. I hear you've had our baby.'

I went from shock to outright annoyance in seconds. It *had* been our baby. Then Simon had left and it had become *my* baby. All the frustrations of the last few weeks were on the tip of my tongue. I wanted to put him straight, to tell him where to go. Then I thought of the little pink creature in the cot next to my bed and I relented. It wasn't the time.

'Yes,' I said, 'I've had the baby. He's healthy, he's beautiful and I've called him Ben.'

Then I placed the receiver back in the cradle and walked gingerly back to my bed, head buzzing with anger, resentment and something else.

After three days I was allowed to leave. The doctors were happy with Ben's progress and the nurses seemed convinced that I could look after my child. I wished I shared their confidence. The second I stepped out of the hospital and I felt Ben wince as his first taste of fresh air buffeted his tiny little face, I froze. Was he dressed appropriately? Had I put enough clothes on him? Was I holding him correctly? All my insecurities came flooding back.

Mum saw instinctively what was going on and put her arm around me. 'Come on, Kerry, love. You're doing just fine.'

Back at Sandy Lodge, I just wanted to be with Ben but the doorbell wouldn't stop ringing. Word had got around the village and relatives and friends traipsed in and out for several days. A lot of my old school mates popped by. They were really pleased for me, although after the obligatory baby chat, they couldn't help mentioning they'd be shopping and clubbing later that week. Obviously I wouldn't be joining them. For one second I felt a pang of jealousy. I was a mum now. I couldn't see myself ever going out again.

After the first rush of guests had been and gone I had another pair of visitors. Or rather Ben did. It was his paternal grandparents, Cliff and Audrey Ward. They'd rung first and we'd agreed it was fine for them to come over. I didn't have any beef with them – in fact, they were both really nice. Initially, at least, it was quite awkward. Then I saw how much they were already in love with their grandson and any doubts were washed away.

They knew Simon wasn't supporting Ben so they did what they could. Instead of unloading a carload of toys and games that we'd never have got round to playing with, they gave me practical gifts: three months' worth of nappies, talcum powder, milk formula, bathing creams – essentials that they knew I'd have trouble affording. They were so very thoughtful. I just wished their son had half their class.

Ben was blessed with four of the best grandparents a child could wish for. But as wonderful as my dad, Cliff and Audrey were, I don't know what I would have done without my mother. From the moment Ben was born she was there. She was with me every step of the way in hospital, reassuring me, guiding me. She knew I was terrified of making a mistake. She also knew how tired I was. So when I had to get up at two in the morning for a feed, she got up with me. Then again at five and at eight. She could comfort Ben while I prepared the formula, or I changed a nappy while she did it. Even if she did nothing, just having the moral support was amazing. She was worth ten nurses. She really made me feel I deserved to be a mum. And I knew my son would never have a better person in his life than her.

Once the pressure of getting everything right subsided, I realised how much I loved being a mum. I'd always adored dolls, and for all my moaning I'd loved helping Mum bring up Danny, so I knew I had it in me. It was what I'd been put on earth to do, what I'd always dreamed of. I just hadn't expected it to happen quite so soon.

Christmases are special times for children. Ben's first was spent at Sandy Lodge. Danny was only ten and Stephen was still at school too, so there was a proper family environment. Cliff and Audrey came over with gifts on Boxing Day and the whole holiday period was high-spirited and fun, with good food, good company and thoughtful gifts. At the centre of it all was an oblivious little boy who couldn't have been more loved.

As we moved into 1990, I began to enjoy a little more freedom. Mum offered to look after Ben for the odd morning or afternoon and, after a few days agonising about it, I agreed. I didn't go very far the first time, even though I knew Mum and Dad would look after him as well as – if not better than – me. Gradually, I learnt to put the guilt aside and embrace my personal time. I started taking myself off to see friends or go shopping, or to just get some fresh air along the beach. After being cooped up for so long, having a few moments to myself was a godsend.

Other times I'd take Ben out in his pushchair to show him off to friends. They all thought he was cute but most of them were barely eighteen, like me, and even more immature. They couldn't imagine having a baby. Most only saw the negatives. They had no idea how someone so tiny and so young could be the best thing that had ever happened to me.

As I got more confident in my parenting skills I started travelling further afield. The first person I wanted to see down south was Grandma. Popping down to Sheffield to visit her, Granddad and my aunties and uncles became a regular occurrence. In the other direction, I had friends as far north as Mablethorpe, including my old boyfriend Darren Seabrook and his sister, Karen.

Once I had worked out which combination of buses would get me there, I set off.

After a lovely afternoon with them, I was heading back to the bus stop when I bumped into another new Mablethorpe resident. It was Shaun – Jane's husband and, more importantly, Simon's brother-in-law.

As much as I disliked Shaun, it was impossible to avoid him. So I said hello and enquired after his family. He seemed to take great relish telling me that they had a house guest I might be interested in: Simon.

'I know he'd love to see his boy. Why don't you come back with me?'

I should have ignored him. In the end, the idea of proving to Simon what he was missing out on – and with no parents to intervene – was just too tempting, and I followed Shaun home. A surprised Jane welcomed me in.

'I've come to see Simon,' I said, by way of explanation.

Jane looked at Shaun then back to me. 'Didn't Shaun tell you? Simon was staying but he's gone back to Wales.'

I didn't know who to be more cross with: Simon or Shaun. But Jane didn't let her husband's behaviour bother her, so I ignored it as well.

What I couldn't ignore was when Jane mentioned that Simon had been living there with another woman. My face must have told her everything.

'Oh my God – you didn't know?'

Jane didn't know where to look. As the apologies tumbled out of her, I caught my breath and calmed her down.

'Please, Jane, it doesn't matter.'

'But...'

'Seriously, I don't care. I've got no feelings for Simon anymore.' I looked down at the little bundle in my arms. 'I just thought he deserved to see his son.'

I was putting on a brave front, but that part was true.

Jane decided to ring Simon and for the first time since our hospital call we spoke. He said if I waited there he would come straight back. Like a fool, I said, 'Okay.' But afternoon passed into evening and evening into night. If he'd set off when he'd claimed he was going to, he could have walked it. At six in the morning I scooped Ben into his buggy and walked back to the bus stop. Letting me down was one thing. Letting his son down was something else.

One of the disadvantages of living in a bungalow is that sound travels. I'd heard the doorbell and vaguely registered Dad calling out to say he was answering it. I was putting Ben down at the time so my mind was elsewhere. Suddenly, there was a crash as door smashed into frame and I knew exactly who had called.

'The bloody cheek!' Dad was fuming. 'That was Simon. After all this time. He thinks he can swan up and play being a dad after leaving you in that pigsty! He's got another thing coming.'

'Where is he now?' I asked.

'What do you care? I slung him out. Told him to crawl back under whatever rock he's been hiding under for the last six months.'

I went back to putting Ben down and thought little more about it. Two days later, we had a call from Cliff. He said Simon was staying there and he felt his son should be allowed to see Ben. Would we mind having a family-to-family meeting to discuss the way forward? Dad's answer could be summed up in one two-letter word, but Mum and I outvoted him. I didn't want to fall out with Cliff and Audrey. And, as much as I hated Simon, it wasn't my right to deny Ben a father. He might have two 'mums', but a dad would be important later on. Especially for a boy.

The meeting began frostily but Cliff could calm any waters. I agreed that Simon should have access to Ben – within reason. He could either come to the bungalow or I would take Ben to his grandparents' house where Simon was staying. My only concern was that someone should be around. It had taken me weeks to gain the confidence to look after a baby. I knew Simon would need help, whether he admitted it or not.

Over the following weeks and months I saw more and more of Simon. We never once discussed what had gone on before. He acted like it had never happened and I preferred to pretend it hadn't. Then, one day he said he'd made a terrible mistake leaving me and would I ever consider giving him another chance?

I said yes.

I couldn't have been thinking straight. It's as if Simon had the power to bewitch me. I was so desperate to give Ben a father I thought it would be easier if we were all together. And I knew I couldn't stay at Mum and Dad's for ever, but I also knew I didn't want to be alone. Getting back with Simon just seemed to make sense. Even if the love I'd had for him was gone.

Leaving Mum and Dad was harder this time. They'd had the initial reactions I'd expected, then calmed down. I had to make my own decisions and my own mistakes; that was always their policy. This time, however, there was a real sadness in Mum's eyes, almost like I'd betrayed her. Because it wasn't just me leaving home. I was taking Ben, her beloved Ben. I couldn't have hurt her more if I'd tried.

Simon got a job with his brother's decorating business and we secured a two-bedroom council maisonette in the Norfolk Park area of Sheffield. It wasn't a palace but it was clean and it had white walls. For someone with the right imagination it was perfect, a blank canvas, and Simon certainly had ideas. The first thing he did was put up a wall blocking off the lounge and dining area so we had two separate rooms – Dad loved knocking walls down, and I'd found a man who loved doing the opposite.

Animals intrigued Ben. He liked pointing at dogs and cats and birds when we were out and about, so we decorated his room with pictures of wildlife and jungle creatures and put a shelf near his bed for his fluffy toys. At five months, he liked playing with his bed sheet as much as the cuddly bears people had bought him, but I could see where his interests lay.

Ben was too young to say if he missed his Nan and Granddad but I know I did. You're not meant to say this, but rattling around in a maisonette every day with just a baby for company can get on top of any mother. I could see my grandma or Jane, and Mum was only a phone call away but, most days, from the time Simon went out in the morning to the point he returned, I often didn't speak to another adult. The only other children we saw were at the park every day. I admit, I was lonely. But it was my choice and it was the best for Ben. I had to remind myself of that. Ben's security had to come first.

I tried to fill our days as much as possible. I thought he'd like going to the rare breed animal park to see the pigs and sheep and miniature ponies, and mostly he enjoyed it. The huge pigs with tusks scared him. I don't know if he thought they were dangerous or whether he decided they were just ugly. If they came close he'd squeeze me hard and bury his face in my neck.

Bearing in mind how we spent our days together, I wasn't surprised to hear Ben's first word: 'Mum'. I knew it wasn't an accident. He was looking directly at me with his big blue eyes when he said it. I was so happy I spent the rest of the day trying to make him say it again.

Within a few weeks he had quite a vocabulary based on what he could see. 'Bott' – short for 'bottle', because he didn't have a dummy – was another early word. Of course, 'cat' and 'dog' came out very early, along with 'bick bick' – biscuit – and 'toast'. And Simon got the shock of his life one evening when he came through the door and Ben cried out, 'Dada!' It's almost worth going out just so you can see the delight on a baby's face when you return.

Apart from my loneliness, I think we were genuinely a happy little family. Simon was conscientious about his work and he always had the time and inclination to do things around the maisonette at weekends. What had happened before was still unspoken. I just knew he wanted things to be right for us this

time. When he came home one day with a present for me, I realised how much he wanted it.

'What's this?' I asked, although I could see it was clearly a
ring box.

'I thought we should get engaged.'

'Well, that's romantic.'

I couldn't hide the sarcasm and we both laughed. It wasn't
exactly a scene from Mills & Boon. Even so, it's not every day you
have a marriage proposal, so of course I said yes.

Did I love him? Once again, I was putting my family first. At
the same time, I was putting my roots down further in Sheffield.
But I knew that if Simon and I were married, there would be no
chance of me ever returning to my family's home.

*Maybe that was behind Mum making a decision that would
soon change all our lives for ever.*

It was Ben's first birthday and everyone came to spoil him
rotten at our house. He wasn't that bothered about presents but
he did love being the centre of attention. He loved the radio being
on. He'd pull himself up against a chair or hold my hands and just
bop around. Doing it for an audience seemed to be his favourite
thing in the world. The more people looking and laughing at him,
the more he would carry on giggling and dancing. He was a little
star in the making.

We'd had a lovely day and Mum and I were washing up when
she announced, 'I need to tell you something. We're moving to Kos.'

'What do you mean you're moving there? You've only just
got back!'

Ben and I had left Chapel St Leonards in March. In June, Mum
and Dad had taken the boys to Kos for a fortnight with Mum's

sister Anne and her husband Terry. It was the first time ever the family had been abroad. I was really happy for all of them – even though I knew that if I'd still been living at home, Ben and I would have been put on a plane as well. On the other hand, had we never have left Chapel, maybe that holiday might never have happened. I got the feeling Mum was so hurt by me taking her grandson away she wanted an escape. Where better to escape to than a Greek island in summer?

They'd sent postcards and come back raving about it, so I knew they'd enjoyed their trip. Mum even said she wanted to move there. But who hasn't said that after a brilliant vacation? There is a difference between loving a holiday and emigrating to the place. It was an infatuation. It would wear off, I was convinced of it.

Only it hadn't. Mum had become depressed when they'd returned and started nagging at Dad to move to Kos. Like me, he'd dismissed it as post-holiday blues. But as the weeks passed, Mum continued to ask the same thing over and over:

'Well, why can't we?'

Then one day Dad answered. 'I don't know. Let's do it.'

They sold up, bought a large caravan and an old Land Rover to tow it, then Dad spent a couple of months refurbishing both in his spare time. Finally, at the start of December, they were ready. Ben and I went up to wave them off. I needed to see it with my own eyes.

I was trying not to cry but you'd never have guessed. Mum and I were in floods. Luckily, Ben only had eyes for his uncles in the back of the Land Rover and their new travelling companion – a corgi they'd rescued, who happened also to be called Ben.

Eventually Dad prised me and Mum apart and they got going. Even as they pulled away I saw Mum repeat the words she'd said so often over the weeks:

'Come with us.'

She knew I couldn't. She knew I had a life of my own in Sheffield with Simon and Ben. Maybe that was her final shot at saving me from that life.

I'd broken my parents' hearts by running away from them. Now they were running away from me.

Christmas Day, 1990. I remember it clearly as the first I'd ever spent away from my family. Even though we had a great time with Simon's brother Steve and his wife Diane at their house, there wasn't a moment I wasn't thinking about my parents.

Ben had a lovely Christmas and received a lot of presents, including various Dinky toy cars and cuddly toys. His favourites were animal-related: a plastic set of sheep, cows and ducks. He couldn't stop playing with them and making the animals' noises. He was walking by now – barefoot if he could get away with it; he hated shoes – so he also managed to do his own physical impressions. I could have watched him all day, it was so funny. The only downside was knowing that Mum was missing out.

She wasn't the only one.

I'd been jealous of my family the second they set off. Within a week I wished I'd gone with them; after a fortnight I was having serious doubts about my decision to stay in Sheffield. My family had played such an important part of my adult life. I saw them at least every other weekend and we spoke most days on the phone. They'd always been there for me, even when I'd appeared to be fleeing in the opposite direction. Now I was the one left behind – and I hated it. The idea of not seeing them for months or years was heartbreaking.

At least I knew they were thinking about me. Via postcards and letters I was able to track my family's movements through France, across the Alps into Italy and down towards the Greek border. On a good day I got a photograph as well. On 12 January 1991, I received a snap of my brothers splashing around in the sea with the caption: 'Having a bath, Mediterranean style!' I loved having this window into their adventure but at the same time it was killing me not being part of it. Each morning that passed without a note from Mum was another day that dragged by.

Finally I got the message I'd been waiting for. They'd arrived in Kos and parked the caravan on Ramira Beach, the first stretch of public space they'd come across. After a few days, Dad had done his usual trick of finding a man who knew a man who said they could move officially to a space in a field in a coastal area called Paradisi.

'Honestly, Kerry,' Mum wrote, 'it's Paradisi by name – and Paradise by nature.'

Occasionally Mum would say she'd phone on a certain date. Knowing the international switchboard as I did, I was in place at the phone box an hour early and at least that afterwards if Mum didn't ring. But when she did get through I'd spend most of the time in tears. She did, too. Our blubbering cost her a fortune! There were some words I always made out: there'd be a sniffle then quiet, then Mum would say, 'Come out and join us.' I laughed every time. I couldn't join them. I had my son, my fiancé, my home and my life. Why would I want to give all that up?

Instead, I'd promise to send her packages of Oxo cubes and Branston Pickle, and other home comforts they were missing.

Then one day I surprised us both by saying, 'Okay, I'm coming out there.'

'You're what?'

'Mum, I'm bringing Ben to Kos.'

She was over the moon, of course, and we spent an excited hour making plans. Mum told me how to apply for a passport, what to pack, where to buy tickets. She even said she'd send over the money for our fares. At the end of it all she said, 'What about Simon?'

I didn't know what to think about him. Right then, I wondered whether to tell him anything at all.

'You can't just leave without a word,' Mum said. 'That's an awful thing to do.'

'You're right, it is horrible. But he did it to me.'

CHAPTER FIVE

I'VE LOST HIM

I swear Gatwick Airport was bigger than any town I'd ever been to. When you've just got off an overnight, five-hour National Express coach journey, it seems even more alien. Although it was pitch-black outside, the whole building was illuminated like a film set. I was nineteen years old and completely out of my depth.

Ben took it all in his stride. Dressed in his favourite red dungarees, a little white shirt and trainers, and clutching his favourite cow from his farmyard animal set, he just toddled alongside me as I tried to fathom where to go. I don't think he'd ever seen so many people in one place. He loved it. He kept stopping, pointing at one of the brightly lit shop fronts, and saying, 'Pretty.' He was such a content little fellow. Nothing fazed him.

I wish I could say the same for me. I kept repeating, 'We're going to see Nana, we're going to see Nana,' as much to remind myself of why I was putting us through this ordeal as to comfort him.

I'd not so much as set foot on a boat before, let alone a plane. I was terrified, but I couldn't show it. If Ben got a sniff that I was scared he'd be uncontrollable. I had to make him think that whatever was about to happen was the most normal thing in the world. Like a bus with wings.

That's easy enough when you're strapping yourself and your little boy in. It becomes a lot harder when you hear the roar of the engines, you're flung back into your seat and all you can think is, *How is this huge lump of metal that's bigger than the coach we travelled down in ever going to get off the ground?*

The air stewardesses were lovely and because there were spare seats either side of us, they let Ben have his own one until landing, when he'd have to go back on my lap. Keeping him occupied for four hours was a challenge but we had his animals and colouring-in books, and there was a meal that was more distracting than filling. By the time he fell asleep after it, I was exhausted.

As I looked out of the window across the vast expanse of white clouds, I thought about what I was doing. Was I mad, upping sticks and travelling to a country I'd never even visited? It was one thing Mum and Dad doing it. They had careers, skills, experience, a bit of money behind them. I was a teenage mum with a toddler. What on earth was I going to do there?

At least I'd have Simon. I'd relented and told him about my plans and he hadn't exploded. He knew how much I missed my family and how it was breaking my heart being separated from them. Even so, when I asked him to come and start afresh over there, I was surprised when he said, 'Okay.' Maybe I was even a bit disappointed. Still, with all three of us going, the excitement in the house for a few weeks was tangible.

We agreed that Simon would stay and sell up our larger belongings, then join me and Ben when he'd settled everything. That might take a week, maybe a month. At least with his building background, he wouldn't have trouble finding work.

If take-off had been challenging then landing was an ordeal

from start to finish. Ben was still sound asleep when the seatbelt signs went on. I managed to scoop him up and got him safely belted in, and I just hoped he'd stay asleep till we touched down. I didn't want him to see me panicking.

Mum had warned me what to expect but nothing can prepare you for that sensation as the plane slows and starts to sink through the clouds, leaving your tummy higher up. *We're going to crash!* was all I could think. When Ben woke up screaming I thought at first he knew something I didn't. He was clutching his head and I realised his ears must have popped like mine as the cabin pressure dropped. Even asleep he must have felt it, but unlike me he didn't have a boiled sweet to suck on. He freaked out, inconsolable. There was nothing I could say or do to comfort or distract him; not pointing out the view of white buildings for as far as the eye could see, not even saying over and over, again and again, 'We're going to see Nana, we're going to see Nana.'

At least it took my mind off crashing, although even as I held my breath then gasped as the wheels of the Monarch airliner bounced down and the brakes squealed into action, I knew what Ben didn't.

We'd be doing it all again in a couple of hours' time.

It was 21 April 1991 and, as far as the tourist industry was concerned, still 'closed season', so there wouldn't be any direct flights to Kos until the demand picked up later in the year. Consequently, Mum had told me to get to Athens then buy a domestic flight ticket to complete the journey. It sounded pretty straightforward. Mum said I had enough cash for a taxi to the domestic terminal and for flights to Kos. There wouldn't be much change so I had to be frugal. That's why we'd brought a packed lunch.

Ben was still upset as we reached the exit on the Monarch. Then the heat off the runway took his breath away and he just stared with wonder. I was doing the same. Even that early in the year, it was very, very warm. By Sheffield standards, it felt like stepping into a bath.

We went through passport control and found our luggage without a hitch. There was a rank of taxis immediately outside so we climbed in one and began stage three of our journey. I couldn't get over how blue and uninterrupted the sky was, even so close to the terminal. I had such a good feeling about everything. We just needed to get through the trial of one more flight.

In fact, there was another hurdle much closer at hand.

As we pulled up outside the domestic terminal, I counted 2,000 drachmas from the small bundle in my purse. That was how much Mum had said the fare should be. That was how much I'd budgeted for. I lifted Ben out and we joined the cab driver at the boot of the car. As he flipped up the lid he said, '4,000 drachma.'

I'd already handed it over before I realised he hadn't said 2,000.

He looked at the notes in my hand and shook his head. '4,000.'

'That's not right.' I couldn't think of anything else to say. 'It should be half that.'

He shrugged and closed the boot again – with our bags still inside.

'4,000,' he repeated.

I felt like the wind had been knocked out of me. I'd only been in the country ten minutes and I was messing it up already. I could feel the tears welling. I wanted to be so strong for Ben. Now it was all going wrong. If I handed over another 2,000 drachmas, would I still be able to afford an aeroplane ticket? But what choice did

I have? We hadn't packed many things, but the bags in that boot contained all the possessions Ben and I had left in the world.

Welcome to Greece.

Ten minutes later, with Ben in one arm and dragging our bags with the other, I managed to find the ticket queue. According to the departures board in the hall, there was a flight leaving in under an hour. I took a deep breath and forced myself to picture Mum's smiling face when we arrived. 'We're going to see Nana.'

When I reached the desk my worst fears became a reality. I was exactly 5,000 drachmas – about £11 – short of the ticket price. Not only had I overpaid the taxi driver but in my fluster to find the inflated price, I must have dropped some notes from my purse. The woman behind the counter waited for me to pay but I couldn't even move. I just stood there, shell-shocked, disbelief and rage fighting to be uppermost, as I stared at the space in my purse where the rest of the money should have been. For a few moments the world disappeared; Ben, the sales assistant, the airport itself, all vanished as I tried to think what to do. Then the dam burst and the tears came gushing out. I was so angry with myself for ruining everything. We were never going to get to Kos now.

It was all that cab driver's fault. I hated him. I hated Greece. I hated Greeks. I wished I'd never come.

Then I felt a hand tap me on the shoulder and I turned to see a man in a suit gesturing past me towards the cashier. They had a brief conversation, then he reached into his pocket and pulled out 5,000 drachmas and pressed it into my palm. I was stunned. I watched it happen, I felt the warm squeeze of his hand in mine and I couldn't take it in. *This isn't happening to me.* But it was. I was still crying but laughing at the same time. I must have looked a complete mess but I didn't care. This wonderful, wonderful stranger had just saved the day and with it, it seemed to me, my whole life. I hugged him as hard as I could with one arm then, clasping our tickets like they were gold, I ran over to the check-in with a couple of minutes to spare. I'd changed my mind about the locals. They were incredible!

There was a visible military presence everywhere inside the terminal so I wasn't surprised to see a soldier stationed near the desk when I arrived, still panting. But the breath I had left was well and truly knocked out of me when he put his arm out in a 'stop' gesture.

What have I done now?

I realised the soldier was standing close enough to the ticket desk to have seen what had just gone on. Did he think I was a conman? That I'd duped the businessman into handing over money? Was I going to be arrested? What would happen to Ben?

So many questions in so short a time, and all the while the soldier still had his hand reaching out. Confused, I noticed there was something in it. *Money.*

'Good luck,' he said, in a thick Greek accent, and held out another 500 drachmas. Yes, he had seen everything and he felt sorry for me.

My natural response was to hug the life out of him. One look at the machine gun across his chest stopped me so I just smiled, wiped away the tears, and said, 'Thank you.' Ben was disappointed. Long after the soldier was out of sight, he was still saying, 'Gun. Gun. Gun.'

With a send-off like that I felt capable of flying the ninety minutes to Kos on my own. Once I saw the tiny propeller-powered

Olympic plane waiting on the runway, I wished I could. But it was fine. Nothing could ruin things now. After what I'd just experienced, after twenty-four hours of travelling, I really felt we were on our way to paradise.

I thought I knew the sea. I'd lived by it for long enough and spent all my teen summers in or near it. As the little Olympic Airlines plane left the beigey-white expanse of mainland Greece behind, I realised the brown dishwater waves of the North Sea around Skegness were unrecognisable compared to the turquoise carpet of ocean beneath me now. It was blue, blue, blue for as far as I could see. Goosebumps ran down my arms. I wasn't cold; I was excited.

Landing passed without incident and we made it through the customs checks and into the arrivals lounge. But where was our welcoming committee? I scanned the whole hall and couldn't spot a single familiar face. I tried to keep cool but after everything else, I was panicking. I knew my parents' address but I had no money for a taxi or a bus to get there. Then I wondered, *Is something wrong?*

Fighting the growing desire to scream, I put my bag down by a pillar and walked as far as I dared in every direction. For a second I thought I saw someone who looked like Stephen with long hair, but I dismissed him and carried on scanning the faces. Ben was amazingly cheerful if not very helpful. He kept saying, 'Where's Nana? Where's Nana?' which just made me feel even more uptight.

Just about holding it together, I trudged back to the bags – and saw my dad, my mum, Danny and Ben the dog, followed by a long-haired Stephen. It *had* been him! They all looked so amazingly healthy. Glowing tans were one thing, but they all had the look of people without a care in the world. You could tell just by looking that they were happy, and not just because we'd arrived. Whatever new lives they'd carved for themselves on Kos, it was working. I'd never seen bigger smiles on anyone in my life.

Ben nearly fell out of my arms as he flung himself towards his nan. His little legs were running in mid-air just trying to get to her. I thought I was all cried out but I could feel a few more drops coming. This was where I was meant to be.

We all piled into the Land Rover and drove back to Paradisi and the caravan. It was a forty-minute journey but it felt like seconds. Everyone was in party mood, talking fifteen to the dozen. Ben was being barraged by questions left, right and centre but he just wanted to talk to his namesake in the back. I couldn't take my eyes off the scenery: olive trees covered the hills, while rows of pure whitewashed-brick villas lined the streets. The further we got from the airport, the more I started spotting old women dressed head to toe in black. It was like a uniform. My family, all sporting shorts and T-shirts, couldn't have stood out more. Above it all was the light blue sky, as endless and unspoilt as the ocean had been on the way here. If I weren't holding Ben so tightly I would have pinched myself. It was like stepping onto Fantasy Island.

Greek drivers like to use their horns every couple of seconds, so it was a relief when Dad finally pulled off the road, turned down a short drive, then parked outside a familiar-looking caravan. The last time I'd seen it, it was looking the worse for wear outside their home in Chapel St Leonards. Now it was surrounded by olive and fig trees on one side, the driveway at the front and fields everywhere else. It might not have been everyone's cup of tea, but to me it looked magical.

What Dad had rented was originally an overgrown patch of field. A few months later, their little domain was worthy of an episode of *Grand Designs*. Dad and Stephen had hacked down the foliage and cut back all the trees and bushes, leaving the caravan in a picturesque clearing with views of green whichever way they looked. They'd put up a cane fence all the way round and turned it into their own private haven, with large vegetable patches on one side and a beautiful seat carved out of a tree on the other. They'd even built a shelter so they could sit outside without danger from the sun. Mum hadn't been exaggerating – Paradisi really was idyllic.

Ben saw it, too. As soon as he was released from the Land Rover he pulled his shoes and socks off and ran off to explore. He hadn't got far when he turned and called out, 'Nanny, get me, get me, get me!' Greek grass, as he had just discovered, wasn't like English grass. It is coarse and spiky and quite vicious if you have such tender young skin. After that experience, Ben wouldn't go anywhere without company. And certainly not without his shoes and socks.

Mum was relieved when she finally caught up with him.

'Look what I've got for you, Ben.'

She led us to the other side of the shelter where the grass was shortest. There was a paddling pool, already filled with water warmed by the sun, a tricycle, a pushchair, a cot, buckets, spades – you name it, Mum had it ready for us. After the generosity I'd experienced that day, very little could have surprised me, but this took my breath away. Mum had borrowed everything from friends whose own children had moved on to other things. Ben didn't know what to play with first.

Eventually, Mum managed to drag us into the caravan for the guided tour.

'This is where Nana lives, Ben,' she said, and let him run into her bedroom. Then she led us into the lounge and explained to Ben that the sofas there would convert into beds later on. 'This is your and Mummy's bed. Can you imagine it?'

I was worried about space but Mum said, 'Stephen hasn't slept in here for weeks.' It was so hot he preferred to take his pillow and sheet and sleep on the roof of the empty chicken coop at the back of the caravan, like Snoopy.

Ben and I were so tired that after a light meal outside we snuggled down for the night in our new home. I'm sure I was still smiling as I drifted off.

Hearing Ben squeal with laughter was a wonderful way to wake up. I lay listening to him for a few seconds before I sat bolt upright, head spinning round. Where was I? I couldn't help smiling as I remembered.

If anything, day two in Kos was even better. The caravan was fifteen minutes from Psalidi beach, so that's where we all headed. As many happy memories as I had of the dunes and shelters at Chapel, Psalidi was out of this world. Watching Ben busy with his bucket and spade, or making friends with the few other people out in April, made my heart swell. He was so content, so happy to mess around in the surf with his uncles, or introduce himself to strangers. There could not have been a prouder mummy.

Each day passed like a scene from a blissful holiday postcard. In the evenings we would eat out at local tavernas. I'd never heard of dishes like *souvlaki* or *saganaki* but before long they were my regular order. Greek people, Dad explained, rarely ate at home. Because the weather was so nice, they preferred to dine outside, at restaurants or bars, with as many other people as possible. They were an incredibly sociable people. I saw families of twenty eating out together on a weekday night, children in tow. There was no special occasion. That's just how they were.

Ben slipped easily into that lifestyle. As soon as he'd finished his meal he'd be wandering around the other tables making friends with any other children present or just smiling and giggling at the grown-ups. He had such a cheeky face he was always met with a tickle or a pat on the head. What he liked most, though, was seeing all the stray cats and dogs prowling around the taverna entrance. As quickly as the bar owners and waiters were shooing the animals away, Ben was snatching meat from his plate or those of strangers and throwing it over to the nearest little kitty.

Despite the age gaps – ten and sixteen years respectively – Ben, Danny and Stephen got on like brothers. If Danny could have skipped school to play with Ben he would have done (although he probably would have skipped school even to wash up, given half the chance). Danny loved playing his Elvis CDs and Ben would dance away. With Stephen, Ben had a harder choice: go exploring for animals or have little rides on the back of Stephen's 50cc motorbike. They'd only pootle around the caravan site at about two miles an hour, with Stephen keeping a firm grip of Ben, so there was no danger of accidents, but to look at Ben's face you'd think he was breaking the sound barrier.

By day four I can honestly say I hadn't thought of England once. Kos was my home now. I was with my parents and I was with my son. My fiancé would be joining as soon as he could. Even if he didn't, there was nothing for me at home any more.

Dad and Stephen had found building work on some of the many half-finished properties in the area. Poor Danny was enrolled at a school for Greek children, which he hated. That left Mum free to spend time with us. She was also free in the evenings, and soon offered to babysit Ben if I wanted to go out with Stephen. My brother had already scouted the local hostelries and had a few he wanted to take me to. Most of them, it seemed, were on a stretch of road called 'Bar Street', for obvious reasons.

As the season was still barely alive the bars weren't that full: the customers they did have were mostly Greek. That didn't matter. After sharing every night under the same roof as Ben from the moment we'd left Sandy Lodge, it was just so refreshing to get out of the house, to have a bit of time to myself, to let my hair down.

Kos wasn't expensive by any means. Still, it wasn't fair to expect my parents to keep me and, after asking around, I heard there was a job going about a ten-minute walk from the caravan. The Palm Beach Hotel was looking for someone to work breakfast and evening shifts in the dining room, as well as spend afternoons frying and serving poolside snacks. I obviously said something right at the interview because not only did the manager, a young guy called Manos, offer me a position, he also agreed to take on my mum as well.

The last thing I wanted was to be away from Ben but without Simon around to support us, what choice did I have? In any case, Ben was just as happy playing with his grandparents and uncles as he was spending time with me. If I'm honest, he probably enjoyed having a break from seeing my face all the time. I know Mum in particular would have looked after him every minute if I'd let her. She loved having him.

We quickly fell into a routine. If I was working lunchtimes, I'd push Ben over to Mum's, leave him there and go to work. If I stayed to do the evening shift as well, then Ben would sleep at the caravan. Or if I was on breakfasts, I would drop him off the night before. Mum only worked the lunchtime shift and never when I was on, so there was never a problem with childcare.

Far from resenting me working, I think Ben enjoyed it because of the perks. Manos insisted that my family feel free to use the hotel's facilities at any time so, while I sweated away dishing up French fries and burgers, I was able to watch my son bobbing up and down in the water in his arm bands while either Stephen, Danny or Mum kept him company. I once saw him take a stray cat into the shallow end with him, much to the cat's displeasure – Mum was laughing too hard to stop him.

When I wasn't working, I'd take Ben to the beach. Mum would usually come and so too would her friend Athena and her son, Alex. Alex had just turned three so it was mostly his toys and clothes that Mum had acquired for Ben. Athena and her husband Dino were lovely people and it rubbed off on Alex. Watching him and Ben play together, they could have been brothers.

Ben loved the beach. It was like being at the swimming pool but the water was bigger and better. Before he could go near either, of course, he had to be covered in sun cream. The Greeks used to say the April and May sun was worse than summer so it was important to keep children covered. I think Ben was drilled a bit too well. I was watching him toddle around one time, in his own world, when he stopped next to a couple of sleeping sunbathers.

I turned for a second to get Mum's attention. When we looked back, Ben had found a tube of lotion from somewhere and was slapping it extremely liberally onto his chest and arms. By the time I got over there, the sunbathers had woken up – which was not surprising, considering the amount of cream splattered over their legs. I was so embarrassed at my tiny little tealeaf, but they laughed it off. Then, as I stood with them, Ben found someone *else's* bag and dived down into that instead. It was a full-time job keeping him out of other people's belongings. To strangers he must have looked so cute helping himself. I only saw the mischievous little urchin who'd disobeyed my instruction.

On days when I worked afternoon and evening shifts, I'd spend the hour in between diving and sunbathing. After the evening shift I would often stroll over to the bar and have a beer with the two guys who ran it. Martin and Peter were both English, so they got on well with the mostly British clientele, but they were also nice lads. It was really great to be able to unwind with them when my shift finished at ten o'clock. I'd sit at the bar, they'd be on the other side, and we'd put the world to rights for half an hour or so until I began the walk home.

Mum didn't last long at Palm Beach. I think she preferred looking after her grandson to working. Fortunately for the family, Dad and Stephen won a new contract at the same time Mum was handing in her notice. Dad's sociable nature had so far been responsible for them getting the plot for the caravan, acquiring all the kit for Ben from friends and getting my apartment at a knockdown price. Now he had met a man in a bar who had a proposition. His wife's family had a rundown farmhouse up in the hills in a village called Iraklis. It was her dream to renovate the property to its pre-war glory. And it was her husband's lot to do whatever she wanted.

The man was called Michaelis Kypreos and he really was a good sort. As well as providing jobs for our two men, he said Dad could move the caravan up to the site and take advantage of the free water and electricity connections that ran to the dilapidated cottage. Not only would they be getting a wage and free utilities, they wouldn't have to pay rent on the premises – and they'd never have an excuse for being late for work.

When you're nineteen, you don't always appreciate how fortunate you are. Looking back, everything seemed to be falling into place. We didn't need to earn much to have a decent lifestyle in Kos. Even when drachmas were tight, the sun and people's happy faces more than compensated for it. As the weeks passed and the temperatures rose, the hotel got busier as all of Kos seemed to come alive. It was like being back in Chapel again with the weekly or fortnightly turnover of fresh blood, the only difference being the ones arriving here were pale and those heading home were tanned – or burnt.

As more tourists arrived, the harder the bars worked to get you in. There were some great offers on cocktails and beers, and I have to thank Stephen for not being slow in exposing me to this side of the island. There is nothing in the world better or more satisfying than being a mum. But at nineteen there was a part of me that was fulfilled just being out with people my own age, having a drink, having fun, having conversations with strangers you'd never see again. As Stephen said: 'It's all very well having lovely friends like Athena and her husband Dino, but they're our parents' age. You're missing out. You need to be out with people as young as you.'

My only experience of clubs and bars had been when I was a schoolgirl. It made such a change to not have to lie about my age. I'd pretended to be eighteen then. Now I could go in with my head held high (and laugh at the dozens who were clearly underage).

In the space of four or five weeks I went from a timid little housewife to a fully rounded woman with my own personality. I really came out of myself. I acquired some confidence I never knew existed and, once or twice a week, I let my hair down, enjoyed the company of others and felt like Kerry Needham for once. I hadn't felt this free since my days of boob tubes and braids, during my Madonna and Boy George phase.

I'm sure my happiness spread to my role as a mum. I've met so many parents who can't help taking out their frustrations on their children. They feel held back somehow. I was lucky. I could indulge myself every now and then and know that Mum was looking after Ben with as much care as she'd ever looked after us.

Occasionally Mum and Dad went out as well. Normally this didn't affect me. Ben and I would be at our apartment, none the wiser. But one day I arrived for dinner at the caravan as planned. I was on breakfast duty the next day, so Ben needed to be there overnight. When we arrived, everyone was rushing around and Mum announced she and Dad were going out straight after eating. Normally I would have gone back home, but she said would I mind stopping over? Obviously, I didn't need to be asked twice. We had a lovely meal under the stars as usual, then I put Ben to bed and waved off my parents. The fact that Danny and Stephen went with them was the only thing that upset me. *I know I couldn't go anyway, because of Ben, but my whole family's having fun and they haven't even invited me.*

73

I reminded myself that I had my own family now and settled down for an early night myself. I don't know how long had passed but it only felt like minutes till I heard Mum and Dad clattering back in. You never got privacy sleeping on the lounge beds but it was as though they were trying to wake me. I rolled over and looked at the bunch of gigglers in the doorway. It took a few seconds before I realised there was one too many.

'Simon?'

'Hello, Kerry. Surprised?'

So that was where they'd all gone – to pick Simon up from the airport. When my brain eventually woke up, I realised I was surprised: he'd done it. He'd cut our ties back home and come out to start life afresh with me and Ben. In other words, he'd put as much distance between him and his parents as I'd had between me and mine. I honestly never thought he would.

After showing Simon around our little corner of the island, we settled into a proper family life. Ben treated him as though he'd never been away. Like so many other things, he took Simon's absence and sudden reappearance in his stride.

Confident that we were serious and happy about staying, Dad drove us about ten minutes away to a place called Kako Prinari – or the 'Turkish village' as it was known. A friend had a small apartment to rent at 'mate's rates' and so for about 10,000 drachmas a month, we got our own little slice of paradise. It was virtually the extension to his friend's house and it was very basic and small, but if it kept me in Kos then I was happy. There were three rooms – bedroom, living area and bathroom, all divided by a curtain rather than a wall – plus the smallest kitchen I'd ever seen, tacked onto the living space. It had a cooker with one ring and a single baby saucepan. I couldn't even comfortably warm a tin of soup on it. Mum's kitchen in the caravan was bigger.

Size didn't matter to Ben, or to the army of ants that marched through the apartment each day. Ben thought they were his pets. He loved scooting them along, saying, 'Hurry up, hurry up,' or letting them climb up his hand. I tolerated them until the day I realised they were pouring from the sink and the drawers, and even the cupboard where our food was stored.

Dad helped Simon get a job on a building site and we soon settled down to a proper family life. We both worked, Mum was on hand to look after Ben whenever necessary, and there were even times we could go out together at night. That was a treat we had never experienced when we lived in Sheffield.

Whether it was my new self-confidence or whether Simon felt out of his depth, the honeymoon period didn't last long. He began arguing with his employers and was soon seeking a new position. Within a couple of weeks, the same thing happened again and suddenly he was out of work. That was the point at which he seemed to resent me going to Palm Beach every day. The more he sat at home twiddling his thumbs or – worse – looked after our son day after day – the greater the theories of what I got up to grew in his head. Especially when I didn't return from an evening shift until midnight.

Almost inevitably, the arguments began. Although Simon started the fights, usually late at night when I came home, I admit I rarely bit my tongue. So what if he didn't like being stuck with a child to look after? It was his child, and I'd done it for eighteen months. Now it was his turn.

I could see Simon wasn't enjoying life in Kos as much as I was but I wasn't prepared to compromise. I couldn't be held responsible for his failure to fit in. Still, I don't think I realised how hard he was taking it. The crunch came when I was on an evening shift and I heard a commotion in the hotel foyer. With the open-plan layout, sounds carried, and I couldn't help picking out Simon's voice from the din. I also knew he was drunk.

By the time I had made my excuses to my colleague and run to reception he'd gone, but Manos, the manager – and the owner's son – was nursing a sore nose and eye. Simon had accused him of having an affair with me. That's what the fuss had been. Manos had laughed the accusation off, obviously, which had goaded Simon into punching him. He must have regretted it because he fled immediately. I tore out onto the road but there was no sign of him. He'd either sprinted away or was hiding. He clearly didn't want to see me. At least, not the new, confident, self-sufficient me.

Simon arrived on the island on 12 June 1991. Within a month he was making plans to return to Sheffield. So much for our new life. But he hadn't given up on us. He wanted Ben and me to accompany him. For all his stupid behaviour, I couldn't bring myself to dismiss the idea out of hand.

'If you go back, get yourself a job with prospects – none of your door-to-door selling, and you find us a home – a proper, decent, respectable home – and you call me, I will come back. But I'm not giving up this life for what we had before.'

I was firm. I was also convinced I'd set the bar so high I'd never hear from him again. And if he did achieve what I'd requested, well, I'd face that dilemma then.

Then, on 22 July I said, 'See you later,' to Simon and walked Ben to the caravan as usual. Mum drove Simon to the port and she and Ben waved him off. As the ferry began its voyage to Athens I was probably serving a dozen *souvlaki* and chips. By the time I got home after the evening shift, he would have been back in the UK. I didn't give it a second thought.

My concern, obviously, was Ben. I didn't want to tell him Simon was gone for good so I explained that Daddy was popping home to see his brothers and sisters. That seemed to work. Walking to Mum's over the next couple of days, Ben was as chipper as ever. I suppose Simon hadn't been in his life as much as he could have been. It would have left a larger void for him if my own dad had disappeared.

Life very quickly settled back to normal. I didn't work the evening shift on the 23rd so Ben and I stayed at the apartment together. In keeping with the Greek style of children staying up with their families till ten, eleven, even midnight, then catching up on sleep with afternoon siestas, Ben and I went to bed quite late. Normally, he wouldn't stir till about eight or nine the next day. On this particular day, he decided to have a lie-in. For the afternoon shift I needed to be at Palm Beach by eleven, which meant leaving Ben at Mum's thirty minutes earlier. That, as I looked at him dead to the world at half past nine, was looking less and less likely. Despite me making as much noise as possible as I showered and dressed, he somehow slept through.

When Ben eventually came to, the last thing on his mind was my time-keeping dilemma. The second he opened his eyes he just wanted to play and no amount of me asking him to get dressed had any effect. Even when I picked up his clothes for him, he ran off giggling around the other side of the bed. It wasn't the hugest flat in the world but when you're chasing a toddler it could feel like it. I managed to pin Ben down and get a vest over his head and socks on his feet. By the time I pulled on his shorts the socks had been torn off. I gave it one more go then admitted defeat. It wouldn't be the first time he just wore sandals without socks.

Obviously, that was the day Ben's pushchair was at the caravan so I had no comeback when he demanded to ride on his bike instead. I was aware of the clock ticking away but what was being a few minutes late to work compared to the happiness of my son?

Ben's bike was actually a tricycle which was still slightly too large for him. As his feet couldn't quite reach the pedals, Dad had tied some rope to the handlebars so I could drag it along. Ben seemed happy enough with that, although typically this was the morning he saw more butterflies and crickets and cats and cows than usual, and he wanted to stop at every one. Eventually I realised there was no hurrying him that day so we arrived at the caravan after the time I was meant to already have left. It wasn't the end of the world. It just meant I'd need to prepare the salads and crockery for the lunchtime snacks in half the time. I wasn't going to skip breakfast with Mum and Ben for that.

I had a coffee and a happy fifteen minutes chatting while Ben tackled a boiled egg and bread soldiers. It was just as well he wasn't dressed properly as most of it splattered everywhere apart from his mouth. Mum put a tea towel round his neck as a bib but that didn't stop him smearing his whole face. And hands. And lap. He couldn't have been happier, but I was glad I wouldn't be tidying up.

Before I left I asked Mum what her plans for the day were.

'Oh, I don't know. I was thinking of visiting Athena. Or we might pop into town. I haven't decided yet.'

'Okay, well, have fun.' I kissed her goodbye then tried to do the same to Ben without getting too much egg on my face. 'Love you, both.'

Walking, I'd be half an hour late for work. If I ran, it would just be fifteen minutes. Electing for somewhere in between, I jogged along, smiling at the memory of Ben sitting with his tea towel bib and a big, yellow smile. If I'd known that would be my last memory of him I would have concentrated harder.

The day passed without incident. Manos had raised his eyebrows when I hurried in but nothing was said. The snack bar opened on time and my brother, Stephen, popped by in the afternoon for a swim in the hotel pool, then went over to have a drink with Martin at the bar. He often did that. By the time I nipped out for a dip between my shifts he had already left. I got dressed and waited on the tables in the restaurant as usual, then cleaned up. Afterwards, I went over to join Martin and Peter at the bar for my customary bottle of lager before making the journey home. Despite arriving late, it felt like a long day.

I'd barely taken a sip when I heard a commotion coming from inside the main hotel. For a second I thought it was Simon again. Then I remembered he was safely back in Sheffield. A moment later Jorgas, the night porter, came running out.

'Kerry, Kerry, come, come!'

I put down my lager and pulled a face at Martin. Jorgas could really get on my case when he wanted to. No doubt I'd left an oven on or a pan not looking as spick and span as it needed to. As usual, I'd go over, take my punishment, then come back to finish my beer.

When I reached the main building, however, Jorgas led me past the restaurant and through to the brightly illuminated reception area. The first thing I noticed was the two tall policemen standing by the desk. But they weren't making the noise. That was my mother who was sobbing on the steps outside the door. She took one look at me and crumbled even more. That's when I realised she and the police were together. My heart flew into my mouth. Had something happened to Dad or Stephen or Danny?

'Mum, what is it? What's going on?'

'Kerry, it's Ben.'

'Ben?' I asked. It hadn't even crossed my mind that he could be in trouble. 'What about him?'

'He's gone. Ben's gone.'

She fell into my arms.

'I've lost him.'

CHAPTER SIX

HE'S STILL OUT THERE

These are the events of 24 July 1991.

Apart from it being about 110 degrees, it had begun as just another normal day in paradise for my family. Dad had driven the Land Rover up to work on the farm as usual, and Stephen had gone on his motorbike. Then I had arrived at the caravan and set off for work, and Ben and Mum had had the whole day in front of them.

After I'd left, Mum got Ben washed and changed in the clothes I had brought with him. I'd pulled out little shorts, brown sandals and a white shirt with a hint of a green pattern. Mum was very close to catching a bus into Kos Town but at the last minute decided it would be nice to push Ben up to see his granddad and uncle working at the farmhouse. Iraklis was about a forty-minute walk and most of it was uphill. Mum was fit enough. Danny wasn't at school and he'd be okay with the distance. In fact, Mum was more worried about Ben the corgi's little legs managing the walk with them in the midday sun.

It was a picturesque route and Mum was in no rush so they actually took closer to fifty minutes. Ben alternated between spotting the animals in the fields with Danny and bashing two toy Dinky cars together. They were all covered in sun cream and

Ben had the shade from his buggy roof, so it was just a lovely, idyllic day.

After about half an hour they reached the fork where the road continued one way and a dusty old lane led off in the opposite direction. Mum turned off and struggled with the pushchair on the loose-stone surface. Greek roads aren't magnificent at the best of times. This wasn't even a road. It led past a handful of houses at the bottom, a building site where a villa was being constructed from scratch, then an odd-looking villa raised above road level and finally the loose-chipped driveway leading off to Michaelis's property at the top. The only thing past there was forest.

The farmhouse was set back about twenty yards from the lane so Mum released Ben from the pushchair and he and Danny and the dog scampered over to surprise Dad and Stephen. It worked. Michaelis saw them first.

'Eddie, you didn't tell me your lovely family was coming.'

'I didn't know myself!'

It was an exaggeration to call the building a farmhouse because it was so rundown, but that is what it used to be and hopefully would be again. It was a single-storey building that looked out towards the mountains in one direction and fields and woods in the other. Everything needed repairing or replacing. There were no doors, just frames, which had left it at the mercy of the weather and any passing animals for years. The overgrown garden had had to be hacked back even to access the place. The kitchen and bathroom all had to be stripped out and the walls, ceilings and floors were all going to be virtually rebuilt. It was a massive project, guaranteed to keep Dad and Stephen busy for the best part of a year.

Ben loved the place immediately. For a start, the fields in the distance had goats and cattle. Also, with no doors or furniture in the way, he could whizz around the place with his cars while the men worked outside on the guttering. Best of all, Dad and Michaelis had bags and boxes of the most exotic-looking tools. As soon as one of them stepped up a ladder, Ben dived into their kit and took out a clamp or a spirit level or trowel. Mum was never more than a few feet behind, always reminding Ben, 'Put that down. It's not yours.'

Michaelis had a different response.

'Christine, let the boy play. As long as it's not sharp, I'm happy for him to have it.'

The typical response of the laid-back Greeks where children were concerned. Whether Ben was raiding their tool bags, pinching their sun cream or asking for pork from their plates in restaurants, they all said the same thing: 'It's okay, it's no problem.'

It was nearly lunchtime anyway, so there wasn't much trouble for Ben to get into. Mum had brought a few things to eat but Michaelis saw it as a special occasion. He sent Stephen out on the motorbike to a shop in the village where he had an account. We all knew the shop well. It was run by a woman called Xanthippe – or Sissy as she liked to be called – who dressed more like a lawyer, even though she spent her day cutting hams and selling lilos to tourists. We often shopped there. Whenever we went to or from the beach, we had to pass Sissy's shop and Ben would always ask for the same thing: 'Ice cream!' Sometimes he got his way. On other occasions, particularly if lunch or dinner weren't far away, I'd say no. Usually that was fine. Once or twice, however, Ben decided that wasn't good enough. He screamed the place down until Sissy came out with an ice cream for him. After that, whenever she saw him she would hand one over. It was a really sweet thing to do, although annoying if I'd already said no.

Sissy was surprised at the size of Stephen's order of cheeses and meats.

'You are hungry today?' she said.

'It's not all for me!'

He explained that Mum and Danny and the two Bens had paid them a surprise visit. Then, loading up the water and food, he sped back up the mountain to the farmhouse.

They all sat down on chairs or boxes and had a typically Greek lunch. Ben was eating on the go, too excited to stay still longer than it took to pick up half a cucumber or a tomato. Then he'd wander off eating them like an apple, popping back for some bread and olives when he ran out.

It was a blissful afternoon. Those who wanted the sun sat in it and those who didn't had the shade of the trees. And it was so peaceful. Earlier in the day there had been a digger truck transporting rubble from a building renovation at the bottom of the lane to the top. The driver had to pass the farmhouse to dump the hardcore ready to be used to improve the dirt track before driving back down again, kicking up a trail of dust with its heavy wheels as it went. But now building work had stopped there for the day, and they were able to eat undisturbed.

By coincidence, it turned out to be the perfect day to visit. Michaelis had ordered a shipment of supplies for the roof but the delivery truck hadn't arrived first thing as promised. By the time they finished lunch, the men had pretty much written off any hope of it arriving that day at all. It was frustrating for them, but it did mean everyone could enjoy their food and conversation without hurrying.

'We'll give it another hour,' Michaelis sighed, 'and then you may as well go home early, Stephen.'

So they waited and ate some more, and all that time they were royally entertained by a tiny jester. Ben had discovered a water barrel and after he'd skimmed his cars along the surface he'd started scooping bowlfuls out to mix potions with dirt and leaves. When he tired of that, the next scoop was tipped straight over his own head.

I suppose it was pure instinct to try to cool down in that savage heat. Even so, the look of shock on Ben's face as the water soaked him made it look like he'd jumped into a shower of ice.

Stephen saw it happen and burst out laughing. Everyone else joined in when they saw the drowned rat dripping in front of them. That was enough for Ben. That boy lived for laughter. He thrived on it. So, uncomfortable as he was, what did he do?

Scooped another bowl of water onto his head.

The laughter was even louder this time, more so when he yelled, 'I'm so funny!' Of course, he carried on dousing himself until Mum put a stop to it and dried him off. She hung Ben's shorts from a tree to dry and told him not to get anything else ruined because there were no spares. Ben didn't care about wearing only a T-shirt and little buckled sandals any more than he did about being wet. He just loved being a showman.

With that little performance over, Ben moved onto his next escapade. This involved jumping on the gravel mounds, then taking handfuls of the stuff through the house and dumping them out the other side. Every couple of minutes he'd be back. Even when he wasn't in sight, his laughs and imaginary conversations with his tools could still be heard.

Finally, Michaelis gave up on the hope of the delivery arriving and told Stephen to go home early.

'Even if the materials arrive, it will be too late to start.'

Dad agreed, adding, 'Grab the jerry can, son, and fill it up at the garage.' They would need the diesel for the generator in the morning.

Stephen disappeared behind the house where the vehicles were parked. He didn't have to hunt for Ben because his nephew came trotting over, and not to say goodbye. The only thing Ben loved more than his toys was other people's – and Stephen's motorbike was top of that list.

'Bike! Bike!'

Usually Stephen was as weak as the rest of us when it came to turning down a request from his nephew – Ben pretty much had us all wrapped round his little finger half the time. But not today. Stephen had an errand to run and the sooner he got it over with, the quicker he could enjoy his rare few hours off.

'Go back to Granddad, Ben,' Stephen said. 'No rides today.'

He shooed Ben away and made his escape. From the other side of the farmhouse, everyone heard the little 50cc engine fire up and the fading volume as Stephen sped away down the lane.

It was about two minutes after that Mum said, 'Ben's gone quiet.'

Dad laughed. 'He can't be up to any good.'

'I'd better go and check. He's probably cuddling a stray cat to death.'

Mum left the others and walked casually through the house. She didn't call Ben, not at first. She expected to see him crouched down with his bucket and spade and mound of ants or a pile of sand. Things like that could hold his attention for ages. It was perfectly normal that he'd go quiet.

Ben wasn't where Mum expected. *Where is the little bugger?* She could see where he'd been so she didn't panic. *He can't have got far.*

Mum got her bearings and scanned the horizon. Everywhere she looked was mostly fields. She could see for miles in most directions and either it was so wide open that she would have been able to spot Ben in an instant or it was too overgrown for him to have dared to venture. That only left the lane. She walked to the top of the driveway, checking the hedges along the way. At the end she looked both ways, with no sign of him.

Well, obviously he went round the house while I came through it.

That was the only plausible explanation.

She trudged back up the driveway and walked the opposite way around the dilapidated building. Dad, Michaelis and Danny were exactly where she'd left them.

'Has Ben been back in?' Mum asked.

'No.'

That was when she felt her stomach clench for the first time. This was the only place he could have been. If Ben wasn't with Eddie and Danny...

She forced out the words she didn't want to have to say. 'He's not here.'

'What do you mean he's not here?'

'He's not outside.'

'Have you checked the driveway?'

'Yes.'

'Have you looked in the fields?'

'Yes, yes!' Mum was getting annoyed now. More out of worry than anger. 'I've looked inside and out. If he's not with you, then I don't know where he is.'

Her voice was shaking and Dad could tell from her face she was serious. He leapt up and sent Danny one way, asked Michaelis to help him check the outbuildings, and told Mum to look again at the road in case he'd made it that far.

They all set off calling Ben's name and shouting and hollering for him to come back. Their best bet was on the goat sheds and chicken coops. Ben loved animals so much it made sense he might have wandered off to feed them.

In between the sound of them all calling out, there was the occasional putt-putt of a distant scooter or slow-moving truck crawling up the main road. There were no other human sounds. Just the wind and the animals puncturing the silence.

Meanwhile, Mum put her rising sense of terror to one side and tried to visualise Ben reaching the lane. Uphill soon became inaccessible for a toddler, so that took seconds to check. In any case, she decided, if Ben had gone anywhere it would only have been in an attempt to catch Stephen. With the dusty, barren road stretching emptily out before her, Mum started jogging, scanning the ditches either side, even though she knew he wouldn't be in them. Ben was too timid to have tackled their intimidating wild weeds – certainly not without making a noisy fuss.

As she reached the sharp bend in the lane, Mum eased her speed. She'd already covered more ground than she imagined Ben could have travelled in such a short space of time. The second she turned the corner she was confident her grandson would be in sight.

He wasn't.

Mum stared again at the sheer unbroken nothingness of the unmade lane. There wasn't an animal, a vehicle or a person to be seen. And definitely no sign of a little boy. Ben was only twenty-one months. It was inconceivable he could have made it that far, let alone gone any further. And if he had, he would have answered her shouts.

She trudged back round to the house and waited for the others to return. They all shook their heads. How could a toddler just disappear? There was only one other explanation.

Stephen must have taken him.

I can hear my dad's voice now: 'The stupid little idiot. Fancy not telling us he was taking Ben for a ride.'

Ben didn't even have a helmet. What was Stephen thinking?

They kept on running through other ideas but this was the only one that made sense. No one had heard any other vehicles. None of the other landowners had arrived to feed their animals that afternoon. There had been no comings or goings at the house opposite, where the lane met the driveway. Stephen had to have taken him.

'He's probably taken him to visit Kerry,' Dad said. 'Palm Beach is on the way to the garage.'

Reckless of Stephen though it was, they were all desperate to believe something and that was the most convincing conclusion. They could relax now. Michaelis and Dad had some clearing up and preparation to do for when the building materials arrived, so they'd be another hour. Mum said she wouldn't wait.

'I'll take the dog and the pushchair home. Stephen and Ben will probably be back by now.'

There was no sign of anyone at the caravan but Mum did spot the jerry can full of fuel for the generator. Obviously Stephen had been back, but Mum assumed he and Ben had gone to the hotel for a swim. She began to prepare dinner. It was almost five o'clock. Ben had last been seen at half past two. Unless he ate at my snack bar, the little fella would be hungry by now.

Dad and Danny arrived back twenty minutes later. Dad wasn't worried, but he wasn't happy either.

'I'm going to wring Stephen's neck,' he said. 'He can't just take Ben off gallivanting whenever he feels like it.' Dad said he'd drive to my apartment and if no one was there, onto the hotel, the only places the pair could be.

Ten minutes later, Dad pulled up outside my little flat. We all had keys for it and, as he turned the key in the lock, he let out a sigh of relief. He could hear the shower. They were there.

Dad poured a glass of water and made himself comfortable on the small sofa. A few minutes later the bathroom door opened and Stephen stepped out.

Just Stephen.

'All right, Dad? Have you come for a shower as well?'

'No, I haven't. Where's Ben?'

'What do you mean?'

'Is Ben with you?'

'No. Why?'

'You didn't bring him here on your bike?'

When he had processed the question, Stephen was offended at the idea. 'Of course I didn't, Dad. He hasn't got a helmet. I never would.'

Dad's mind was jelly as the horror set in. He started shaking. Stephen picked up on it a few seconds later. Mum and I were still in the dark.

'Get dressed. Let's go.'

As they ran out to the Land Rover Stephen said, 'I left Ben playing by the door, Dad. I swear I did.'

Dad said nothing. He knew it was true but he didn't want to believe him. If his son hadn't whisked Ben off, then what the hell had happened to him? Toddlers don't just disappear. He felt sick.

Mum crumpled when she saw Dad and Stephen return alone. One minute she was holding a knife and plate. The next they were both on the floor.

'No, no, you must have him, Stephen, you have to have him.'

But she knew from her son's face he was telling the truth. It could only mean one thing.

'Ben's still out there.'

A state of frenzy descended on the caravan. Somehow they held themselves together enough to plan. Dad and Danny would return to the farmhouse in the Land Rover. Mum and Stephen would take his motorbike to the police station in Kos Town. It was six o'clock in the evening. Ben had been missing for three and a half hours.

Dad and Danny were silent as they drove to Iraklis. As they pulled up Dad said, more to himself than his son, 'Ben must have wandered down the lane. Someone must have found him. They'll be trying to return him home.'

That was the thought that kept him sane: Ben had toddled further than Mum imagined possible and then a neighbour on the main road or a passing car had come to his rescue. They'd probably be attempting to locate his parents right now.

Danny said, 'Shouldn't we tell Kerry?'

Dad agonised over that. 'What's the point of worrying your sister? Ben will be safe and sound before she finishes her shift.'

I think he truly believed that.

They reached the farmhouse and began to go over the same ground they'd already scoured, just in case Ben had found his way back. If anything, it was even quieter so the faintest noise would be heard. But the light was fading. They didn't have torches. Dad was furious with himself.

Meanwhile, Mum had reached the police station. For Stephen's sake she managed to hold herself together. Her son seeing her in distress wouldn't help anyone. Mum's mood worsened in trying to make herself understood. Even though the duty officer spoke English, it was a slow, painful process. When Mum finally got him to understand, his first response was, 'The baby is with the mother.'

They always called him 'the baby'.

'No, his mum's at work.'

'Then his father has him.'

'No, his dad's in England. Look, he was in my care and now I can't find him.'

The policeman wasn't convinced. It was the height of the tourist season. He probably saw more than his fair share of excitable British women. He told Mum to go home, look again. Like Ben was a toy fallen down the back of the sofa.

Mum was losing it. 'He's not there. We've searched and searched and searched.'

Finally the officer asked the all-important question.

'When did the baby go missing?'

'I'm not sure. About half past two.'

He did the maths. In a second, the case had gone from a probable drunken tourist leaving her baby in a bar to a serious case of a missing child. Suddenly it was action stations. Two officers were despatched to follow Mum to the farmhouse.

It was six thirty. Ben had been missing for four hours.

Having the police on site was a comfort. It was also an admission that something was wrong. Very wrong. Still no one was admitting to themselves or each other what it could be.

Dad was relieved when he saw the patrol car following the motorbike up the dust track to the farmhouse. His faith was tempered when he realised they'd arrived without food, drink or even torches. It was seven o'clock. In an hour it would be dark.

The police began by going over the same ground that everyone had already checked several times. Their next move was to call Michaelis. He was the owner; he should be there. Dad couldn't see the point but it would at least be good to have a Greek and English speaker on their side. Already, he was beginning to feel the police had their own agenda. At the very least, they weren't listening to anything he had to say.

After Dad recounted the events of the day – again – one of the police said to Stephen, 'So you took the baby on your motorbike.' Fact, not question. Stephen denied it, of course, and Dad told them to leave him alone. They did – for now.

The farmhouse felt like the middle of nowhere, although there were one or two secluded homes dotted around. Across from where the lane joined the driveway stood the strange-looking villa. It wasn't just high, it seemed to have been built back to front. You had to go round the rear to enter – as the police discovered when they decided to pay a call.

An old lady Dad had seen once or twice answered. She confirmed that she had been in all day and had, crucially, seen Stephen leave on his motorbike.

'Was the baby with him?'

'No, the baby was playing. Over there.' She pointed to the back of the farmhouse. To exactly where Ben was last heard.

The search continued down the lane to where the new house was being built to replace a ramshackle square building that stood nearby. It was little more than a room, and clearly no one was at home so Dad and the police split up to investigate the various outbuildings and hen houses.

With the light fading and desperation growing, Dad saw one of the policemen call his partner over. They were crowding around a yard bin when Dad arrived behind them. Was he imagining it or didn't they want him to see what they'd found?

Pushing past, Dad watched, heart in his mouth, as the first officer lifted a black sack from the bin. It was still light enough for him make out the dark red liquid seeping through the bottom of the sack. There was only one thing it could be.

Dad spun round, partly to catch his breath, mainly to ensure Mum was nowhere near. He could not allow her to see this. Turning back, he forced himself to watch. As the second officer stood back, the first held the bulging sack at arm's length then dropped it unceremoniously to the ground and tentatively kicked at the flap to hook it open. He got it first time. The sack peeled back – and an eye stared out.

Dad's body reacted first and he felt the bile rising in his throat as he dropped to his knees. Tears, screams, words would follow in seconds. Then suddenly the officer's shouts of concern turned to laughter. Dad concentrated, and just made out one word.

'Goat.'

The eye belonged to an animal. What it was doing in a sack in a bin would have to wait. All that mattered was the simple, brilliant fact that it did not belong to Ben.

By now, Mum and Dad were beginning to concede that Ben could have reached the row of houses right at the bottom of the lane. Even though the police agreed, they refused to knock on anyone's doors – and they wouldn't let Mum and Dad either. They said it was an invasion of homeowners' privacy calling so late at night.

It was nine o'clock, barely dinner time for Greek people, and Ben had been missing for six and a half hours.

According to Mum and Dad, the police seemed surprised that Ben hadn't been found. They acted as though it was just a matter of time before he appeared. Nearly three hours after they'd arrived, they were none the wiser and a lot more anxious. As a result, they started going over questions they'd already asked.

'Where is the father?'

Mum told them again about Simon. Greek families tend to place the male at the heart of the family. Both men pulled a face at this. A man's place was with his family.

'Where is the mother?'

'She is at work.'

'Why isn't she here looking for the baby?'

Mum explained how they thought they were protecting me. It would be awful to be told your son was missing one minute, then have him returned unscathed the next. That's genuinely what she thought would happen. The policeman shook his head. 'No. She must be here.'

So that's when they'd come for me.

I didn't have a clue about any of this as I rushed over to Mum on the steps outside the hotel. Disturbed by the noise, Manos appeared in the lobby – he wasn't normally there so late – and spoke to the officers in Greek. A few minutes later, Martin and Peter arrived. They'd left a waiter tending the bar.

'Kerry, what's going on?'

'I don't know,' I said. 'Something about Ben.' Mum was making no sense. Luckily Manos had got more from the policemen. He explained that Ben had gone missing from the farmhouse. That the family were up there searching for him. And that they had no supplies and, crucially, no torches.

Martin spoke to Manos, then knelt next to me and Mum.

'Kerry, go with the police. We'll follow with torches and food and water for your family.'

I nodded. That was all I could manage. I wasn't panicked, I was in a daze. The words 'Ben's missing' refused to filter through to my brain. I was hugging my mum and telling her everything would be all right because I believed it. Nothing had happened to my son. Nothing ever would. How could it?

Mum was still sobbing as I slid in next to her in the back of the white Citroën police car. The policemen were silent and stayed that way until we pulled up at the farmhouse. I'd never been there before. The car's headlights illuminated a low-rise building that had seen better days. A few seconds later, the figures of my father and brothers appeared in the glare.

It was half past ten. Ben had been missing for eight hours.

Even when Dad explained the events of the day to me, I didn't crumble. I knew they would have looked after Ben as well as I would have. Nothing bad could have happened to him. He'd walked down the lane and some kind old local had taken him in from the scorching heat. He was probably tired and hungry so they gave him a bite to eat and bed to lie down on. They probably had a good look around the area and saw no one. They didn't want to disturb Ben so they planned to take him to the police station first thing.

A few minutes after I arrived, Martin and Peter pulled up on Martin's scooter. They'd brought as much as they could carry: food, drink, blankets and torches. They'd even packed a first-aid kit, in case Ben had fallen down somewhere.

We all split up and covered the ground that everyone had been over. Using one of the torches I surveyed the landscape. It just looked empty. It was the worst place in the world to play hide-and-seek. There was nowhere to go. Which made me think, *How can you lose a child up here?*

I took one look at my mother and knew I could never say that. She was still inconsolable. I think that was one of the reasons I was still being strong. She needed an arm around the shoulder, not hurtful accusations. That wouldn't help anyone, and it certainly wouldn't help find Ben.

The odd flashes of the other torch beams criss-crossing else-where in the darkness gave the whole site an eerie feel. We were all calling out for Ben, waiting to hear his cry or those words, 'Mummy!' or 'Nana!' Deep down, though, I didn't want him to be there. That would have meant he'd been injured and alone and scared for the best part of nine hours. No, I preferred the theory that he'd wandered off and had been rescued by a confused but kindly passer-by. The morning would reveal all. I was absolutely convinced of it.

I think the police clung to the same idea. Close to midnight, after a fruitless two hours with flashlights, they said they needed me to come to the police station. They also wanted a picture of Ben and a copy of his passport. Dad said he would drive me to the caravan and pick them up, then take me to Kos Town. Even though I knew in my heart that Ben wasn't up there any more, it felt like a betrayal leaving – like I was walking away from him, especially when the others stayed. But the police were insistent.

It was half past twelve. Ben had been missing for ten hours.

CHAPTER SEVEN

WE'RE ON OUR OWN

On any other night I would have looked with envy at the bright lights of the bars in Kos Town and the revellers laughing and drinking outside. Not this night. My mind was still in Iraklis, as good as blank. I didn't notice Dad weaving around the partygoers who had staggered into the road or the din of the mashed music booming from each venue we passed. I didn't even realise we'd stopped until Dad said, 'Kerry, we're here.'

In the shadows, Kos police station looked like a fort. It had battlements and turrets and an imposing doorway two storeys high. You expect knights on horses to come out on a drawbridge. Only the sound of the sea lapping in the harbour across the road reminded me where we were.

We went in at the less ostentatious reception entrance and the officers from earlier came in. I handed over the documents and waited while they were copied. Then there was silence. We waited for them to talk. They looked like they were waiting for us. For the first time, I realised they didn't have a clue what to do next. I thought about the last two hours. We'd reported a missing child on an isolated roadside. What had they done? Sent two police officers. Two officers for a child who had been missing for four hours in 110 degree heat. I know it's years later, but when twelve-year-old Tia Sharpe was reported missing in London in 2012, there were eighty officers involved in looking for her from day one. Where was our backup? Where were the sniffer dogs? And where were the torches? It had been dusk when they left the station. Most of Kos is without streetlights. What were they thinking?

I was only nineteen, but I knew there was more that they could have been doing.

Finally Dad said, 'What now?'

One of the policemen shrugged. It made it look like he didn't care, but I knew that was a typical Greek mannerism. 'We will check the ports.'

He explained that there was one ferry to Athens a day – or night – and there was still time to catch it.

His colleague nodded. 'Yes, you meet us at half past two at the port. The ferry leaves at three. We will check the vehicles together for the baby.'

Dad agreed to join them and we left. But I was dazed. Why were they even thinking of the ports? Ben wouldn't be there. He'd wandered off somewhere, he'd fallen. He was sleeping now and in the morning someone would hand him in. He wasn't in a car. He wasn't leaving the island. He was asleep, safe in a Good Samaritan's house. I knew they existed. I'd met two at Athens airport.

We drove back to the farmhouse in silence, the cacophony of Kos's nightlife growing fainter in the distance. As I stepped back out onto the now familiar gravel, the only sounds I could hear was a distant dog barking and occasional bursts of cicadas in the far-off forest trees.

I hated the police for suggesting that Ben might have been snatched. I was desperate to prove them wrong. I stared out into the darkness and imagined the people asleep in the houses further down the lane.

Ben must be there.

I decided to do what the police should already have done. With Stephen, I walked back down the lane to the row of nine or ten houses at the bottom. They weren't visible from the farmhouse but if Ben wasn't up there, he would have to have passed this way. Anyone seeing a toddler in the searing afternoon heat would naturally have taken him inside. The police said it was an invasion of privacy to disturb the locals. I didn't see it that way. There was a child missing, for God's sake. My child.

It was half-past one in the morning when I knocked on the first door. When there was no reply I knocked again. I didn't care about the time. I didn't care about anything except finding my boy. Finally a light went on and a middle-aged man emerged blinking behind the half-opened door.

Getting his attention was the easy part. Getting him to understand was harder – and it was nothing to do with him being still half-asleep.

I hadn't prepared anything. I just said, 'Have you seen a little boy?'

The guy did the shrug and hid further behind his door. He was looking at two teenagers dressed for midday, not midnight, and he didn't understand a word we were saying.

I started to mime 'toddler' and pointed up the hill. Then I remembered the policemen called him a 'baby', so I said what I hoped was the Greek word I'd heard them say – 'Meecro' – and gestured to my eyes. Looking back, it was a surreal nocturnal game of Charades but somehow it got through. The man repeated, 'Micro?'

I nodded, eager to hear.

'No *micro*.'

And he closed the door.

It was the same story for the whole row. Some of the residents understood a few words of English, but mainly we had to act out our message. Whether they followed or not, everyone closed their doors with a shake of the head. 'No baby.'

Hands on hips, I stood outside the final villa and looked down towards the main road. Compared to the lane up to the farmhouse, it was as smooth as a billiard table but by England's standards it was still little more than a narrow, winding country road. I'd only been along it in darkness but I couldn't remember any houselights for a couple of miles. There wasn't anything until you reached the village and Sissy's shop. I imagined Ben picking his way past the roadside thistles and weeds and stopping to look at every lizard, every bug and every bird that crossed his path. I hadn't heard more than two vehicles in the hours I'd been there. I wasn't worried about an accident. Not like I would have been in Sheffield. In fact, traffic was my only hope of finding Ben. Any driver who'd passed him that afternoon would have stopped – the second you saw a toddler on his own on that uninviting stretch you'd investigate. You'd find out who he was with. And if it was no one, you'd take matters into your own hands. That's the natural thing to do. I knew Greeks loved children. I knew I could trust them to have done the right thing.

Back at the farmhouse, Dad was just getting ready to leave for the port. I didn't see the point, but he was determined. He was going early in case the police started without him. Mum was sitting by the building, rocking and crying, as Dad pulled away. It broke my heart to hear her sobbing, 'It's my fault. It's my fault.' We all tried to comfort her but nothing was working. Only when Danny sat next to her did she calm down. Danny needed her. She would be strong for him.

I honestly don't know what we did for the next three or four hours. We'd been over every inch of the farmland several times. Peter and Martin returned home with my blessing. They'd done so much, been so thoughtful. They left the torches and supplies and promised to check up on us the next day.

'And don't even think of coming into work. We'll tell Manos.'

Work? I hadn't given it a thought.

The passing of time in darkness is almost impossible to chart. Only when the first cockerels started crowing and the birds in the trees began their chorus did we have a clue that dawn was approaching. The sun was peeping over the horizon when we heard the familiar sound of the Land Rover rasping over the loose-chipped lane.

I knew Ben wouldn't have been at the port. Even so, when Dad emerged alone from the car my heart sank. If possible, it sank even further when he revealed what had happened.

'The police didn't show up.'

Stephen kicked the Land Rover's tyre. 'But it was their idea!'

This time it was Dad's turn to shrug. 'I know. I was there at half-two. The ferry started loading at three. No one came.'

On his own, Dad didn't have the authority to board the boat or ask anyone to open their boots or trailers. So he'd run around the queue of cars making their way to the mainland, staring in at the windows, focusing on any kids in the back seats. It had been impossible. The light was against him. Even with a torch the glare off the glass stopped him seeing much, and parents weren't happy with a desperate stranger beaming light in their kids' faces. So after two miserable hours he'd come back, beaten and feeling betrayed by a police force that didn't seem to care.

'Let's go home,' he said. 'We'll start again tomorrow.'

I've let my family down enough times and they've always stood by me. That's how it is with us. When one member is down, the others rally round. So, as distraught as we all were by Ben's disappearance, watching Mum's heartbreaking deterioration before our eyes couldn't be ignored. She needed us as well. I couldn't imagine – I still can't – the guilt she felt.

Mum didn't say a word on the way back to the caravan. We virtually had to walk her to bed. She wouldn't eat, drink or talk. Her face was completely blank. It was like having a zombie in the room. I was worried.

No one felt like eating or sleeping but we'd been up almost twenty-four hours. Getting ill wouldn't help Ben so I made toast and coffee for everyone. Dad downed about a dozen cups. It was killing him being so impotent. It wasn't just my son who was missing. It was a grandson and a nephew.

No one could relax at the caravan. At seven o'clock, we all set off for the police station. If we were going to get answers from anywhere, it would be here. *Or so we thought.* On the way we dropped Danny off with Mum's friend, Monica. She had a son, George, the same age. It was Monica who had given Ben the paddling pool and buckets and spades. We agreed Danny should be protected as much as possible.

At night, the police building had towered sinisterly over the small harbour where daytrips and the hydrofoil jetted to and fro. By day it was no less imposing. It was six storeys high in places, with a clock tower, crenellations and, just behind it, the famous Tree of Hippocrates – where the 'father of medicine' is said to have taught his pupils. Tourists with cameras were already wandering around there as we pulled up. The whole world, it seemed, was oblivious to our pain.

Including the police.

The grand two-storey entrance was reserved for the judges, public prosecutors and court personnel who shared the same building. We went in once again via the more understated door to the left. Dad spoke for us at the reception kiosk and was told, 'Please wait.' A few minutes later, a man in a nondescript, grey suit introduced himself as Christos Bafounis. 'I'm chief of security police.' He gestured towards a door. 'Come.'

Bafounis had very curly black hair, almost afro-like. He was in his forties, average height, average weight, with very dark eyes. The overall impression as I traipsed behind him down a gloomy corridor was that he seemed very stern-looking. He certainly suited his surroundings. He led us through a door and suddenly we were back in daylight. Like all ancient castles, the police station had a large quadrangle at its centre, surrounded by four walls.

If the design was mediaeval, the morality behind its use was just as out of date. The whole ground floor looking out onto the square was jail cells. Some were empty, some were inhabited. It was intimidating walking past, seeing the prisoners watching us. I didn't know what any of them had done, but it didn't seem right that their cells were exposed to the elements. They didn't have glass or plastic screens; there were just metal bars, floor to ceiling, just like you'd see in a Wild West film or cartoon. Even with my mind full of my worries, I couldn't help finding the scene barbaric, backwards even. I hoped the chief of security police would be more enlightened.

I was disappointed. Bafounis was of a generation and a culture where men spoke to men and women knew their place. Even when he stopped outside an office on the first floor, pointed and said, 'In,' it was addressed to Dad.

The room had a couple of desks, bookcases and wooden benches on one wall. Doors led through to other offices. There was an open-plan feel to the place. People wandered through all the time.

Bafounis pointed again. 'Sit.' We all took a place on the bench and waited for him to speak. He didn't, at least not to us. He barked into a phone and a few long, silent minutes later an officer in uniform appeared. He was one of the ones who'd come out to the farmhouse, although he made no attempt to acknowledge us. Maybe he was intimidated by his boss. They spoke in Greek for what seemed like ages. Then the copper disappeared and Bafounis started on his paperwork. Not once did he look at us.

About ten minutes later, another uniformed officer came in. He spoke to Bafounis then offered us refreshments. It was such a relief to have someone acknowledge us, especially in English, that we took the opportunity to vent our frustrations on him.

'What's going on?'

He spoke in his native language to Bafounis, waited for the reply, then said, 'Your baby has not been handed in.'

'Have you checked the hospitals?' Dad asked. My blood froze at the thought of Ben being a patient anywhere. But he had to be somewhere.

Another conversation with the boss. 'We are doing that now.' Apparently the officer who'd been in earlier had been dispatched to the Kos hospital. Why he couldn't phone I didn't know. But, we were assured, he'd return soon.

Tea, coffee and water came. Bafounis still didn't look up. Ten, twenty, fifty minutes passed. A couple of times he left the room then returned to his desk, without acknowledging us. It was excruciating. I assumed he had a team of officers combing the island. I couldn't begrudge that taking his attention.

Suddenly there was a noise from the main door behind us. A woman and teenage girl were being led into the adjoining office. The girl looked about seventeen, eighteen. She was crying, absolutely distraught. Her mother was just about holding them both together. As they were shown to seats, I noticed that the girl's clothes were torn and hanging off her in places. The officer dealing with them was as brusque as Bafounis. He dealt in gestures and shrugs. Even when he glanced over at us, it didn't occur to him to close the door. Privacy, it seemed, was not something his clients warranted.

I wish he had closed that door. Then we wouldn't have had to listen to that poor girl's account of being raped in the early hours by three local men. The women were Scandinavian. The only language other than their own that they spoke was English and so we followed every agonising word – and every inadequate response from the Greek policemen. For the first time in twelve hours I put my own problems aside. It was torturous watching this poor lass pouring out her heart to a man who just shrugged and made occasional notes. As far as we were concerned, he couldn't have appeared more uninterested if he'd tried. If I'd learned the accused were his own brothers, I wouldn't have been surprised.

From the basic English responses he gave, he didn't believe for one minute that Kos boys could do what the girl claimed. She must be lying.

'You drink too much. You make love to the boys. Yes?'

The girl cried, screamed, 'No, they raped me!' but her words were met with stone ears.

At some point the officer left for ten or twenty minutes, as usual with no explanation. He returned with a book of photographs.

'Look. Find the men.'

That was it. His investigation extended to searching a file of previous occupants of the downstairs cells.

In England, even in the late 1980s, there would have been a female police officer present. There would have been a change of clothes. At the very least there would have been some privacy. But we saw and heard every word of that poor girl's testimony. At the end, we all looked at each other, the same thoughts running through our minds.

If they can treat a victim of rape so off-handedly, how on earth are they going to treat us?

Dad picked up his glass of water and, ignoring the looks from the officers, took it over. The women had been offered nothing. That told us everything. We were terrified. Absolutely terrified.

On his way back, Dad closed the door. He glared at Bafounis as if to say, *You should have done that*, but the chief of security police didn't look up. He did, though, when Dad went over to the desk and leant down on it. He was very close to losing his temper.

'I went to the docks last night,' Dad said, as calmly as he could manage. 'Where were your officers? They said they would be there. Where were they?'

There was no clue on Bafounis's face that he'd understood a word. He picked up a phone and, a moment later, the second of the previous night's officers appeared. Greek words were exchanged then the officer said, 'There was an emergency last night. The Albanian gypsies got out of control. We all had to help.' He looked at Dad's unimpressed face. 'I'm sorry.'

Throughout it all Bafounis hadn't said a word. But, I realised, he'd obviously understood Dad enough to summon his officer. So why wouldn't he speak to us? Not even to Dad, a man?

It's fair to say we were losing patience and, with it, respect for the way Bafounis and his team were conducting the investigation. What was the point of them covering every inch of the island with officers – as we assumed they were doing – if they went on to treat us like this? Why tell us to 'sit' and then pretend we weren't there? Would it have hurt Bafounis to at least tell us what he and his team were doing?

Another half-hour passed and then the first of the previous night's officers returned. He spoke to his chief, nodded at us, then addressed Dad.

'Your baby is not at the hospital.'

Then he smiled a goodbye and left.

'Of course he's not at a hospital,' I said.

'So where is he?' Dad asked.

'He'll be here soon. Someone will hand him in. Whoever found him will bring him here soon.'

And then I relaxed back onto the hard bench.

We stayed there for another two hours. Then there was another commotion from the main door. This time it was a voice we all recognised. But why was it coming from the hall?

'Hello, everyone!' The irrepressible figure of Xanthippe Aggrelli – Sissy from the beach shop – burst into the room. Sissy was about six foot, slim with dark hair, pretty fair skin for a Kos native, vivid red lips and a high-pitched voice. As usual she was dressed in a suit more fit for a courtroom than a tourist shop. For the first time it didn't look out of place.

She hugged us all and expressed her condolences, then spoke to Bafounis. A few minutes later another figure entered the room. He was older, in full police uniform with badges and epaulettes. He looked like he was in charge.

'This is Chief Dakouras,' Sissy explained. 'He is the boss.'

We shook his hand and he disappeared in a show of theatrical gestures. Then Sissy said, 'Mr Bafounis would like to interview you all. I shall be your interpreter.'

The odds of our local shopkeeper just happening to arrive to translate our statements were implausibly long. Under interrogation from us, Sissy eventually revealed that she hadn't been invited to help at all. She'd seen Monica with Danny and George and had learnt of our tragedy. She'd put a call in to her good friend Dakouras, and offered her services. That was an hour ago. Now here she was, ready to act as our go-between.

Dad went first. He followed Bafounis and Sissy into another room, then emerged half an hour later. Then it was Mum's turn. For the last six hours, she hadn't said a word. She'd barely acknowledged Sissy's arrival, even when she was forced into a hug. Dad helped her to her feet and encouraged her to the door. Sissy was all smiles and sympathy as she escorted Mum into the room.

Another half-hour passed. I don't know what they got from Mum. She sat down silently and stayed that way as Stephen was called in. Finally it was my turn. I sat down opposite Bafounis. Sissy was on his left. Bafounis asked a question in Greek, Sissy translated it into basic English and I replied. The first questions were standard identification information: name, address, parents' information, address in England. Nothing, to my mind, that could help anyone find my son. Finally, they asked me what had happened the day before. I told them what I could, which was very little. As Sissy relayed it to Bafounis he wrote it all down in small, wiry Greek script. My statement barely covered a page. Dad, who knew more than anyone, said his testimony covered just four.

Bafounis showed little interest in anything I said. Only when he asked for Ben's full name did he look up. Via Sissy, he said, 'What is the baby's name?'

'Ben Stephen Needham.'

He wrote it down and repeated slowly, 'Ben, Stephen, Needham.'

Then he looked at me, his charcoal eyes burning into me. I sank into my seat. I was frightened. The way he was glaring made me feel guilty – of what, I didn't know. What was he going to say?

'Stephen is the father's name?'

It took me a couple of goes to explain. 'No, his father is Simon. Simon Ward.'

Bafounis consulted his notes.

'Your brother is called Stephen.'

'Yes.'

Something was troubling him. It was written in his face. I wished my dad was with me.

'Stephen is not his father?'

'No, Stephen is his middle name. My brother is also called Stephen. It's a coincidence.'

Sissy explained as best she could. Greek boys usually take their fathers' names. Bafounis was struggling to comprehend why Ben was named after his uncle and not his dad. I don't know what was going through his mind, but I did know it wasn't helping find my son.

Before I left the interview room I asked Sissy, 'What's going on? They're not telling us anything. Where are they searching?' She spoke to Bafounis and relayed his reply. 'They're looking, they're looking. You must wait.' Then she smiled and shooed me out.

We sat on the wooden benches for another two hours and nobody told us a thing. Slowly the message got through: there was nothing to tell because they were doing nothing. There wasn't an army of officers tearing Kos apart. There was no island-wide manhunt. It was a joke. They were just waiting, like us, for someone to hand Ben in. That was their idea of police work.

If I had known they weren't looking, there's no way we would have wasted a whole day sitting in the police station: we'd have been out knocking on doors. Asking people, doing something, anything.

Dad snapped first. 'I've had enough of this. They're doing bugger all. If we want things done, we'll have to get proper help.'

No one seemed bothered that we were leaving. An officer asked if we'd be at home overnight and Dad said yes. Then we left and drove straight to the Palm Beach Hotel. I wanted to update my friends. Dad wanted to make a phone call.

Manos was happy to let us borrow the phone in reception. Most of the customers were in the restaurant so there wasn't a problem with noise. After a few minutes' flicking through the phone books under the desk, Dad dialled a number.

'Hello, British Embassy.'

Dad spoke to someone for five minutes. He explained every-thing that was going on, ending on how unsatisfactory the police response had been so far.

The embassy man listened. Then he asked, 'Have you been interviewed?'

'Yes,' Dad said.

'Was there somebody to translate for you?'

'Yes. Although she was only a shopkeeper.'

'Is your daughter by herself?'

'No, she has me, her mother and brothers. We're all together.'

There was a pause. Then the man said, 'Okay, well, it sounds as though everything is being done correctly. There's nothing we can do.' He wished us luck and rang off.

Manos spoke very good English but I doubt he knew half the words Dad came out with as he slammed the phone down. The air was blue. I hadn't seen Dad this livid since my days dodging school.

'You're told that the British Embassy is there for you if you get into trouble abroad,' he raged. 'Well, that's a joke. They don't want to know.'

The man had been brisk, unsympathetic and, in Dad's opinion given the situation, borderline rude.

Dad reached his arms around all of us. The huddle calmed him down and reassured the rest of us.

'The police aren't doing anything and the embassy doesn't want anything to do with us,' he said. 'We're on our own.'

CHAPTER EIGHT

THE FATHER HAS HIM

That was the night I cried.

We were back at the caravan. Ben had been missing for thirty hours. All the rational explanations were being tested to their limit. If he'd been rescued, he should have been handed in to the police by now. If he'd been injured, the hospital should have been alerted. So where was he?

Monica came over to drop Danny off. I'm sure she had questions but one look at our faces told her everything.

'Have you eaten?' she asked.

Someone said 'No.'

'I thought so. I've brought soup.'

No one felt like eating but we needed to. I hadn't touched a thing since a slice of toast at breakfast. As I broke off a piece of bread to dip, my mind went to the tea towel wrapped around Ben's neck the previous morning. That was the last time I'd seen him. He was sitting, eating exactly where I was now.

I don't know what happened to my bowl afterwards. I think Monica must have washed them all up. I know she took Mum in hand. She got her clean and ready for bed. Somebody needed to, but none of us had the strength. We were all barely clinging on ourselves. Monica was a godsend.

It was when she'd gone and I was curled up on the bed that I noticed my pillow getting damp. The tears came and they wouldn't stop. I hugged my knees in to my chest, shuddering silently under the thin sheet. I didn't want anyone to hear me. I needed to be strong. For Mum, for my brothers. For Ben.

We all managed to sleep. The next morning I made breakfast for everyone. Only toast again, under the small gas grill. I didn't mind if it was eaten or not. I was acting on instinct, going through the motions. I just needed to be busy. Mum stayed in bed. It was Day 3.

The sun was already beating down by ten o'clock but no one had any inclination to leave the caravan. Where would we go? What would we do? Then, at eleven, the sound of a vehicle slowing along the short gravel driveway had us all scrambling for a window.

It was a police car.

'Ben!'

I was off the sofa in a heartbeat and at the door in two. Stephen, Danny and Dad were close behind. I'd moved so quickly the white Citroën was still parking. By the time the driver opened his door I was halfway to it, the short prickly grass that jabbed into my bare feet barely registering. I stopped at the gravel, ignored the driver walking towards us and instead studied his partner, still easing out of the car. The glare of sun on glass meant I couldn't see in the back of the car. The bead of sweat on my forehead wasn't due to the temperature – any second now, that policeman would open the rear door and scoop out my baby.

But he didn't touch the handle. He didn't even glance behind as he slammed his own door and followed his partner to where we were all gathered, breathless, waiting, looking in his arms, looking behind him, looking in the car. He seemed oblivious to his audience. If anything, he stared more intently at Stephen's motorbike than he did us.

'Where's Ben?' I called out. 'Have you got Ben?'

They both shrugged. The pain in my feet bit. My knees buckled. I sank into my dad's chest. Elation to emptiness in seconds. If they didn't have him, why were they here? I felt sick.

'Has there been an accident? Is he all right?'

The policeman who had been driving raised his hand. 'We have good news.'

He ushered us to the shaded seats under the canopy. I took a few deep breaths and tried to focus.

'We have had a sighting,' the officer began. 'A lady in a cigarette kiosk saw your baby.'

'Where?' Five voices at once.

'At the airport.'

The airport? What would Ben be doing at the airport? My hands were white where they gripped the arms of the plastic chair. It was a joke. *How could he get there? He's not even two.*

Then I heard what the policeman was really saying, and my nightmares started.

They had taken a photograph of Ben to the airport and shown it around. This had been that morning. Not on the 24th, not even yesterday. Still, the lady who ran the cigarette concession had taken one look at the picture and said, 'He was here.'

She swore it was Ben. He had been with an older boy of about eight, who'd asked in English, 'Could he have some chocolate?' – and gestured towards the toddler.

At that point, the younger boy had repeated – in English – 'Choc choc.'

'Of course he can. Do you have any money?' the woman had replied.

The older boy shook his head.

'Well, go and ask your parents and then come back.'

They never did return.

I didn't know what to think. The woman was adamant it was the boy in the picture. But that meant someone would have had to have taken Ben there. And why? To take him on a plane somewhere? From the way the older boy had said '*he* wants some chocolate', the cigarette vendor had assumed they weren't related, although they both looked the same, with their mops of blond hair. And, I had to admit, 'choc choc' sounded very much like Ben's work for biscuit, 'bick bick'. Could it have been him?

Part of me wanted to go straight to the airport. Another part insisted it was futile. The woman was mistaken. Ben would be back soon. But the seed had been planted.

In the end, the decision of what to do was taken out of my hands. The policemen said, 'Christos Bafounis will see you now. Come.'

So back we went to the police station, once again via Monica's to drop off Danny. Apart from Mum, we didn't travel in silence for once. For Dad, the fact that the police had left it two whole days before bothering to check the airport was unforgivable. What about all the flights that had left yesterday or the day before? Did the Kos police have the power to check all the passenger logs?

I wasn't so concerned by that. I had to believe Ben was still on the island. The alternative was too painful to bear. At the end of the day, the kiosk woman had identified Ben from a photo after the event. She didn't know if he'd boarded a plane or left with an adult to come back to Kos Town. And as she hadn't seen the strawberry birthmark on his neck or the one on his knee, could we really trust her word, anyway?

On the plus side, we were thrilled that something was being done. *At least they're looking...*

Sissy was waiting with Bafounis when we arrived. She informed us that Danny was required for an interview, so Dad set off to collect him. In the meantime, they asked for Stephen to give another statement.

'Why me? I told you everything yesterday.'

'Just come, Stephen.' Sissy said. 'One more interview.'

I was left with Mum. If anything, she'd retreated further into herself than yesterday. If I touched her arm she looked at me. The rest of the time I don't think she knew I was there.

Danny arrived just in time to see Stephen come storming out. Sissy was trying to calm him. He shook her away and stood in front of us, tears in his eyes.

'They accused me.'

'Accused you of what?' Dad said.

Stephen could barely get the words out.

'Of killing Ben.'

'Killing...?'

I couldn't even repeat it. What the hell was going on?

Stephen recounted his ordeal. Via Sissy, Bafounis had told Stephen what had happened on the afternoon of the 24th.

'You see the baby, take the baby for a ride on your motorbike and the baby falls off. He dies. You panic and bury him.'

They had just come out with it. Stephen is Ben's uncle, for God's sake. He loved him like a brother, like a son. Stephen would take his own life before letting a hair on Ben's head be harmed.

'The indicator on your motorbike is broken,' Bafounis had continued. 'My men noticed it this morning.'

'So?' It was all Stephen could do not to laugh, the accusations were so preposterous.

'It broke when you crashed with the baby.'

'No, it didn't. It's been broken for ages.'

Bafounis went on. 'You crashed, the bike smashed, the baby died. You buried him.'

'Have you seen how hard the earth is round here?'

No response.

'What, I just happen to have a shovel on my bike, do I?'

Bafounis ignored the sarcasm. 'You buried him and drove to the hotel,' he insisted.

'No, I didn't!' Stephen's hand smashed onto the table. Sissy jumped, Bafounis glowered. Another officer came in to check on the noise. Bafounis waved him away.

'Tell the truth.'

'I am telling the truth.' He pleaded to Sissy. 'Tell him, please. You know I didn't do it.'

I hated Bafounis for putting my brother through that. This boy wouldn't harm a fly. He loved all creatures. And I know he loved his nephew.

I stood up and hugged him. There was nothing I needed to say. He knew I didn't blame him. None of us did. None of us ever would.

We sat there again for the whole day. Sissy was ever-present with her placatory words. 'They make enquiries, they're looking, they're looking.' I was relieved when Bafounis called me back into the interview room.

If he'd dared to ask me about Stephen's broken indicator I would have told him where to go. There was no way my brother could have been involved. Instead, Bafounis had another name for me.

Simon.

We went over once again the fact that Ben had my family name and, by coincidence, his uncle's as a middle name, and not his dad's. Then Bafounis put his pen down and fixed me with his penetrating glare.

'His father has him.'

I explained that wasn't possible. Simon had left two days earlier. Bafounis just shrugged.

'Maybe he left. Maybe he came back?'

I shook my head. Simon and I hadn't parted on the best of terms, but he would never do anything to harm Ben. He knew that Ben couldn't live without me and my parents. No, he wouldn't have done that.

'We will check,' Bafounis said.

I left the room in a daze. So far that day, the police had accused Stephen of killing Ben, Simon of kidnapping him and a stranger of smuggling him abroad on a plane. I needed to face facts: they didn't have a clue what was going on.

We weren't in a good way. As soon as we were back at the caravan, Stephen took himself out to the hen house. He wouldn't talk. *Couldn't* talk.

I wasn't doing any better. Physically I was there; mentally I was miles away. It was Friday evening. Ben had been missing since Wednesday afternoon. I am amazed I held it together so long.

Monica came again with more food, and dealt with Mum again. I don't recall how long she stayed. I don't remember saying a word. All I could think about was what had happened that day. Whichever way I looked at it, the police weren't expecting Ben to be handed in. Not today, not tomorrow, probably not ever.

They thought he'd been kidnapped or, worse, killed.

I didn't eat anything that night. I didn't say anything I can remember and I didn't cry. There were no tears left. I was hollow, empty. Drained of everything. Dad had to order me to bed. I couldn't even manage sleep. My head was full of the same images of Ben's smiling face. How could he have been stolen or killed? It just wasn't possible. The police were wrong and that was the end of it.

The pressure affected us all differently. With me fading fast, Stephen in hiding and Mum out of the loop, it was left to Dad to hold the fort. He felt as guilty as Mum about Ben's disappearance but someone needed to be alert if the police arrived with news, and someone had to think about Danny.

But by Saturday morning, even Dad had snapped. Although we didn't know that then.

I woke up at about half past eight, determined once again to take on the day. Danny slept in till nine. Mum emerged a few minutes later.

'Where's your father?'

It was the first time I'd heard her speak for a day or two. If Dad wasn't in the bedroom, I didn't know. I hadn't heard him leave. When Stephen came over for some coffee he mentioned hearing the Land Rover starting up early.

'Maybe he's gone to see Bafounis,' he said. 'I know he was angry about them accusing me yesterday.'

That made sense. It was on all our minds. As Bafounis preferred to speak to men, Dad was the obvious one to go there. We tried to eat breakfast. Mum went back into her room. Danny played outside with Stephen. I stared at the wall.

I don't know how long I sat there but suddenly Mum's door opened and she asked again if Dad had returned.

I shook my head.

'He's not at the police station,' she said, some emotion in her voice, and retreated once again.

Before I knew it, the afternoon sun was already beaming down. I decided to go to the hotel and see my friends and explain events. I needed to remember that my family weren't the only people worried about Ben. Manos couldn't have been more sympathetic and he offered to speak to Bafounis on our behalf. I regret not letting him now. But he'd done enough letting Martin and Peter help in the search and – even though it was the last thing on my mind – promising to hold my job open until I was ready to return. 'Besides, we have a translator, our friend Sissy.'

I joined my friends at the bar. There were no jokes or laughs like there used to be. Even the jollity of the rest of the customers didn't make an impression on me. I just wanted to be among people. We were all going stir-crazy in the caravan. A distraction – any distraction – was a life-saver.

The sun had set by the time I left to go home. I still arrived at the caravan before Dad. It was nine o'clock. He'd been out for fourteen hours. Whatever line of enquiry he was pursuing had to be serious. Then, an hour later, I heard footsteps shuffling through the gravel outside.

I heard and smelt Dad before I saw him. Mum was ahead of me.

'You're drunk,' she hissed, as he pulled himself up into the doorway. 'Get to bed.'

After three days of being on another planet, Mum was well and truly back with us, trembling with fury at Dad. He was rambling in his drunken state, saying there was something wrong with the Land Rover, that he loved everyone: the usual baloney. Mum wasn't impressed. She frogmarched him into their room, then slammed the door.

The atmosphere as the rest of us turned in for the night was strained. For Mum, it brought back the bad memories from when we were young of him putting a drink with mates after work ahead of his family; going to the pub instead of coming home for his dinner. She also said he was selfish for just leaving us alone.

I couldn't be too upset with Dad. He may have absented himself physically, but Mum had as good as disappeared mentally over the last few days. I was just as disappointed with her for abandoning us. But I didn't mention it. We all needed to be pulling together as a family, not tearing each other apart.

The following morning we left Dad sleeping it off in the caravan and took the Land Rover out. Dad wasn't lying about something being wrong with it: we eventually found it stuck against a tree down the lane. Luckily it wasn't damaged, and we drove to Monica's. Instead of just dropping Danny off, we all stayed for the day.

Monica was amazed at the transformation in Mum. I wasn't. Mum was back to herself because with Dad going off the rails, someone needed to be on them. They were a good partnership. If one wasn't on top of things, the other would step in.

As it was a Sunday, Monica cooked a big family meal for everyone. I don't think I ate a thing. Without having Mum to worry about, I felt myself sinking. I couldn't shake the insinuations Bafounis's scattergun-approach was coming up with: kidnapping, injury, death. How dare he suggest it? I realised I was shivering. It wasn't cold. I excused myself and stood outside in the warm air. I needed to be alone.

I don't think anyone was looking forward to going back to the caravan. Mum's mood darkened as we approached. Dad was outside, lying in the shade when we pulled up. There could have been the mother of all rows. Instead, Mum just gave Dad a look and went straight into the caravan. He stared after her, then at us, then at his feet, shame written all over him. More words weren't necessary.

But Dad did have something to say. One consequence of his day out was that he'd poured his heart out to a lot of people. One of them, Tony, a regular at the Sandy Lane Hotel across the road from the caravan, had something very interesting to say.

'I saw your Simon last week, Eddie.'

'Oh, yes. What was he up to?'

'He was going in the bank in Kos Town. I said hello.'

'He's back in England now,' Dad explained. 'Christine dropped him at the ferry on Monday.'

Tony sipped slowly from his beer bottle, then placed a hand on Dad's arm.

'That can't be right, Eddie.'

'Why not?'

'Because I saw him on Tuesday.'

CHAPTER NINE

I WANT TO TELL
THE WORLD

Without the sound of the cicadas chirruping, I might have thought my ears had stopped working. Even Ben the dog was silent. Dad's words and their implications hung in the air. Then Mum broke the spell:

'Well, that's impossible. Ben and I waved him off ourselves.'

'Did you see him actually get on the boat?' Stephen asked.

'He waved to us from the deck as it pulled away. He definitely left Kos.'

'And then he came back,' Dad added.

'No,' I said. 'Bafounis has made you think that. He's making us turn on each other. He's already tried to make us point the finger at Stephen.'

I wiped the perspiration from my forehead. This whole conversation had got me worked up and I couldn't put my finger on why. Was this the excuse my dad had been waiting for to turn me against Simon for abandoning me so cruelly when I was pregnant? Or did he genuinely believe there was a chance he'd taken Ben?

'Dad, are you sure you're remembering this right? You did have a drink yesterday.'

There was a noise like a harrumph from Mum, but she said nothing.

'I know what I heard, Kerry. I think we should consider it seriously.' He stared at me and, voice low and earnest, said, 'Can you honestly say you don't believe Simon has it in him?'

I paused. As upset as I had been, I still hadn't wanted my parents to know about the callous way he'd walked out on me. The way he'd made me wait at Jane's and not shown up until three days later. He was Ben's father after all, and I had wanted to be loyal. Even so, what would Simon have to gain from kidnapping Ben? Surely he didn't think he could just take Ben back to Sheffield and then I'd just follow him home?

Once the idea was planted, it took root very quickly. There would be no going back for me and Simon if he was responsible for Ben's vanishing act. On the other hand, part of me prayed that he *had* taken him. At least my boy would be safe with someone he knew and loved. It wouldn't be long before he was back in my arms.

'What are we going to do, Dad?' I said.

'You need to have it out with him. We'll call him tomorrow.'

I nodded. 'I'll know if he's lying the second he opens his mouth.'

Whether he was involved or not, Simon had a right to know what was going on. It was now Day 6 since Ben had gone missing. It was time we told the family. Simon has told me since that we had spoken a couple of times since Ben disappeared, but I was so distressed I can't remember the calls or what was said. He definitely didn't know about Ben. The conversation I will never forget is the moment I told him Ben had gone.

On Monday morning, Simon called me at the hotel. Dad was there with me and we were grateful for the use of the phone, but I wished it wasn't such a public place. Phones in 1991 still had leads, so Manos dragged it as far as the cable would stretch to give us as much privacy as possible. Even so, anyone coming to reception for anything would have seen and heard us.

I really didn't want to tell Simon. I realised I was in a state of denial. Saying what had happened, putting it into words, felt like it would make the nightmare real. When I heard his voice, I struggled to hold myself together, and took a deep breath.

'All right, Kerry?' he asked.

'I don't know how to tell you this.' More deep breaths. My throat felt like it was made of paper. 'I don't even know where to begin to explain.' Another breath. I closed my eyes and held the receiver against my forehead, willing the words to form. 'It's a long story,' I said eventually, 'but, basically, Ben's gone missing.'

Silence. Simon's turn to be lost for words. Then, quietly: 'How?'

I started with the details, as matter of fact as I could. Simon took it all in calmly. Then he asked when it had happened.

'Last Wednesday. The 24th.'

'The 24th! You waited a week to tell me?'

I had to let him rant. I tried to say we thought we were doing the right thing. That there was no point worrying him if Ben was going to be handed in the following day. That that was genuinely what we had thought would happen.

'You couldn't have done anything and it would have been cruel to tell you. I thought we were going to find him.'

'So why are you telling me now?'

'Because...'

I couldn't finish that sentence. Why *was* I telling him now? I realised the line had gone quiet.

'Simon? Simon? Simon!'

His voice crackled back into life. He was sobbing uncontrollably. I could barely make out the words.

'I'll call you back!' he shouted, then hung up.

I was shaken. Simon's reaction had rocked me. Maybe he didn't have anything to do with Ben's disappearance after all. Dad took the phone and called his sister, Nancy, and her husband, Derek. He relayed the same facts I'd said, as unemotionally as possible. His voice sounded small.

'Eddie, do you want us to come out?' Aunty Nancy said.

Dad went silent. He thought of Mum, so fragile and only recently talking again. He thought of me, trying to be strong, to remain positive. And he thought about his own binge, so pathetic a way of hiding the pain.

'Please,' he said.

That was the last phone call either of us wanted to make, so Dad arranged for Nancy to call everyone else. There was one more conversation I needed to have, though. And as soon as the phone started trilling, I braced myself.

Simon was back in control of his emotions. He asked for more information and I told him as much as I could about the police investigation. He said that he would try to get a flight and come out. I was about to hang up when I remembered something.

'Simon, the police asked if you could bring your ferry and aeroplane tickets.'

'Why?'

'I don't know. They just asked.'

'Fine,' he said. Then he hung up again for good.

I sat with my knees up to my chin, my arms wrapped round my legs, holding two of Ben's little plastic cows. The adrenaline caused by making those phone calls had carried me home. Then I'd crashed. Dad and Stephen had made the daily trek to the police station for an update. If I closed my eyes I could see Ben. Strange as it sounds, that hurt. I didn't want to see him in my dreams; I wanted him in my arms.

Saying those words to Simon – 'Ben's gone missing' – had somehow made it worse. I hadn't told anyone before. It was no longer a bad dream. By articulating it, I'd made it real.

Mum spoke to me. Danny spoke to me. Ben the corgi tried to scramble onto my lap. I don't remember saying or doing anything. Not even when Dad and Stephen returned. They didn't have any news. I knew that before they opened their mouths. What was the point in listening?

The rest of Day 7 passed in the same despondent fug. Day 8 was a landmark. It was Wednesday 31 July. Ben had been missing for a full week.

It was also a full week since I'd been back to my own apartment. I couldn't face it, not even to use the shower. There were too many reminders of Ben in that place. I didn't want to be there alone. I wasn't strong enough to be anywhere alone.

Unfortunately, being around the others wasn't much help either.

Looking at us, you'd have thought a decade had gone by. I hadn't seen Mum eat more than a slice of toast in the time since Ben had gone. The rich suntans that Dad and the boys had when

I'd arrived seemed to have faded. The bags under the eyes, the drawn faces, told their own story. We were zombies. Existing, not living. We'd been gradually losing it mentally, now our bodies were catching up with our minds.

I remember walking with Mum to the shop, being surrounded by holidaymakers without a care in the world, buying food I didn't care about and she wouldn't eat. We were barely going through the motions of normal family life. We didn't feel like people any more. Life, as we all knew it, was on hold.

The previous day, Mum and Dad had had a chat about his disappearing act on Saturday. Mum had told him in no uncertain terms that he needed to be strong.

'You're the dad; you're the man of the family. You need to be here for us, and for Kerry.'

Dad had agreed and so far had been true to his word, but what could he do? If we weren't sitting miserably outside the cara-van, we were nursing a coffee in the café next door to the police station. Dad was as frustrated as the rest of us. He was suffering as much as anyone. There was no law that said he had to handle it better than me or Mum or Stephen or Danny.

Over the weeks that followed, the café became a home from home for all of us. As we were never made to feel welcome in Bafounis's office, the café next door was the next best place. We spent a lot of time there just sitting, staring at the harbour, nursing cups of coffee or juice, and waiting. Always waiting. Sometimes all of us would pop in to see Bafounis, or usually just Dad or me would make the journey. Then we'd go back to our coffee until it was time to go home.

*

There was a TV in the caravan that had never really been used because it only picked up local programmes, and most of family life was lived outside, anyway. For the last week, however, it had been on pretty much constantly. The gabble of Greek newsreaders and game-show hosts was somehow more soothing than listening to our own thoughts.

I remember at one point noticing the ten o'clock news was on. It didn't matter to me one way or the other: time had lost its value for us. If our caravan beds didn't have to become sofas in the mornings, I don't think I would even have bothered getting up. The hours and now the days were blurring into each other. If anything, sleep was the only release we had. But I hated falling asleep in case I missed the moment someone knocked on the door.

Right on cue, there was a knock on the door.

'Ben!'

I couldn't help it. It was the response I had to everyone and everything. Why else would there be someone outside at that time of night? It had to be good news.

Dad opened the door and we looked down on a tired-looking guy with neat, blond-brown hair, dressed in jeans, a shirt and jacket. He smiled when he saw us.

'Eddie Needham?'

'Yes. Who are you?'

'My name's Martyn Sharpe. I'm a journalist. I want to tell the world your story.'

I've had my fingers burned many times over the years by reporters and newspapers and gossip columns. People tell me I should be more guarded. Maybe I would be if my first experience of the media wasn't as nice as Martyn.

He said he was from the *Sun*. He wanted to write the story of Ben's disappearance. He said the publicity could help find him. It wasn't just in the UK that the *Sun* was massive. I think everyone who came to Kos read it, even if it was two days late by the time copies arrived.

We had nothing to hide. Even so, did we want a journalist in our lives? Would the police want us to do it? Probably not. That was all the persuasion we needed. Christos Bafounis made us feel like we were inconveniencing him every time we turned up. And, besides, Martyn was a Yorkshireman. We knew who we'd rather trust.

We invited him into the caravan and watched while he got his notebook and pen out, and made himself comfortable at the table. There were no Dictaphones in those days and he didn't have a camera. When he looked up, there were five washed-out faces staring at him like he was an exhibit in a zoo. I'm sure he had a long list of questions, but Dad went first.

'How the hell did you find us?'

Martyn laughed. 'Palm Beach Hotel. The night porter gave me directions. It's been quite a journey.'

I watched him warily. The idea of a national newspaper being interested in us was mind-blowing. We were just a family.

Then Martyn asked his first question and any doubts about co-operating vanished. The whole story poured out. Dad led the answers but we all chipped in, with Martyn scribbling in his book like crazy to keep up. I think he only asked a couple of things and we just spoke and spoke until Danny was asleep in Mum's arms. The rest of us weren't far behind.

It was such a relief to feel like we were actually doing something positive, even if we were just talking. I saw my family come alive for those few hours. I felt alive as well. I had to thank Martyn for that. He was a saviour for my family. We'd all been rotting for so long, withdrawing into ourselves and dying from the inside. We could barely seem to get a flicker of interest from the Greek police two miles away and this guy had flown out all the way from the UK to hear what we had to say. Somebody who spoke English who wanted to help. I swear him arriving kept us alive a few more days.

The only downside came as Martyn was leaving, and Dad asked how the *Sun* had even heard of us.

'I heard about you on *Calendar*,' Martyn said. 'Otherwise I would never have known.'

Calendar is a teatime magazine programme broadcast by ITV's Yorkshire Television. On Tuesday night they had run an appeal for money by a man who desperately needed the airfare to get to Greece to help search for his missing son.

That man was Simon. He'd been approached by the press and had agreed to an interview.

It turned out Martyn Sharpe wasn't the only journalist who watched *Calendar*. Over the next two days, the entire British media descended on our caravan. The *Daily Mail* were there at breakfast, the *Daily Mirror* at lunch, and the rest gradually over the next twenty-four hours. By the time the Sunday papers arrived, they were looking for new angles. I remember the *News of the World* only wanted to speak to Stephen. To each one we said the same things. I doubt we were very impressive. We were numb inside, talking on autopilot. I'm sure they wanted us to be excitable and entertaining, but we didn't have it in us. We had the facts, no more. The pain had wiped out any emotion.

The *Mail* was the first paper to ask for photos, and not just of us. They asked to see the farmhouse and the area where Ben could have wandered. Dad offered to go with them, but in the end we all piled into the Land Rover with him. It was unspoken, but I think on some level we just wanted to be together: no one should have to go to the farmhouse on their own.

In the end, there was a queue of photographers calling out instructions, asking us to do this, turn there, all the while click-click-clicking away. Posing like we were at a family wedding left an unsavoury taste my mouth. Worse, though, was to come.

Malcolm Brabant was the BBC's Athens correspondent. Obviously he hadn't seen Yorkshire Television's programme, but the news industry must be a small world because he turned up shortly after the last English paper. Talking to a television camera is incredibly nerve-racking: you have to think so much more about what you're going to say. You have to select the right words first time and make sure you get your message across. I think Malcolm spoke to Mum and Dad first. I was panicking by the time my turn came. I just thought, *Right, deep breath, stay focused and composed, get everything out that we want to say – then collapse.*

I just about managed it. Then Malcolm asked one final question.

'Kerry, if the people who have got Ben are watching now – what would you say to them?'

The bastard. There was no way I could answer that and stay composed, and he knew it.

'Bring him back. Please, bring him back! I don't care why, how, just please, please bring him back to me!'

As kind-hearted as he was, when it came to his work Malcolm could be utterly ruthless about getting what he wanted. And what he wanted was me crying on film. He'd waited, put me at ease with the early questions and then lit the fuse and watched the fireworks.

Over the years, I've been lucky enough to be interviewed by Malcolm many times and he always knows which button to press. It feels horrible at the time but I suppose it makes for dynamic, unforgettable television. And if it prompts one person to reveal something they know, it's worth it. To this day, that has remained my approach to the media: I will do anything to keep them interested in Ben's story, regardless of the personal cost to myself.

As the English press interest died down, attention from the local media grew. One or two of the interviews were conducted outside the caravan as usual. Some TV crews, seeking a bit of local flavour, filmed us down at the Tree of Hippocrates – perhaps they hoped some of his wisdom would rub off on the police force a stone's throw away. We certainly did, although perhaps it wasn't helpful to have said as much in the interviews. We probably could have been more tactful when talking about the Kos police to their compatriots, but we were just being honest.

We didn't turn down a single interview but there were times it seemed like a never-ending process. Just when we thought we'd seen the back of the media, another stranger with a notepad or a camera would appear at the caravan door. I know in their way they wanted to help but by Friday afternoon I was drained. We were all exhausted, mentally as well as emotionally. I felt like the roadkill I saw lying in the street every day, being picked over by scavenging birds. The birds just do what they have to, but at the end there's nothing left. That's exactly how I felt. I poured out my soul again and again, relived the horror time after time. It was intrusive and I wished afterwards none of them had ever come.

It was just one more reason to mistrust Simon. After all, without him, they would never have known.

The initial mood spike created by having the British press take an interest eventually plateaued. Once they'd gone, having taken their pound of flesh, we were left again with the crushing emptiness of our own thoughts.

The only thing that kept us going was the hope that once the national coverage started filtering down in the UK, the authorities there would take notice and get involved. The British Embassy in Greece might have seemed to have washed its hands of us, but they didn't speak for our country. It was only a matter of time before Britain sent the cavalry. Or so we thought.

What we actually got was Simon.

I got back to the caravan to one day discover a note pinned to the door. It was from Simon, asking me to meet him at the apartment. Without any means of contacting him, I had no choice but to turn up with the key at the suggested time.

The British people had excelled themselves. Simon's fare had been paid in full by generous strangers. I don't know if they donated enough to pay for two extra tickets, but his brothers, Paul and Chris, turned up at the apartment as well. They were all riding colourful scrambler motorbikes as none of them had a licence for a car.

I remember staring hard into Simon's face, looking for a sign. I'd told myself that I would know the second I laid eyes on him whether he'd been involved. When the time came, I honestly didn't have a clue.

'Have you brought your ferry and plane tickets?' I asked.

'Yeah, I've already dropped them off at the police station.'

'Great,' I said. But I was thinking, *How convenient*. Had he really brought them, or was he lying? How would I learn the truth?

'Are you sure you don't want to come in?' Simon said.

'No, I need to get back.'

'Well, maybe we could go out tonight? You and me. Have a meal, get a drink, and have a proper chat about everything?'

'Do what?' I felt the blood rushing to my head. 'Do you have any idea what I've been going through here? We've been suffering, Simon, every minute of every day. I don't even know what food is any more.'

By the time I finished I realised I was screaming, but I couldn't stop. I felt my knees buckle and I hit the floor hard on my palms. I'd used up all my strength shouting. All I had left were tears. I lay my head on the tarmac and sobbed my heart out.

I don't think Simon knew what to do. He kept saying, 'What's wrong, Kerry? What is it?' It was his brothers who scooped me up, sat me upright on a wall and tried to calm me down.

Gulping for air between sobs, I managed to force out how Simon had been spotted in a bank in Kos Town the day after he was meant to have left. He looked at me like he'd seen a ghost.

'That was Monday, not Tuesday. I swear.'

I said nothing.

'Kerry, you believe me, don't you?' He was kneeling in front of me, his hands on my shoulders. 'I went to the bank on Monday to get money to buy my tickets.' He stood up, kicked the wall. 'Kerry, don't you trust me?'

Now Simon looked ready to cry.

'I don't know, Simon. I don't know.'

*

The next day Dad made his regular trip to see Christos Bafounis. Uncle Derek and Aunty Nancy had arrived the night before. While Nancy stayed at the caravan to look after Mum, me and Danny, Derek went with Dad into Kos Town. They returned with news.

'Bafounis says he's seen Simon's ticket.'

'And?' I said.

'And nothing. He says it's just as Simon says. He caught the ferry then the plane on Monday. He wasn't here Tuesday.'

'That can't be right.'

'That's what Bafounis says. And, by the way, he wasn't too happy about it, either.'

'Why not?'

Dad shrugged. He'd obviously been spending too long at that police station. 'I think he'd pinned his hopes on it being Simon.'

Bafounis wasn't the only one. My shoulders slumped and I put my hands over my face. I realised how much store I'd put in that theory. If Simon had him then of course Ben would be perfectly looked after. I had no doubts about that. Ben probably wouldn't even know we were worried about him. Simon would have just said, 'We're going on a little holiday. Mummy will be coming soon.' Just like I'd told Ben so many times about visiting his Nana.

I would never have forgiven Simon if he had taken Ben, but at that moment I really wished he had. Because if Simon didn't have Ben, then who did? Simon had had nothing to do with Ben's disappearance. The truth was far, far worse...

There was nothing to do but cry again.

CHAPTER TEN

THE BIRDS WILL COME

Simon wasn't the only person now interviewed by the police. After the Ward brothers had flown home as frustrated by the police investigation as the day they'd arrived, we began to hear from all our island friends and colleagues that they'd also been called in one by one. Monica, Athena and Dino, Manos, Martin, Peter, Dad's drinking friends – everyone. I didn't understand what Bafounis was playing at. They couldn't help with the abduction. Some of them had only recently discovered the news. So what was the point?

'Character references,' Dad explained. 'Bafounis wants to know what we're like as people.'

'How does that help him?'

'It tells him if our friends think we're the sort of people who might have done something to our own flesh and blood.'

I gasped for fresh air. The very idea of people suggesting that made me sick. I know the police have to do their jobs but this was poisonous. They should have been out looking for Ben, not scratching around for gossip about us. Still, we had nothing to hide.

Throughout the day, however, the poison seemed to spread to us. We couldn't help picking over every potential permutation.

What had people said about us? Were they judging me for being an unmarried mum, for leaving Ben while I went to work, for being a teenager with a child? Dad had similar thoughts, Mum too. We were already wrecks, emotionally barren and physically stretched. Now we were paranoid as well.

Bafounis wasn't just speaking to friends. He and his men had also interviewed everyone who could possibly have any information about Ben's whereabouts. Michaelis was called in for his version of events, as was Dino Barkas, the driver of the digger that had been dumping hardcore earlier in the day. Even Sissy was called to give her own account, as she had spoken to Stephen that day.

The first we knew of this was when we made our daily pilgrimage to Kos Town the following day. Dad and I went straight up to see Bafounis while the others made their way to the café as usual. The chief of security police never seemed happy to see us but today he actually looked up. I could tell he had news. An English-speaking officer told us Barkas had reported seeing a white car parked along the lane on the day Ben had disappeared. He couldn't identify the passengers but he could tell there were two men in the front and a woman in the back.

'They took your baby.'

It was the news I'd been dreading and praying for at the same time. On the one hand it was evidence that Ben had been abducted. On the other hand, it was a breakthrough in the investigation. Finally we had something to go on.

Dino had not been able to confirm whether there had been hire car signs on the number plate or bodywork but it had looked like a Suzuki, a popular model with the rental companies. The police were going to check for cars reported stolen and ask Avis and

Hertz and other firms to scour their records for anyone who had previously hired a white vehicle. It would be quite a task: every other hire vehicle seemed to be white.

'Who do you think was in the car?' Dad asked the officer.

He shrugged.

'We are looking.'

He picked up a piece of paper from Bafounis's desk. On it was a picture of Ben and a lot of writing. It was a 'Wanted' poster. I knew it was coming because we'd written some words for it. Seeing it for real and knowing the police would be putting it up around the island was another matter. Even if it had all been translated into Greek, seeing that poster was just another harsh reminder of the fact my baby boy was missing.

Dad and I went back to the coffee bar to update the others. I don't remember walking there. I couldn't take in what we'd just heard. After all the whispers and shrugs, to have the police come out and say, once and for all, that Ben had been abducted was sickening. The idea of strangers laying their fingers on my precious boy turned my stomach.

Dad relayed the news.

'He's been kidnapped?' Mum said. 'Who'd kidnap Ben? We haven't got any money. We can't pay a ransom.'

'Whatever it is we'll find it somehow and we'll pay it,' Stephen said. I loved him for that.

It was Dad's turn to be quiet now. Finally he said, 'I don't think it's that kind of kidnapping.'

'What do you mean?' I asked.

'If Ben's been taken, it's not to get money out of us. It's to sell him.'

'Sell him? Who sells children?'

It was the most preposterous idea I'd ever heard. People didn't sell children. Had Dad been drinking?

'I'll tell you who,' he said. 'Gypsies.'

He went on to tell us what certain people at the pub opposite the caravan site and also in Athena and Dino's coffee bar had been saying to him since they'd read about Ben in the local press.

'I've heard it from too many people. It's the gypsies. They sell children for illegal adoption. Sometimes they even sell their own.'

I couldn't believe what I was hearing. Kidnapping was one thing. This was human trafficking. *You can't buy and sell children like they're bags of sugar.*

It got worse. Dad reported the various whispers from his friends. If the snatched kids were lucky, they were sold to the highest bidder and raised with their new family in another country. The less fortunate ones were used as organ donors – whether they could spare the organ or not.

I was in a nightmare that I couldn't wake up from. What was Dad even saying? Did he really believe his own words? He'd lived the Irish Traveller life for years. In England, gypsies were unconventional, they had a reputation for petty crime. But they didn't abduct children to harvest their organs. What made him think Greek ones would?

'These are not gypsies,' he said. 'They're scum.'

Dad was a man on a mission. As we sat in the café one morning, he announced, 'I can't sit here waiting. I need to be looking.' What we didn't know was that various friends in various pubs had pointed out to him the sort of locations in Kos where a kidnapped boy might be smuggled without too much fuss. Conspiracy theories abounded, I knew that much. But we also had no idea that several people had suggested Dad take up their offer of acquiring a handgun. The people he would be coming up against wouldn't think twice, he was assured, of using a weapon to protect themselves. Mum and I were blissfully ignorant of all this. We just knew every morning he packed a lunch and disappeared for the day, again and again and again.

I only had coffee in front of me but I couldn't drink it. I couldn't even face water. Nothing would stay down. My stomach, like my mind, was in turmoil.

I stared out over the harbour, at the day-trippers hopping between islands and fishing boats returning with their overnight hauls. Even if the police had checked the main port, there were so many other vessels leaving from smaller harbours like this one or inlets all around the island. I watched every boat depart and wondered, *Is Ben on that one?*

Eventually, we made our way back to the caravan. On the way we called into the hotel bar opposite. A couple of Mum and Dad's friends were there. It didn't take much prompting for them to repeat what they'd already told Dad. He hadn't been exaggerating. Everyone we met seemed to know the rumours that children were snatched to order. Yes, sometimes it was for organ theft. Other times it was because a couple couldn't have a child for whatever reason and so bought one from the gypsies. The way I understood it, the kidnappers presented a menu of options and prices. Apparently blond, European-looking boys and girls fetched the premium prices. They could be passed off as American, Australian, Scandinavian, northern European. But not Greek. That in itself told a story.

After the hideous suggestion that children were being taken to have their kidneys removed, the idea of a couple so desperate for a child that they were willing to break the law to get one didn't seem so terrifying. The purchasers would have to be rich and they'd have to want a child more than anything. When the police finally tracked Ben down, he would at least have been cared for by people rich enough and wilful enough to look after him.

But there was so much about the abduction theory that didn't stack up. Ben couldn't have been taken to order because no one knew he was going to be up at the farmhouse that day. Even I didn't know that was Mum's plan that morning. What's more, the farmhouse was in such an out-of-the-way location that nobody could have just been passing. It's a dead end. If you were cruising around looking for targets, you wouldn't go up there, not with the beach and the busy back roads elsewhere.

And where did this leave the white car? Was it gypsies in the car? Dad didn't think so.

'They'd have a truck, probably a flat-bed with a tarpaulin over the rear.'

'So where does that leave us?'

'I don't know. But, first thing tomorrow, I'm going back to Bafounis.'

The next morning Dad presented the villagers' consensus about the gypsies. Bafounis and his English-speaking officer listened then, of course, shrugged.

'It is not gypsies,' the officer translated Bafounis's words matter-of-factly. 'Kos gypsies do not cause trouble.'

According to him, anyone from Kos was incapable of committing a crime. We knew that was the official view from the way the

Swedish rape victim at the station had been treated. If you believed the locals, Kos inhabitants never even got a parking ticket.

Dad wouldn't let them get away with that as an answer. Too many people were suggesting it as a genuine possibility. They wouldn't have just made it up to hurt us. Bafounis said that he would speak to the leader of the largest gypsy camp on the island.

'But it is not them. They steal livestock, maybe, but not babies.'

Looking back, one thing was still clear. The police didn't have a clue what to do. If Kos had never suffered a single crime then obviously they had no experience of solving one. Certainly not a case of child abduction. Even so, they were still experienced officers. Why didn't they ask for assistance? The Athens police could have advised. Even the UK police would have sent bodies over if requested. I don't know if it was Bafounis or his boss Dakouras or someone more senior dragging their heels, but they were wrong. They should have made the call.

Knowing the police were groping in the dark made everyone a potential suspect. I found myself studying every adult with a blond child, thinking, *Is that him? Have you got my Ben?* I lost track of the times I saw a little toddler turn around and felt my heart hit my boots.

It wasn't just children. I couldn't see a little white car without my neck spinning like an owl's. I think we all did it, sitting in the café, watching the traffic like a tennis audience. Left, right, left, right.

We weren't the only ones chasing shadows. Michaelis had a theory of his own (a theory we did not for one minute believe). He rented some of his land out to a farmer to raise cattle and goats.

After he'd suggested Dad move his caravan to the farmhouse, Michaelis had informed the farmer that he'd have to find somewhere else for his animals. The man hadn't taken it very well. Maybe he had snatched Ben to get back at who he perceived had stolen his property.

It made as much sense as anything else. But one theory I could not contemplate was that Ben had died on that farmland on 24 July. Sadly, following the release of the 'Wanted' poster, that seemed to be the only theory anyone could come up with. Mum's friend Monika came straight out with it and said Ben must have had an accident at the farmhouse and died up there. Other people were more tactful, but their surmising of the situation was just as offensive.

'He climbed into the bucket of the digger and fell asleep,' one so-called friend of Dad's said. 'Then Dino started work again without realising.'

'He slipped and fell under the rubble,' another pessimist guessed.

For the most part these were people who hadn't seen the farmhouse and based most their information on the news reports, gossip or the poster itself. I shouldn't have let them get to me. After all, we'd searched that farmhouse and its grounds day and night. Even so, the following morning at the police station, I planned to ask Bafounis what he thought. I knew I could rely on him not to pull punches. I had also had a proposition from Malcolm Brabant.

In the end we actually saw Bafounis's boss, Mr Dakouras. At least he spoke English. I asked him outright if he felt, honestly, that Ben had died on that hillside in Iraklis. When he shrugged, I explained that Malcolm had offered, via the BBC, to organise specialist equipment to search the area. This time Dakouras shook his head and tutted.

'No need, no need,' he assured me. 'If the baby is there, the birds will come.'

As macabre as it was to hear, it made sense. That's how farmers know if one of their livestock dies in the field: the birds begin to circle, like vultures, overhead. They never had. We would have noticed.

Which is why I was surprised one morning when Dad and I called in at the police station for our usual non-update and sensed there was something we weren't being told. Eventually an officer admitted, rather matter-of-factly, that the army had been to Iraklis and searched the farmhouse site.

'Why weren't we told?' I said. 'We could have helped.'

A shrug.

'Well, did you find anything?' At that moment, I wasn't confident of being informed even if Ben was found.

'The army searched every inch. Fire brigade divers even searched the well. No sign of the baby.'

We learnt later that the army involvement had come about after pressure from the British Consulate in Athens. Perhaps they weren't as unhelpful as they'd seemed on the phone. They certainly hadn't been too impressed by Dakouras's theory. Either way, someone should have told us it was going on. Dad put aside his personal investigation for the day and drove straight up there.

The idea of the army scouring the area filled us with hope. We pictured the way the UK police conducted countryside searches, dozens of officers in a line, walking in unison, beating the earth and bramble with sticks, combing every square inch of the target site. We didn't want Ben to be found there, obviously. A child could not have survived on his own for that long. But the fact they were applying such resources was a massive confidence boost. Finally, the authorities were acting.

When Dad reached the site, he spoke to the neighbours who'd seen the search and he knew we were back where we'd started.

According to the couple who lived across the lane, there had been army troops at the site. Some, but not a battalion. No more than half a dozen, Dad was told. Worse than the number had been the attitude. Our witnesses said the troops sat in the shade the entire time. Unless Ben had been hiding underneath one of the deckchairs by the farmhouse, those soldiers were not going to find him.

It's hard to hear information like that and not blame the messenger. Dad was furious. More lies. More laziness. More Greek behaviour.

He forced his way over to the well, down the field from the farmhouse. The amount of prickly bracken meant there was no way Ben, who was timid even about the harsher grass, would have dared wander that way. He certainly could not have scaled the three foot needed to climb over the wall of the well. Later that night Dad returned with Stephen. Stephen was a fully qualified diver. He took one look at the narrowness of the well, pictured himself squeezing down there with his air tanks and diving apparatus, and said, 'Dad, there's no way a fire brigade diver has been down there. Anyone who says they have is lying.'

We called the Consulate and also spoke to Dakouras and Bafounis. They all gave the same response. The search had been thorough and conducted to the best possible standards by the highest qualified experts. That told us everything.

In the immediate aftermath of Ben's disappearance, I was strong for Mum and Dad. They needed me. Then, as Mum recovered some of her strength, I began to withdraw. By the time the whole town was offering an opinion on my son's whereabouts I knew I was going mad. Every hour I spent staring into the distance at the caravan or watching the waves at the harbour, I just had the same phrases echoing around in my head: 'he's kidnapped', 'it's gypsies', 'he's dead', 'sold for organs'... I couldn't make them stop.

Mum saw what was happening to me and tried to fix it. Ben had been missing for almost three weeks, Derek and Nancy had left and Dad was scouring another part of the island. It was down to us to help each other once again. She said to me one morning, 'You're not going to Kos Town, we're going out.'

I didn't fight her. I didn't have the energy. I barely had the strength to get into the Land Rover. We drove about eight miles outside Kos Town, then Mum parked and led me down a pretty steep walkway to a rocky beach. I could see the steam coming off the water pools even before I reached the bottom. We were at the island's famous Thermal Beach, where the water is heated by volcanic action deep below.

'Just for today,' Mum said, 'you are going to let your hair down. You're not helping Ben by getting ill.'

I know I had an amazing day because Mum took pictures and tells me I dived into the hot spa pool then the cold sea, then back into the steamy pool. The problem is I don't remember a minute of it. The second we returned to the caravan I think I must have switched back onto autopilot. I love Mum for trying to help but it was going to take more than a paddle and a splash to stop my descent into inertia.

We were all suffering, and not just mentally. Ben had been missing for almost a month and money was running out. We weren't eating, although Mum was still making small meals, and we tried to force ourselves to have lunch somewhere so that cost a bit. Then there was caravan rent and petrol for our daily ping-ponging journeys to Kos Town. Without money, we faced the very real possibility of having to leave Kos – there was no social security safety net like we'd get in Britain. No money, no home, no food. It was as simple as that.

Dad saw a way to kill two birds with one stone. He decided to go back to work.

'We need an income.'

He was worried we would judge him. Nothing could have been further from our minds. In fact, the following day I ended up back in my old job as well.

I hadn't made a conscious decision to return. I'd gone to use the phone at Palm Beach to update my grandma; if I could face it, I would call Simon as well. He'd been back home more than a week. As soon as I stepped inside reception, Manos took one look at what I'd become and said, 'Why don't you come back to work? Take your mind off things? You're around friends. It might just make it a little bit easier for you.'

'I can't. I need to be contactable in case there's news.'

'Here you have the telephone,' Manos said. 'The police can reach you in seconds.'

He had a point. What was I achieving rotting away outside a café or the caravan all day, every day? So I said yes. Manos couldn't have been nicer. I got a choice of shifts and I think he even told Jorgas not to give me any grief during dinner service. Everything was set up for me.

And I still hated it.

It started okay. Knowing that tourists don't want to be served by a physical wreck gave me a reason to get washed, change my clothes and put make-up on. Even my hair, which hadn't seen a brush in a month, soon looked the part. As soon as I set off on the walk to work, however, no amount of personal grooming could stop the pain rushing back, at least for those fifteen minutes I was on my own. I didn't have to worry about keeping my feelings in check in case I upset Mum or Danny. It was a time of contemplation, an opportunity for my own thoughts to come to the fore.

I'm not religious, but on my first day I looked at the beautiful blue sky and heard myself say, 'If there is a someone up there, why are You doing this to me?' I couldn't understand what I was doing and I couldn't stop either. It sounds stupid now. I was trying to reason with fresh air, begging for help from an entity I didn't believe in.

'Please, God, please, stop this pain. By the time I've finished this shift, please let him be back at the caravan. Please let Ben come back.'

It was the same story on the way home. Luckily, I straightened myself out and wiped away the tears before I reached the caravan. Then, the next morning, I looked back at the sky again and said, 'Okay, today then. Make it today. Please let somebody come to the hotel today to say they've found him.'

In between my rants at the Almighty I somehow managed to fry a few chips, serve burgers and pizzas and I even made an effort to engage with the customers. But it was all an act, a front, a smokescreen. The guilt came after every shift. What right did I have to distract myself from thinking about my missing son? What did that say about me as a mother if I wanted to forget what had happened, even if only for a few hours?

I think it was good for me to get out on my own, but there were a lot of mixed emotions. The final straw came when I heard whispers from locals that I shouldn't have gone back to work. Greeks say they have a family culture, but they nearly tore mine apart. People I didn't know were judging me for how I was handling my grief, saying I was betraying my son. In Greece you never stop mourning. I think some people wouldn't believe I was hurting until I dressed head-to-toe in black and began wailing in the streets. The gossip was mean, none more hurtful than the growing accusations that I'd abandoned Ben to be looked after by my mother. Greek mothers married their child's father. They stayed at home, they didn't work. It never occurred to some people – including the police – that there was another way. I couldn't cope. I lasted eight days at the hotel and then I said goodbye for good.

Dad didn't even make a week.

He came home the first day with his hand bandaged up. The second day a roof beam fell close to his head. Another foot closer and he could have been killed. Michaelis couldn't be angry at Dad, but he was concerned.

'Eddie, I don't think this is safe for you. Your mind is elsewhere. Please, just rest.'

But there was more to Dad's injury proneness than lack of concentration. I don't know how long it had been going on, but he had turned to secretive drinking as his way of coping. We were all so busy existing in our own little worlds – even when we were in the same room – he could have grown an extra head and we might not have noticed.

Mum's problem was easier to spot but even that seemed to have crept up on us. She was cooking for everyone else but not

Me at eight months old.

With Stephen, Christmas 1977.

The day we arrived at our caravan to start a new life in Chapel St Leonards.
Left to right: Stephen, Dad, Mum and Danny.

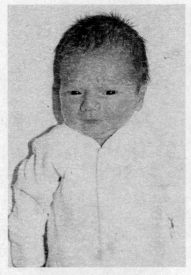

Ben on the day he was born,
29 October 1989.

Ben in a sand pit at the boating
lake in Chapel St Leonards.

Ben's first drink through a straw.

Crawling on the beach in Chapel
at eight months old.

Ben sleeping at his nanny's house.

Loving bath time.

Sat on a mountain at the crazy-golf course, Chapel St Leonards.

Cheeky Ben hiding things under cushions in our home in Sheffield.

Ben and his nanny at Chapel St Leonards.

Ben at ten months, with his proud grandad.

Ben on a winter's day, Sheffield.

Ben with his great-grandma Edna.

Our few happy months on Kos.
Here Ben is cuddling a stray cat
at the caravan.

Ben on Kos, wanting to help
Grandad fix the fencing.

Mum outside
the caravan.

This was the last
photo taken of
Ben before he
disappeared.
He loved Stephen's
motorbike.

A portrait of the family taken for the press coverage one week after Ben went missing. *Left to right:* Danny, Stephen, Dad, me and Mum. And that's Ben the dog.

Me, wandering around near our caravan.

Back home, in Ben's bedroom.

One of the many photos that were so kindly sent in by members of the public from their holidays. Sadly, this also wasn't of Ben.

My beautiful daughter, Leighanna, in September 1995.

My parents have been
tireless in the search for
Ben. Here they are on
Shadows in the Mist on
Greek TV, with Kostas
Hardevellas, where we had
what seemed like a very
promising lead, 1996.

Fundraising for
our airfares.

Leighanna, aged 21 months, taking
part in the reconstruction.

Leighanna has always been a part of
the search. Here she is aged four.

With my beautiful
daughter as she is today.

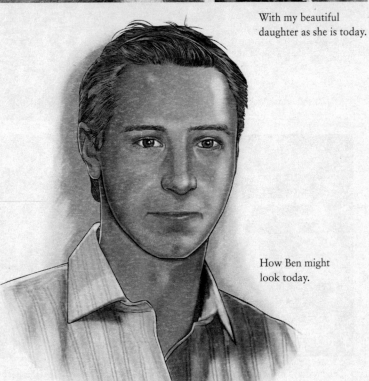

How Ben might
look today.

touching a crumb, except under duress, and was wasting away to nothing. In one month she'd lost three and a half stone.

We all knew that we were dying inside. That's how it felt. Day by day we were getting weaker and weaker and weaker, physically and mentally. I remember climbing into bed one night and thinking, *This is the end. I won't wake up in the morning.* I genuinely thought my body and mind couldn't take any more.

I think the only thing that got me through the night was the realisation that if I didn't wake up the following morning, I would miss Ben coming home. For weeks I thought every night would be my last. Then the next morning I was given another chance.

How many chances would I get, though? One by one we were slipping away from reality. The writing was on the wall. We were all going to die out there, penniless, broken and alone on foreign soil. No one else knew what we were going through. No one could help us. People tried. Mum's sister, Jean, sent money but it just covered basics – it wouldn't pay for the medical aid we were all crying out for – the European Health Insurance Card wasn't in place back then. If we wanted the NHS aid that was due us after so many years of Mum and Dad's contributions, then there was only one place to be.

A week into September, six weeks after Ben had gone missing, Dad took control once again. He looked at Stephen hiding for longer and longer each day in his chicken shed; at Danny, overlooked by all of us when he was just a kid himself; at Mum, emaciated and shattered; at me, broken and destroyed. And he looked at himself, down to his last few drachmas and fighting a dependency on the bottle.

'It's time,' he said. 'We have to go home.'

CHAPTER ELEVEN

YOU HAVE
TWO CHOICES

Even at night, the September air felt like a warm jumper on my skin as I stood on the beach and watched the white horses gallop onto the sand. The waves were hypnotic, entrancing, but I managed to look beyond them, into the darkness of the Aegean Sea. I hadn't wanted to admit it to myself or anyone else before. But now I could. Now I needed to, for my own sanity's sake.

'Ben's not here.'

He wasn't on the island. I had to come to terms with that fact. I probably had done already; I'd just never articulated it in case it looked like I was giving up. I had to face facts. The police didn't have a clue where Ben was. Maybe he'd flown out when the cigarette vendor claimed to have spotted him at the airport. Or he'd been on the ferry that night – when the police hadn't bothered turning up to check. Or he'd been smuggled onto another ship under the tarpaulin on the back of a gypsy's flat-bed truck. It didn't matter. What did matter was admitting he was no longer on the island – and accepting I had no real reason to stay.

From the moment Dad made the decision to take his family home to get the medical help we needed, it was as though a switch in him had clicked. He knocked the vodka and the beer on the head and threw himself into planning our journey. He was dynamic, just like he used to be. I hadn't seen that sort of energy from any of us for a long time.

As it stood, there was no way we could afford tickets back, so Dad once again tried his luck with the British Embassy. This time they were fully aware of the case of Ben Needham. This time they were polite and sympathetic. This time they still said no.

They said they might be in a position to help once they'd means-tested our relatives back home. But it was a process that could take weeks. It was also disrespectful to my grandparents and aunts and uncles. They didn't deserve the embassy poking through their affairs. So Dad, in time-honoured tradition, told them where they could stick their so-called assistance.

A few weeks earlier that would have floored him. Not any more. Dad was a man on a mission. He went back to the caravan and put everything for sale. Finances were tight so unless we could wear it, we couldn't keep it. The caravan, the Land Rover, our television, the boys' mountain bikes, Stephen's motorbike, Danny's little computer game, his records, Mum's gold earrings and even their wedding rings. Everything. They were giving up everything just to get their family home.

I would trade every penny in the world for the return of my son – any parent would. Even so, I wish we could have afforded to return in our own time, not just because our finances dictated it. We had so many other things to worry about, fretting on money was a negative use of our energies. If Ben went missing today, I'm sure the British media would fund at least part of our stay in exchange for a story. Unfortunately, we were completely naïve in the ways of the press back then. We'd given away our whole life story for nothing.

While the great sell-off was going through and with just the Land Rover to get rid of, plans were hatched. Dad said I was to take Stephen to Athens airport then he, Mum, Danny and Ben the dog would follow as soon as the vehicle transaction was completed. The next few days passed, like so many before them, in a blur of packing and tying up loose ends. I still wasn't sure we were doing the right thing but at least we were doing *something*.

On 13 September, Dad and I went to see Bafounis and his team for the last time. They hadn't got anywhere with the gypsy angle or with locating the drivers of the mysterious white car. They saw no reason for us to remain. We promised to contact them with an address as soon as we were settled back in Blighty. In case of emergency, they were told to contact South Yorkshire Police.

'Yes, yes,' Bafounis surprised us by saying. 'We are already in contact with them. They checked Simon Ward's flight record for us.'

So they *had* checked Simon and he was innocent. Why didn't they tell us? If not for my sake, then at least to clear an innocent man's name.

I'd been in two minds about leaving. No sooner had we left the police station than my decision was made. I wanted to get off that island as quickly as humanly possible. Five months ago, I thought I'd arrived in paradise. It had quickly turned into hell. Now I was itching to escape.

Stephen and I weren't the only ones leaving Kos that day. The ferry to the mainland was packed, with no seats inside or out, so Stephen and I stood on the deck and leant on the rail. As the ship pulled away, I scanned the quayside and found Mum and Dad and Danny waving. I raised my arm to signal back but I couldn't do it. It wasn't right.

What am I doing?

'Stephen, I've got to get off.' I was making a mistake. I couldn't leave now. Ben might come back. He'd need me.

I pulled at the collar of my top, trying to get air onto my skin. Out of nowhere, the sweat was pouring down my face. I had to get off. We'd only just left the dock. *I could swim that far.* I looked down at the water churning from the ship's massive propeller, and wondered if I'd survive the jump.

'Don't be silly, Kerry. It's too late.'

Stephen's arms wrapped tightly around me. He sensed what was going through my mind. He was my younger brother, but he was being strong for both of us.

'But he's out there, Stephen. Ben's out there somewhere. I can't leave him.'

'There's nothing we can do here any more, Kerry. Ben's not on Kos. You know that. Whoever's taken him has left the island.'

I felt like the worst parent in the world. Like I was abandoning my son, giving up on any chance of finding him. I knew it was the right decision for our family's sanity. But seeing the shore disappear behind us was too much. I made a desperate attempt to lurch out of Stephen's grip before it was too late. He responded by hugging me tighter. He was crying as hard as I was.

Eventually I felt Stephen relax his hold and he turned his back to the railing and slid down onto his haunches. I stared until the island faded to a dot in the distance, petrified to even blink in case I missed the chance of spotting Ben. Then I hunkered down next to my brother and we held each other until our tears carried us to sleep.

The twelve-hour crossing passed in the same timeless way as the last seven weeks. I don't remember moving, speaking or doing anything. Before I knew it, the unmistakeable sound of horns and shouting from Greek drivers rose above the throbbing of the ferry's giant engines. I was aware of the top deck being suddenly filled by people taking in the night-time view.

Without once looking back at the ocean, I stepped off the ship onto the Greek mainland and felt the Kos lifestyle slip off me like a badly fitting coat. I'd lived there, built a life there. Now I was just another tourist heading home.

Dad, with help from Dino and Athena, had done his research. He gave us an itinerary to follow, starting with directions from the port in Piraeus to a hostel in Athens's Syntagma Square, near the Acropolis. The hostel was basic and cheap, with fifteen beds to a room. I was beyond caring. The next morning, we had to go to Athens airport to buy flights. Dad had no credit card so we hadn't been able to book tickets from Kos. The instruction was, 'Get the first available plane to the UK. Don't wait for us. Don't worry about where it's heading. Just get yourselves home.' Whether we landed in Birmingham, London or Manchester, Dad said that Uncle Derek would pick us up.

Stephen knew about the hassle I'd had on the way out in April. He was as paranoid as me about watching the pennies until we had our tickets in our hands. The odds of there being another generous traveller or policeman to help us out were slim. So we skipped breakfast and hoped the bus to Ellinikon International Airport wouldn't eat too much into our tiny budget.

*

When I'd landed in Athens earlier in the year, I'd had everything to look forward to. It was a trial, but I had the strength to get through anything knowing my family were the prize for completing the ordeal. Five months later, and being informed there were no spaces on any UK-bound flights that day – or for days later – I didn't have that strength. Being told to try again the next day for cancellations was about as much as I could bear. Somehow Stephen managed to lead us the four miles back to the hostel. As well as our one case, he was almost carrying me.

The next morning we repeated the same process – with the same result. What's more, the prices were higher than we'd expected. With another night at the hostel and bus journeys there and back, we'd be lucky to be able to afford to fly and eat in the interim.

'We'll have to stay here,' Stephen said. 'However long it takes.'

The airport had a tree in the departures lounge so we put our case down next to it and made camp there. The day passed slowly, the night slower still. I was hungry, tired, in an emotional drought. I just sat there, stared into the mid-distance and let time wash over me.

I was so drained I barely recognised my own mother when she was standing over me. The plan had always been to meet at the airport if we were still in Greece. I hadn't expected it to work.

With the proceeds of the Land Rover in his pocket, Dad said we deserved a proper meal and a night back at the hostel. Then the following morning we decamped en masse to Ellinikon and had our first stroke of luck. There was a flight bound for Manchester that had five available tickets for us, and one for Ben the dog. Even though it included a scheduled stopover in Yugoslavia and we knew that war had just broken out there, with various states claiming independence, what choice did we have? I couldn't wait to get going. The memory of those Good Samaritans who'd helped me at the domestic airport a few short months ago was long gone. Every moment we were in the country now just increased the pain.

I thought having tickets would be the end of our suffering. After killing so many hours waiting for the flight, we presented ourselves at the check-in desk – and stood open-mouthed as the woman behind the counter screamed.

'The dog! The dog!'

We all looked at Ben and wondered how anyone could be scared of him. But the woman wasn't afraid for herself.

'Where is his box?' she demanded.

Box? Even when we made out what she was saying in her excitable, high-pitched voice, we didn't have a clue what she meant. She calmed down and pointed again at the little corgi.

'The dog can't fly without a box.'

It was the first we'd heard of that. Dad explained that no one had told us anything about a box when they sold us the ticket. Now it was too late to go and buy one. So, if the woman didn't mind, Ben would be coming on as he was.

'No, no, no, I'm sorry, this is not possible.'

'Then I'm not going either!' It was Danny. He scooped the oblivious corgi up and hugged him close to his chest, whispering, 'I won't leave you,' into the dog's ear. I felt my heart break, watching. We'd all coped as best we could over the last weeks and Danny had drawn a lot of solace from the company of his lovable pet. The idea of them being separated now was too much to contemplate.

And there was something else. Something symbolic. This Ben wasn't going to be abandoned like his namesake, not if Danny had anything to do with it. He didn't have to say anything, I just knew. It was an irony too grim to bear. I stared from the dog to the window and questioned again my own decision to leave.

I heard the airline woman call out to someone. All veneer of calm had disappeared. She ran over to another company's desk and even when I couldn't see her, the noise of her voice squealing and squawking carried. It was the same pitch and volume as Xanthippe's – another reminder of the life I was abandoning.

We can laugh about it now but at the time it was horrendous. Danny was distraught. He was not getting on that plane without that dog. And what were we thinking, wandering around the airport with a dog on a lead? It's farcical, really. Did we imagine Ben would just get a seat in economy with us? That he'd have a meal, pop to the toilets when he needed to? It was another example of how we weren't thinking straight at all.

From somewhere a box was produced and, with minutes to spare, we were finally allowed to board. Danny wasn't happy that Ben would be stowed away from us in the hold: part of him was convinced the airline staff were lying. Dad had to physically separate boy from dog, then drag Danny away.

I tried not to look out of the window as we took off over the Aegean, then banked left to head inland towards Albania and beyond. Somewhere out there, down below us, maybe on one of those islands passing underneath right now, was my son. I closed my eyes and tried to sleep.

I awoke as the Olympic 737 made its descent into Yugoslavia. It was the third time I had flown and the first time I'd done it without

Ben. What I would have given to have that small boy sitting on my lap again now. I even missed the screaming as his little ears popped.

The plane was on the ground about an hour. I didn't question it and I was too zoned out in my own little world to notice why. Suddenly, there was a kerfuffle at the front of the plane as three suited officials boarded and spoke to the cabin crew. I didn't take it in even when one of them pointed in our direction and marched down the aisle. Only when the footsteps stopped at the row behind me did I start paying attention. One of the men gestured to Dad and said, in heavily accented English, 'You can't take the dog into England.'

It sank in with Danny before the message reached Dad's brain. My brother was uncontrollable.

While Mum tried to calm him, Dad learned that Ben hadn't been booked in for Manchester.

'You're mistaken. It was done in Athens,' he explained.

'It was never done. Manchester has no papers for the dog. This plane cannot leave Yugoslavia with the dog. You have two choices.'

Danny clawed hysterically at the small side window as the plane finally took off once again. Stewardesses looked over disapprovingly, but they didn't say anything. They knew a child in distress when they saw one, and they also knew why he was upset.

Hundreds of feet beneath us, Dad let poor Ben out of his cage to stretch his legs and answer the call of nature. Danny had tried desperately to get off with them but the officials had not allowed it. Dad wouldn't have permitted it anyway. He read the newspapers; he knew Yugoslavia was not a safe place to be. Troops from both the pro- and anti-independence armies were heading towards the airport at that very moment.

On board the plane, Danny wasn't the only one in tears. We couldn't blame the poor Greek woman too much for forgetting to fax over Ben's paperwork – she'd been busy enough finding his box. Without her, we'd all still be in Athens, and our tickets would have been wasted. Even so, it was torture knowing we'd left someone else behind.

We landed in Manchester not knowing what had happened to Dad. All we could do was wait. We checked the arrivals board and saw a flight due in from Belgrade in four hours. We prayed Dad and Ben would be on it.

They were. Had they missed it, I don't know when we would have seen them again. The next day, Belgrade airport was closed as the warring troops battled for the area. Dad had only just made it out.

It seemed so unfair that all this was happening to us. We couldn't even get home without a drama and without nearly losing one of us – and a dog. That God I didn't believe in had a lot more to answer for.

We picked up our cases and headed for the exit to phone Uncle Derek. Around us there were tearful reunions as family members welcomed travellers home from all around the world. Everyone was so happy – and so oblivious to the suffering in their midst.

I couldn't have hated them more.

CHAPTER TWELVE

IT MIGHT BE HIM

Watching your loved ones in pain can be worse than feeling it yourself. As well as Derek and Nancy, Terry and Anne had also arrived to shuttle us back to Sheffield. I saw each one of them momentarily scan the hall for Ben. They couldn't help it. It was habit. We were all just so used to seeing him.

Dad had arranged accommodation as best he could. He and Stephen would stay with his sister. Mum and Danny would stay with hers. Ben the corgi was in the custody of the quarantine officers for the next six months, and I would be staying with Grandma and Granddad.

We set off there first, in convoy. Mum wanted everyone to hear the full story in person. As soon as Grandma saw me, she broke down. She said what the others had thought. 'I can't believe he's not coming back with you. It's not real.'

It was 16 September 1991. The first day of the rest of our lives.

We'd come back to England partly for medical help, so I set off to register with a local GP. I was still on Grandma's road when a woman did a double-take of me, then walked on. I ignored her, but I had the sense of being watched the whole way there. Just before I walked into the surgery, another stranger said, 'You're Ben Needham's mum.'

I racked my brain trying to place her face.

'Do I know you?'

'You were on the news, love. I'm so sorry for you.' She gestured at her husband and children by her side. 'We all are.'

I was gobsmacked. I'd spoken to every major news outlet while I was in Kos, but I hadn't seen a single headline. I had no idea that the story of Ben's disappearance had been front-page news on every paper and led the national agenda on TV for a week. All of Britain knew everything about us. Naturally, the Sheffield local press had given Ben's disappearance blanket coverage, which explained why I'd felt so many eyes burning into me. I had to get used to the fact that I was a celebrity for the worst possible reason.

The GP knew exactly who I was as well, so I barely had to explain myself. For an instant fix she prescribed a course of diazepam, a strong antidepressant. For the longer term, she booked me in for two therapy sessions a week. She was a trained grief counsellor so if anyone could help me, it was her.

Mum and Dad had the same treatment. Stephen refused. He wanted to work through his problems without strangers.

I could see his point. I understood how medicine could help. Even as I left the first therapy session, I couldn't honestly say that my doctor had done anything. It was only looking back I realised that that is the point.

In therapy sessions, the counsellor doesn't say much. They want to hear from you. It was just such a relief to let it all out. In Kos, we had all lived in each other's pockets. We depended on each other to get through the next hour, the next day, the next week. The last thing Mum, Dad, Stephen, Danny or I wanted to do was hurt anyone else by revealing how much pain we were in. So we had put up brick walls around ourselves so the others didn't know how we truly felt. But of course they were all feeling the same things.

All the pain, all the anger, all the horror that had been locked up, suppressed for the last two months, came tumbling out. I could actually feel the weight begin to lift from my shoulders. Years later, I know those sessions helped me a lot more than any drug. Mum and Dad say the same.

There was also more we could do to help each other. Four weeks after we arrived back in the UK, Dad secured a three-bedroom council house on Tunwell Avenue, in Ecclesfield, very close to where I live now. I loved my grandparents but for those four weeks with them, I felt isolated from the only people who knew and felt exactly what I was going through. Going to bed was the hardest. Alone with my thoughts, I replayed every doubt and misgiving I'd had about coming back. I dreamed about Ben at night and I was smiling when I awoke. Then I remembered.

The new house needed work so Dad said we'd do it ourselves, to get in more quickly. Stephen and Danny tackled the overgrown garden. Me, Mum and Dad worked on the inside, stripping carpets and wallpaper, plastering and painting. With the diazepam, the counselling and the physical labour, we just about got through the days.

As soon as we put our paintbrushes down, however, the guilt loomed large. How was this helping to find Ben? At least the daily routine of visiting the police station or sitting outside the nearby café had felt like we were doing something. Dad had covered hundreds of miles searching around Kos. Over there, I could walk the streets, check alleyways and passing vehicles for a sign. As fruitless as it was, at least we were doing something. Now, 2,000 miles away, we were caged animals. I could not have felt more useless.

We weren't the only ones desperate for activity. Simon's father, Cliff, wrote to his local MP, Sir Peter Tapsell, who passed information about the case to the Home Office. They in turn contacted South Yorkshire Police, who contacted me. I was assigned a liaison officer, the lovely matter-of-fact copper, DS Bert Norburn, who said he would be my point of contact for all matters to do with Ben's case.

'You mean South Yorkshire Police are investigating it now?'

When he nodded I could have kissed him. It was all we had wanted, right from the moment Ben disappeared. It was no shame that the Kos police didn't have the expertise to hunt for a missing child; the only shame was that they were too proud or lazy to ask for help. For the first time, I felt confident the right things would be done.

There was a caveat, however. South Yorkshire Police's remit stopped at the UK borders. Any investigation they did would run alongside the Greek efforts. Any results would be passed onto Kos and it would be up to Dakouras and Co whether they acted. I already guessed the answer to that, but Bert assured me everything that could be done from the UK end would be.

The first thing South Yorkshire Police did was to announce a press conference. Bert didn't pull any punches about what it would be like for me.

'This could be really helpful. But,' he warned, 'I guarantee it will be one of the hardest things you'll ever do.'

He wasn't exaggerating. The Sheffield police station has a large room designed to host dozens of members of the press and television companies – and it was packed to the rafters as I gingerly took my seat alongside Bert and the lead investigating officers. Behind me, on a giant projection screen, were huge pictures of Ben's face. I hated having my back to them but every glimpse I took brought the tears closer.

The detective in charge led the presentation. He gave a synopsis of the events of July, and then outlined the purpose of the conference.

'We're appealing to any British tourists heading to Kos, to Corfu or any of the Greek islands or mainland to be vigilant for a little blond boy who looks out of place.'

As the holiday season was nearing its end, he also had a message for those who had already been away.

'If you've been to Kos, please check your photographs, check your videotapes and home movies. Look in the background: is there a little boy? Have you got a picture of Ben in your holiday album?'

It was powerful stuff. Then the spotlight was turned onto me.

I was absolutely petrified. Journalists called out questions and at first I just sat, too stunned by the whole scene to speak. When I did open my mouth, there was a lightning storm of camera flashes and I had to turn away. I was so annoyed with myself. I had essential information that I needed to give out but it was hard. Flash after flash, question after question. It seemed like a lifetime but it was only an hour. I got through it but I must have looked shocking.

Asking holidaymakers to get involved was a stroke of genius. By contrast, I couldn't see any value in the Q&A session. We'd already been interviewed by every reporter in the land. What difference would this make? What difference *could* it make?

We were so naïve about the power of the media. Two decades later, with reality TV and the internet and social media, I think now most people would know how to get publicity. We didn't have a clue how it worked. Why would a normal, working-class Yorkshire family know we could have asked for payments from the journalists who came over to Kos? We weren't looking to profit from our tragedy, but imagine how different our lives would have been if they'd paid for their exclusives. If we could have afforded medical attention we could have stayed out there a lot longer. Where was the advice from the embassy or the Foreign Office to take advantage of these opportunities?

We just didn't know how to play the game. Shortly after returning from Kos, we decided to get in contact with the children's campaigner Esther Rantzen, so we rang the Childline number in the phonebook. When I told a journalist this years later, she laughed.

'Why didn't you just call the BBC and ask to be put through to Esther Rantzen's office?'

It never occurred to us that that was even a possibility. Normal people don't phone the BBC!

For all my doubts about the press conference, it was only a couple of days later when DS Norburn came to see me.

'It's started,' he said. 'We've had a sighting.'

Bert placed a folder on our dining table and sifted through its contents. I was sitting opposite him, but I felt like a viewer watching on TV. Could that thin, blue folder really hold the key to Ben's whereabouts?

'We've actually had several phone calls,' Bert said.

'What? People have seen Ben?'

'So they claim. We're pursuing each one.'

He warned me not to get too excited. The various calls so far had been from people in many different places. One of them might have spotted Ben, but it was unlikely he'd moved around that much, even living with an itinerant gypsy family.

Bert could have told me all that on the phone. The reason he'd come was in that folder. He slid a glossy five-by-four image across the table.

'Take your time, Kerry. Tell me what you think.'

A moment earlier it had felt like the world had stopped spinning. Now it was in hyperdrive. As I pulled the photograph towards me I thought my heart would burst from beating so fast. Was this really it? Had someone seen my beautiful boy?

My eyes darted over the picture. In the foreground were two children posing on a beach. But it was the small blond figure in the background that the photographer had wanted us to see. I studied the smiling blond toddler then took a deep breath. Bert didn't have to ask.

'It's not him,' I said. 'It's not Ben.'

I didn't need a DNA test or to check for the strawberry birthmark. That wasn't my son. I wished it was but it wasn't. In the space of five minutes I'd been lifted to the moon then dumped back on the ground.

The photograph was just one of the sightings from holidaymakers. The other half-a-dozen leads were just the bones of descriptions: 'Boy, blond, blue-eyed, beach, Zakynthos.' Without a picture there was nothing I could do. These, Bert said, would now go through the channels to be investigated. Unfortunately, those channels could not have been harder to navigate. Bert would send the sightings via South Yorkshire Police to the Foreign Office who would pass them on to Interpol who would redirect them to Athens who would post them to the appropriate island authority. If anything proved how little Greece was co-operating with the UK, it was that: Bert wasn't even allowed to contact them directly.

'What do we do in the meantime?' I asked.

'We wait.'

It could take months for a response, Bert admitted, as frustrated by the process as I was. Once again I wished we had money. However vague one or two of those leads seemed, I would have flown to the four corners of the earth to follow them up.

I barely said another word while Bert gathered his papers. As I closed the front door, his parting words – 'This is just the start, Kerry. We'll find him' – hung in the air.

The reach of the press conference was staggering. The segment shown on *Calendar* alone seemed to have been watched by everyone in Sheffield. So I shouldn't have been surprised to receive a knock on the door one night. I opened it and there was Simon.

I could thank my medication for being calm enough to be civil. It wasn't that I didn't like him, but we hadn't parted on the best of terms in Kos. So estranged were we that it was only seeing me on local TV that had let him know I was even back in the country.

He asked if we could talk and because everyone else was sitting down to their tea, I followed him out to his car. We sat in there for a while and then, as the engine was running to power the heater anyway, went for a drive.

I think 'clear the air' is the best phrase for it. After two hours we were closer than we had been all year.

Knowing that Simon's alibi had been gone over with a fine-toothed comb by South Yorkshire Police had removed all those lingering doubts I'd had about him. They'd seen his passport stamp, his ferry ticket and even a bank statement proving he really did pick up ticket money wired from his father to Kos. I wasn't the only one to have leapt to conclusions. He showed me newspaper headlines from England that had accused him outright of abducting his own son. These had run before he'd even come out to help with the search. Where the press had got their information from I had no idea, although the police could not be ruled out. Either way, Simon must have felt terrible.

Above everything else, I finally appreciated that it wasn't just my son who had been taken. It was his son, too. Our son. We would never lose that connection and it was unfair of me, selfish even, to assume he wasn't suffering as much as me. Simon was in pain too, and he had no one to confide in. Whereas I came from an emotional family, Simon took after his mother, who always managed to seem detached from everything. Cliff couldn't speak about Ben without crying. Whether Simon and his mother had their moments in private or not, it made it easy sometimes to assume they didn't care.

By the end of the night I was thoroughly confused. I had no feelings for Simon as a partner any more and yet there was something there. Like troops who return from the frontline with an unshakeable bond, I felt we would always be linked by Ben. It made sense to stay in touch.

My grandma thought that was the least we could do. She'd always liked Simon and suggested we'd both be happier if we put our differences behind us and rekindled our relationship once again.

'You need each other.'

Mum and Dad had each other, my brothers had each other – why shouldn't I have Simon to lean on, especially with such a trying time fast approaching?

Two years old is a landmark in a child's life. When babies are born they're measured in days, then weeks, then months. But two – that's when you start saying 'years'. On 29 October my son turned two years old, and he didn't even know it. All the diazepam in the world could not have stopped the tears when I thought of Ben not being made a fuss of on his own birthday.

I still bought him a card and I told him in the message how much I loved him. Mum and Dad did the same. Amanda, Donna and Shaun, the children of Simon's sister, Jane, wrote a lovely poem:

> We think about you every day
> We pray for you at night
> We hope that God will keep you safe
> Until that special day
> That you come back to stay.

What should have been a happy time for the whole family was one of the hardest days of our lives. Christmas, as expected, was hell on earth.

It was no surprise to anyone when I moved in with Simon in February 1992. Once again, the place wasn't exactly a candidate for *Location, Location, Location*. In fact, I didn't mind it being a bedsit as much as I was disappointed to have to move to the other side of town again, back to Norfolk Park. It was quite a distance from my family in Ecclesfield. I also fell outside the reach of my GP, which meant an end to her counselling sessions.

I tried to make a go of it, I really did, but I felt a cloud hovering over me every moment I was in that flat. Simon didn't know what to do. When your bed is in your living room it's so tempting not to get up. So I didn't. Day after day passed and I wouldn't leave my bed, let alone the flat. Unless I had a visit from Mum or a journalist, then what was the point?

I also made an exception for DS Norburn when he arrived with replies from Kos about the sightings from last year. To say the island's responses were unsatisfactory is an understatement. Each separate sighting was returned with the note 'No' or 'Not Ben' alongside it. That was it. No explanations, no evidence. What did they mean, 'Not Ben'? What had they done to verify? Seen a birth certificate? Checked the birthmarks? What? I needed details.

I don't think Bert had ever seen such amateur communication from one force to another. It was almost as though Kos was trying to annoy us. He agreed to request more information although, based on this effort, neither of us was expecting to be impressed by the result. Then, as ever, we waited.

On the plus side, new sightings were coming in all the time. Every other week Bert came to the flat with a handful of photographs. I was so grateful to people for taking the time to send their holiday snaps in, but sometimes it was all I could do not to laugh at them. One was as close to Ben the corgi as he was Ben my son.

Bert laughed. 'I only bring you the good likenesses. You should see some of the others!'

Speaking of Ben the dog, more tragedy for our family was just around the corner. With his quarantine period coming to an end, there was the little matter of finding £1,200 to pay for his release. Obviously we didn't have that kind of money. If we did, then as much as I loved that little dog, I would have used it for plane journeys. Danny couldn't understand why we wouldn't hand over the cash. He'd visited the kennels several times. He was desperate to get Ben back.

Dad put out an appeal for help in the local press and it worked – sort of. The kennel agreed to waive most the fee and Aunty Jean paid the difference. After six long months, Danny and Ben were reunited. Sadly, the story had an unhappy ending. Barely a year later, Ben would go missing, just like his namesake. Danny had a theory that the dog was looking for our caravan. He might be right, but we never saw Ben the dog again.

While Bert and the South Yorkshire Police were doing their best to progress the investigation, others were following their own leads. In April 1992 I received a phone call from a *Sun* journalist called Shan Lancaster. She said, 'We've received a report that a boy fitting Ben's description has been spotted on the island of Kefalonia. Do you want to follow it up?'

'There's no way I can afford it,' I said, a dark cloud fully engulfed my mind.

'We're willing to pay if you're willing to go.'

Wow.

A guy who worked on the docks had said that his children came in one night and saw the tail end of the coverage of Ben's disappearance on television. Without knowing the full story, they both looked at the picture on the screen and said, 'We played with him today.'

The father was shocked. Adults can be mistaken and often have a tendency to tell you what you want to hear. But children have no agenda. Why would these kids make up something quite so random? That was what made them such credible witnesses. And that is why Simon, Shan, a photographer and I found ourselves on a flight to Kefalonia the following day.

However blue the sky was outside the plane window, my mood was still very dark. Not even the prospect of finding my son was lifting me. When I had Ben in my arms I would cry with joy. Until then I just wanted to get it over with.

We met the docker and his lovely children, ten-year-old Panayota and her brother Georgos. Shan and Simon did most of the talking to the dad via an interpreter. Then Panayota started speaking and I was rapt.

'I was standing smiling at a blond boy of about three who was waving from the queue for the ferry to the mainland,' she said. 'I waved back and the little boy laughed and jumped up and down. I went to play with him. He was giggling and dancing.'

I clung onto Simon for support. This darling, dark-haired girl was describing exactly how Ben behaves when he finds new play-mates. I'd seen him chuckle and giggle and show off like that more times than I could remember.

There was more. 'He was not Greek but he said some words I understood. When I saw a picture of the lost English baby I recognised him.'

Panayota went on to describe how she and her brother played with Ben till the ferry came. They watched as he got into a red car with two women, then boarded the ship.

The children went over it all again in front of a policeman, and I knew they believed they'd seen my son. I believed they'd seen him, too.

Unfortunately, it didn't help us at all. It had taken two months for the news to reach us. Ben could be anywhere now. The temporary light that had come on in my head began to dim. I wanted to go home.

I don't know what Shan had expected to find. It was a long shot that Ben would have returned to where the children had seen him. It was a dock: people came there to board boats and move on. But, I suppose, she got a story. And, from our point of view, she kept it in her millions of readers' minds. I just wished I hadn't had to endure the crushed expectations.

The *Sun* also paid for hundreds of posters to be put up featuring Ben's face, the message, 'Have you seen this child?' and a contact number – as well as their logo, of course. The picture was almost a year old but it was all we had.

I was desperate to leave but Shan had another lead for us. A village inland called Skala was home to two brothers, Spiros and Stavos Solomon. They had also registered a sighting of a boy who fitted Ben's description. When we showed them the poster they both nodded.

'That is him. That is the baby.'

The only difference, they said, was that the 'baby' they saw had longer hair – and was dirtier. 'He was with some gypsies,' Spiros told us. 'We noticed because gypsies are dark people and he was such a fair child.'

There was that word again: gypsies. If they had snatched Ben, then it looked like they hadn't sold him on. Was that a good thing or a bad thing? I couldn't bear to think about it.

We were in Kefalonia for three days. I don't remember much else except yearning to get back home. To bed.

A week after returning we heard of another series of sightings, this time in a large city on the Greek mainland. Tellingly, it was only a short ferry distance from Kefalonia. A British couple had reported seeing a boy they swore was Ben in a gypsy camp in Patras. When they approached, the gypsies sent the boy inside and scared the couple away. It sounded like the same group who had been in Kefalonia. The trail was getting hotter.

Yet, even though *TV Quick* magazine were offering to foot the bill for my flight, it wasn't enough.

'I can't go, Simon.'

'Come on, Kerry, it might be him.'

I knew he was right. I prayed he *was* right. I was convinced the last sighting was real and there was a good chance the same boy had travelled to Greece, especially if he was part of a gypsy community now. That's why I wanted Simon to go and investigate. We needed to be sure. I just knew I couldn't go with him.

'I'm sorry, Simon. I can't do it. I can't face coming home again empty-handed.'

CHAPTER THIRTEEN

A HOT POTATO

She can't be bothered to go and look for her own son.

What would the gossips in Kos make of that? Those same people who said I hadn't wanted Ben in the first place, who said I'd probably sold him myself, would be having a field day if they'd known I'd turned down the opportunity to go with Simon to investigate a sighting. But I didn't care about them. I didn't care about anything. The cloud hovering over me was becoming the only thing in my life.

I'd been in Norfolk Park for six weeks. That meant twelve missed counselling sessions with my old GP. Just as I never appreciated how much they helped me, I never saw how quickly I crumbled without them.

I know I was impossible to live with. When Simon returned empty-handed from Patras, as I'd dreaded he would, he tried to help. Blaming the bedsit for my ills, he promised to find us somewhere better and in May he succeeded. For the first time, our local celebrity worked in our favour as the council were persuaded to let us have a two-bedroom maisonette that we could get ready for when our son was returned. Not having a room for Ben had seemed so wrong. Like we'd forgotten all about him, moved on.

Before Simon joined us the first time in Kos, he had put what he couldn't sell of our belongings into his brother Steve's loft. As soon as we settled in, he reclaimed our things. Why he thought an ironing board was worth hoarding I'll never know. But the teddies, cars and little toys that belonged to Ben were almost all we had left to remind us of him. Soon after, Simon decorated the spare room with colourful Winnie-the-Pooh stencils and we housed all those toys in there. The room was ready but unmistakeably empty.

Seeing my lethargic attempts at trying to help decorate was the final straw for Mum. She marched me back to my old doctor's and demanded something be done to help me. The next day, a psychiatric nurse came to my new home and we talked. I don't remember what was discussed but for a short while at least, I felt like a fire victim spluttering and gasping gulps of fresh air. I was suffering but I was alive. I looked forward to her next visit.

I hate how depression clipped my wings so tightly. Another promising lead, again in Corfu, came in via *TV Quick* and once more Simon pursued it alone. All I could think about was sleep. I should have gone if only to say thank you to the magazine for putting up a £3,000 reward for information leading to the discovery of Ben – it sounded even better as 1,000,000 drachmas. Both numbers were emblazoned on new posters, which Simon pasted up all over Corfu. For some people, a little financial incentive is the difference between getting involved or not. Hopefully it would make a difference.

When Simon returned two days later I could barely look at him. The hurt in his eyes just exacerbated the pain behind mine. He'd found the blond boy that witnesses had said was Ben and, for the first time, actually had to step closer to be sure it wasn't him.

The likeness was strong and – the telling factor in this instance – the child actually was English. But his name was Christopher and his passport proved it. The whole trip was just another expensive wild goose chase.

Simon attended as many sighting visits as the media would fund, each time with the same heart-breaking result. There was no sign of the calls from the public drying up, especially after a Scottish businessman paid for 5,000 reward posters to be disseminated to UK passengers flying out to Greece. Thomas Cook also publicised the case to their customers, and South Yorkshire Police even launched a series of holiday items – hats, T-shirts, etc – featuring Ben's details. I couldn't help thinking, *If only the Kos police had shown half this interest...*

The ordeals of Ben's second birthday and third Christmas had been almost impossible to get through. Another anniversary threatened to be even worse. As we entered July 1992, the calls from the national media began. Whether they all had the 24th ringed on their calendars or they just copied each other, I don't know, but the phone rang off the hook for a couple of weeks. Everyone wanted to know how I would feel on the first anniversary of my son's disappearance.

The honest truth is, I felt better before I read some of the coverage.

One or two of the bigger papers did their own investigations. The *Sunday Times* sent Carol Sarler over to Kos and the things she came back with made my blood freeze and boil in rapid succession. In a few days, she discovered more than the Kos police had managed in – deep breath – a year. Most startling of all, she even found another family who knew exactly how I was feeling.

On 24 July 1990 – exactly a year before Ben was taken – a young Finnish holidaymaker called Virpi Maria Hunnele was raped and killed on that same Iraklis hillside, according to Carole, no more than 400 yards from the farmhouse. The girl's family went through hell trying to discover what had happened to their seventeen-year-old daughter. They smashed their heads against the same brick wall I'd found myself up against: the Kos police.

The same Kos police who hadn't thought to mention this case to us.

As the *Sunday Times* article suggested, could it really be a coincidence that two youngsters disappeared from virtually the same spot in exactly the same year? Could two seemingly random crimes occur in the middle of nowhere like that?

I knew what Carole was getting at and my head supported her logic. My heart just said, 'No'. To agree with her was to accept that Ben might have suffered like Virpi had twelve months earlier. A mother's brain can't even compute that as possibility. Not without evidence. The Hunnele family had it, even if they didn't have a perpetrator. I couldn't accept it. For the first time, I actually wanted to believe Ben had been taken by gypsies. I wanted him to have been illegally adopted, sold to a rich parent. The alternative was too vile for a human mind to entertain, not even for a second.

I was in bits reading. Then I got to the parts about me. Carole had spoken, she said, to dozens of people in Kos. They virtually queued up to get their two-penn'orth in. And they all said the same thing: 'The family did it.'

It didn't matter that no two people could agree on the same member of the family or the same reason. It seemed good enough for them to sling mud at me, Simon, Stephen, Mum and Dad.

After all, we'd brought shame to their island, the island where no crime ever, ever happened.

I learnt a lot from that article. While most of the people who came forward did so anonymously, I didn't need their names to know who some of them were. The only quote that troubled me came from the local who said Ben was always 'starving and used to come to me for ice cream and chocolate and I would try to feed him'. I had my strong suspicions as to who that might be and, if I was right, why would she say something like that? Her English wasn't always as good as she sometimes seemed to think it was. Maybe she had just got her answer wrong. I hoped so.

I didn't care that some of those interviewed accused me of all sorts of sexual shenanigans. It gives me no pleasure to say that there were plenty of people who judged me for being an unmarried mum. If I looked at a man, I must be sleeping with him. If I had a drink after work it was to find a lover for the night. That was certainly a feeling I got from several of the police investigating our case. *Greek girls, married or not, don't behave like that...*

The accusations against me were so laughable no one in their right mind could believe them. The ones about Ben, however, were daggers in the heart. One is still etched on my memory today: 'A hot potato – I used to call him that because it was as if no one wanted to hold on to him. He was just passed from one person to another.'

I've cried about that quote more than any other over the years. What sort of a person has such blackness inside them that they could say that about a mother who has lost her baby?

Ben wasn't a 'hot potato' – he was loved by so many people, we all shared him. My mum and dad were still young enough to

BEN

have children. Of course they wanted to look after him. They were almost as much parents to Ben as I was. When Simon came out, Ben was with him too. That's a positive. Anyone can see that.

About the only supportive voice in the whole *Sunday Times* article was that of Chief Dakouras. It was nice to see him say, 'I now know this family are not involved in any way with the disappearance of their child,' but why had it taken so long? And why hadn't he done anything to quash the local rumour-mill?

While Dakouras dithered, South Yorkshire Police marked the anniversary by producing a 'new' image of Ben for use on new 'Missing Child' posters. Using the same technology they employ to produce 'photofit' likenesses of criminals, their computer department manipulated one of the most recent pictures of Ben and artificially 'aged' him. The result was a happy-looking boy of almost three years old – and another blow for me.

I shouldn't need a computer to let me see my son grow up.

By the end of July, the press had left me alone once again. There were no more phone calls, no more interview requests. And no more reasons to get up in the morning. I realised it wasn't the bedsit in Norfolk Park that was responsible for my dark moods. Days began to blur once again, the pain of missing Ben grew stronger and sharper. Just seeing his room, his toys and his empty bed brought me lower every day. And then one morning, with the house all to myself, I found a reason to get up.

I walked into the bathroom, took a razor from the cabinet and slashed it across my wrists.

CHAPTER FOURTEEN

WHY COULDN'T YOU BE MY BEN?

I didn't want to die. I just wanted the pain to stop.

If I could have slept, gone into coma or been anaesthetised I would have taken it. I wanted to close my eyes and wake up when Ben was found. That was impossible, so I did the next best thing.

It took the sensation of steel slicing skin to bring me to my senses. I looked at the horizontal cut in my arm, then at the razor. It was like looking through somebody else's eyes, like I'd been hypnotised. Then I snapped out of it, screamed, dropped the blade to the floor and grabbed a towel to stem the flow of blood.

I wasn't badly hurt. It stung for a while but not enough to dial 999. The scar's still there, although faint. It is only recently I confessed to Mum I'd done it. Like so many things, she took the blame on her shoulders for not spotting how ill I'd become.

There was a reason I didn't confide in her earlier. I was ashamed, angry with myself for being so stupid. *You need to get a grip. It won't help Ben if you're a wreck.*

Bearing in mind how much I wanted to sleep, that suicide attempt acted as a wake-up call, loud and persistent. I couldn't let myself be affected by the poison coming from Kos via the newspaper articles. I needed to find the strength to take control of my life again. It was no good hiding any more. I needed to be the one following the leads about Ben.

As my head cleared and I began a personal audit on my life, the same answer repeatedly came up. I needed independence and for that I needed money. In the space of a year, South Yorkshire Police had received more than two hundred sightings. We'd been able to personally follow up the smallest fraction of those. The majority we were forced to wait for disinterested strangers in Kos to respond to them. For the most important ones, we were reliant on the expense accounts of journalists. What would happen if their editors decided Ben's story wasn't shifting enough copies? How would we get to Greece then?

There wasn't much any of us could do for work. We were all on sickness benefits with good reason. It was killing Dad not being able to support his family but he'd been diagnosed with serious arthritis induced by stress. Financial worries just exacerbated the condition. What's more, no one could hold down a full-time job with the doses of diazepam we were on, so Dad started helping out at a friend's scrap-metal yard. The incapacity benefit meant he wasn't allowed to take payment. Instead, his friend let Dad have first call on any of the items discarded, which Dad then took to a boot sale with Mum. It wasn't much at first, but Dad soon developed an eye for possible winners. Not only was he keeping busy now, he was helping a friend and putting a little money aside to fund the search for his grandson.

I needed to do something as well. The volume of letters and well-wishes we received from complete strangers suggested there was enormous support for what our family was going through, so I decided to act on that. With Mum and Danny I made dozens of copies of Ben's wanted poster and a large banner saying 'Help Find Ben Needham'. We packed those, a couple of buckets and a paste-table into Mum's Capri, then at five o'clock in the morning of 16 August, all three of us drove to Knebworth Park in Hertfordshire and set up a little stand. Genesis were playing a concert there that day to an audience of 90,000 people. Even if a fraction of them walked past us, I was convinced we'd make some money. We did. A fortnight later, we set off to Roundhay Park in Leeds and discovered Michael Jackson fans were equally generous, so much so that when we discovered he was playing at Wembley Stadium four days later, we knew we had to be there as well.

Driving down to London was a different proposition to going to Leeds. I'd never been to the capital before. The idea of spending three nights there was a bit intimidating, especially as we'd be sleeping in the car. We went down the night before in order to secure a prime position for the following morning. Ninety per cent of the fans would have to cross the 'Wembley Way' Bridge to reach the stadium, so that's where we needed to be. When a security guard shone his light through the window, I thought we were in trouble. In fact, Mum explained what we were up to and the guy wished us luck and said he'd tell his overnight colleagues to keep an eye on us. When he returned a while later, I assumed it was because he'd been given new orders. He had...

'I've just spoken to my wife,' the guard explained, 'and she says there is no way you're sleeping in that car tonight. You're coming back to ours for tea and a proper bed. I finish in ten minutes, then you can follow me home.'

So that's what we did. It was a phenomenal gesture from a complete stranger. The next morning he escorted us back to the stadium to claim our pitch in good time and again over the following two days. It just goes to prove there are Good Samaritans everywhere.

They weren't the only amazing people we encountered. At one point, a stranger handed over a couple of tickets to that night's gig and said, 'They're yours if you want them, or there are touts here who will take them off your hands.' Then he just disappeared. We'd have loved to have seen the King of Pop in his pomp, but that wasn't why we were there. So I found a tout and a few minutes of haggling later, I had another £100 for the kitty.

Of course, not everyone can be so generous of spirit. As I'd learnt from the anniversary coverage, there are some very mean people out there – and some of them were Michael Jackson fans. One group of lads ignored me when I stood waving my collection bucket at them, which was fair enough. Not everyone can afford to give to charity. Then they saw the posters of Ben, looked at me, and started shouting, 'Ben's dead! Ben's dead!'

They were drunk. They were idiots. And they were quickly told to shut the hell up by the people around them. But Danny saw it all and just started shaking. That's what's most unforgivable. You don't pick on a kid.

Over the course of those concerts we raised about £2,000. I still felt like hiding in bed some days, but knowing the public was behind us gave me strength that I hadn't had before. I felt ready for anything.

The first test of my renewed resolve was just around the corner. A couple of months earlier and I swear it would have killed me.

It began with Bert Norburn asking Mum if she could arrange for everyone to meet at hers. Like all good policemen, Bert was a master of managing expectations. He never wanted to give unnecessary hope because he'd seen the effects of disappointment. This time, Mum said, he was almost excited.

With Dad away following up a lead, the rest of us watched nervously as Bert pulled out a familiar-looking folder. First of all he showed us a selection of photographs that kind tourists had submitted. One or two were pretty close; others stood out immediately to us as cases of mistaken identity. Then he went through other sightings that didn't have supporting photographs, before finally getting to the reason he'd come.

'We've had several reports of Ben in Corfu,' he explained.

'Is there a photograph?' I asked.

'No, unfortunately not.'

'Then what makes this sighting so important?'

'Because it's been reported by seventeen different people!'

According to the many sources, a young blond boy fitting Ben's description had been seen at a taverna in a Corfu resort called Kassiopi every day, as recently as forty-eight hours before. What alerted the vigilant passers-by was the fact the couple he called 'Mum and Dad' were quite old and obviously Greek with dark hair, olive skin and the full repertoire of hand gestures. I could understand why people were suspicious. If you had to pick a family who looked like they'd adopted a child, this sounded like it.

Any sightings without a picture that came via Bert were usually followed up in the same bureaucratically hellish manner. The police certainly didn't have the budgets of large news organisations to ferry us around Europe. Bert was normally a stickler for procedure, but this time he didn't want us to wait for five months while the enquiry took its course.

'I could follow the normal channels,' he said, 'but I think you should get straight over there as quickly as you can. If there's anyone in the press who could help, then make that call. I'd go myself if I had a passport.'

Although there was actually enough money in our Search For Ben Needham account, we all decided that this was exactly the sort of opportunity a news agency would be interested in. It made sense to use our own funds as sparingly as possible.

We'd already enjoyed the generosity of the *Sun* and *TV Quick*, so I made a call to another reporter we'd been interviewed by in Kos. Like Martyn Sharpe, the *Daily Mirror*'s Jim Oldfield was one of the good guys. You can never trust a journalist 100 per cent, of course, because at the end of the day they have a job to do. But when he listened to us in Kos you could see his pain was heartfelt. He wasn't just punching the clock and waiting to get home.

So I contacted Jim and said, 'We don't want to go round the houses – is there any chance the *Mirror* can finance this?'

Seventeen separate sightings and the chance to run the headline, '*Mirror* Finds Toddler Ben'? It was a no-brainer.

I was desperate to go on this trip. Whatever had been pulling me down in April had released its hold. Five months later, I was genuinely excited to be travelling with Mum, Jim and photographer Andy Stenning. We were like school kids on the way over, babbling with excitement. I had such a good feeling. We all did. As I kept repeating, 'Seventeen people can't be wrong.'

Even with all the money in the world, covering 2,000 miles is still a laborious exercise. If you're not waiting somewhere you're about to wait. Airport to runway to take-off to airport to passport control and baggage checks. The closer we got, the longer everything seemed to take and the more on edge I became. I just wanted someone to click their fingers and we'd be there.

We had the address of Yani's, the taverna in Kassiopi where the sightings had taken place, and Jim and Andy got us there in a taxi. As we stood outside, the butterflies in my stomach went into flutter overdrive. I had to take a couple of breaths before I could even think about walking in. As Mum put her arm around me, I said, 'This could be it.'

There was a large outdoor area but as it was midday and the sun was at its most unforgiving, it didn't look suspicious that we decided to sit inside. All the reports said the little boy usually appeared from a door behind the bar, where the taverna linked to the accommodation upstairs, so that is where we needed to be positioned.

At Jim's suggestion, I was wearing a cap and sunglasses, even inside. If it was Ben, we didn't want to risk anyone recognising me and squirreling him away. It was all a bit cloak and dagger for my taste but if it helped, I'd do anything.

I couldn't mask my disappointment as we first stepped in. No boy and no older Greek parents, just a woman and two men in their twenties manning the place. Had we even got the right taverna? Jim confirmed it was the correct address and Mum reminded me that the old couple, according to the reports, owned the place but didn't work there all day.

The first hour passed and gradually our conversation grew more relaxed as we settled into our roles. By the time the second hour ticked by, I'd probably had ten Cokes and about five sandwiches. I barely had the appetite for anything, but for appearance's sake I tucked in. The hardest thing was not staring at the bar. Mum would tap the table if my gaze wandered over for too long.

We were probably worrying unduly. To all the world we just looked like four tourists. What could be more natural than two men and two women in shorts and sun vests having a bite to eat out of the sun?

Then there must have been a change of shift because, suddenly, an old Greek appeared behind the bar, then another, this time a woman. It was them. They were exactly as Bert Norburn's sources had described: fifties, married and undeniably local. We were close, I could feel it.

Just a matter of time.

I have no idea what anyone said from that point on or how many times Mum tapped the table. There was no way I was taking my eyes off that door.

Then I saw him.

In my memory now it's like watching an action thriller where the big finale takes place in slow motion. I can see every blond hair on that little boy's head and picture the giggling face as he runs into view, past our table and out onto the terrace with the old lady shuffling behind him. In real time he was like a whippet. Out in the kitchen one minute, blasting past us the next. It's the trauma that makes it so slow in my recollection. The trauma of taking one look at him and saying to no one in particular, 'That's not Ben.'

I don't know how many chairs I knocked over as I scrambled to my feet and tore out of that taverna. A minute earlier, the bar had been full of hope. Now it felt claustrophobic, like its walls were closing in. I had no breath. I had to escape.

The Greeks in Kos had been waiting for me to go wailing out on the street. Well, today was their lucky day. I was hysterical, absolutely wrecked. I didn't hear the car horns as traffic swerved around me, or Mum as she ran to my side, desperate to pull me to safety. She did her best to calm me down but the tears in her eyes told their own story. We'd invested so much more than money into this. We'd invested hope. I'd allowed my spirits to raise, my guard to fall. And I was paying the price.

I don't know how long I was out there, sobbing. Mum eventually persuaded me to return inside. Jim and Andy were already doing their best to explain why a young woman would sit quietly in a restaurant for two hours then without warning go hurtling into the street. From the looks on the old couple's faces and the way the woman was hugging the boy to her chest so tightly, the message had got through. She was clearly worried I wanted to take her boy.

I apologised to them all while Jim supplied the details. About Ben, about the seventeen tip-offs, about the hell we'd been through. I wouldn't have blamed the bar owners for throwing us out but they were wonderful. They had the look in their eyes of people who knew suffering. Maybe they saw it in mine. Then the woman put her son on the floor and encouraged him to say hello.

'This is Panos,' she said proudly. 'My son.'

They told their story. They didn't have to but they wanted no doubts in our minds. I had none. The boy was two and a half years old, beautiful and with the most twinkling eyes and wonderful smile. But he wasn't Ben.

He was English, however. A Brit had been living in Corfu for many years, enjoying a high-paid job. When she discovered she was pregnant she began to fall apart. The taverna couple said that they would take her baby and raise him as their own. Whether they paid for the privilege or were paid I don't know. But they were true to their word and the little boy calls them Mum and Dad in Greek, the only language he knows. They were all clearly happy but even now the whole arrangement still seems extraordinary to me. Only later on would I realise just how widespread and easily organised such situations were.

As I stared into Panos's questioning eyes I said quietly, 'Why couldn't you be my Ben?' Then I gave him a hug as Andy began to photograph the scene. He was a big, burly man who had captured the worst of society on film over the years, but that didn't stop the tears streaming down his face as he got us all to pose for the story of the century that never was.

I couldn't blame a single person for mistaking that boy for Ben: the whole setup fitted the police description to a T. As we made our way to the airport, however, I knew the trip would take its toll. Whatever strength I'd found to get me there had disappeared completely. By the time we landed in Manchester, I was a twitching wreck. I wanted to go to bed and not be disturbed for a month.

I got one of my wishes.

I was home and hiding under the duvet, eyes dry with old tears, when there was a knock at the front door. I couldn't face getting up. The weight in my head was heavier than my legs. I tried to block out the sound of Simon opening the door and when he came up to the bedroom, I had a pillow over my ears. There was no one I wanted to see or hear.

Or so I thought.

'It's the *Yorkshire on Sunday*, Kerry,' Simon said quietly. 'I think you should come down and talk to them.'

I stared at the picture for the entire duration of the flight. I studied the family faces again and again but my eyes kept going back to the little boy held up to the camera. If it wasn't Ben, then somewhere out there he had a twin, that was for sure.

Like the various national papers, the *Yorkshire Post* had been running its own awareness campaign and someone who had just returned from a holiday in Turkey had sent in this snap. Journalist Iain Lovell was so convinced that it was Ben that he'd persuaded the *Post* to pay for him and me to follow the lead. It was unheard of for the local paper to go outside the county, let alone need a passport. Like so many good people I've met over the years, they were just desperate to solve the riddle.

The only information we had on the photograph was the name of a town. After the harrowing few days travelling to and from Corfu, this took on the scale of hunting a needle in a haystack. Without Iain's optimism, I couldn't have got through it. I wished Mum was there.

We flew into Izmir on the western coast and drove the eighty miles inland and south to Aydin, near where the tourists said they'd taken the photograph in a local market. The problem was, that was as accurate information as we had. Ever the intrepid investigator, Iain contacted the local police station. After the experience I'd had across the water with their Greek compatriots, I wasn't exactly expecting mountains to be moved.

How wrong can you be? As soon as word reached Aydin's police chief, Sevkit Ayaz, he took personal control. Watching him amass a roomful of officers to study the photograph was so impressive, and listening to the animated buzz of their conversations was actually quite thrilling. They were all so focused on helping us.

Then Mr Ayaz and a deputy came over with the photo.

'My men have identified the village as Cine,' the chief said, the pride in his officers apparent. 'My officers will take you there.'

I couldn't have wished for better service. I was escorted to a police car and, with Iain and photographer Paul Barker following in our hire vehicle, chauffeured the twenty-five miles to the village in question. The Aydin police couldn't do enough for me. I felt like royalty. They said they were family men who sympathised with my plight. But the Kos force all had wives and children, and they'd succeeded in making me feel like a streetwalker.

Eventually the road became an unmade lane and the car began to slow. Dust thrown up by the wheels gave the scenery a beigey hue beneath the brilliant blue sky. We were nearly there.

I sat in the car while the policeman showed the photograph to a passing local. There was a flurry of conversation and pointed arms. After another short drive we stopped outside a farmhouse and I was beckoned out. *Time for the moment of truth.*

Knees weak, I followed the officer to the farmhouse. A second after he knocked I heard voices from the other side of the door. A woman's, loud and cheerful – and a child's. He was there. The boy from the photo was inside.

The door swung open and the expectant face of Zayide Sulutas stared back at us. Peeping from behind her skirt was a little blue-eyed face.

I wanted to walk straight back to the car, but the woman deserved an explanation and only I had noticed the truth. Yes, the child looked exactly like Ben – but Ben from the day he went missing, Ben at twenty-one months. Not Ben as he was today, closer to three. And there was something else.

As the mother listened to the policeman, she instinctively scooped her child into her arms. Like the couple in Kassiopi, she thought we had come to take her baby away and I had to step in.

'It's all right,' I told the officer, 'it's not Ben.'

Confused, he relayed the news to the mother who began gushing something in Turkish. Then she slipped her hand underneath the child's top and pulled down the nappy.

'Is girl, not boy.'

The policeman looked shocked but I'd noticed immediately. My own grief turned to concern for Zayide and her husband, Neuzat, who'd come to investigate the commotion. They had to understand that it was our mistake, and nobody was going to take their precious little Saliha.

After a tense few minutes they let me hold the little girl so that Paul could get the pictures for Iain's story. Then we left them there, a happy little family of three. I wanted so much to have what they had. Instead, I'd travelled 2,500 miles to discover a child who was too young and the wrong sex, terrifying a young mum in the process. From Kassiopi to Cine, I'd just brought pain. The last thing I wanted anyone to feel was that I was trying to claim their child. A terrible side-effect of the whole situation was hurting other innocent people. How many more would I make suffer as I tore around the world chasing lead after lead?

Unpalatable though it was, I knew the answer. There was nothing I wouldn't do to bring my son home. *He's out there and I will find him. Whatever it takes.*

CHAPTER FIFTEEN

I'M SORRY

Ben's third birthday and fourth Christmas were even more painful than the previous year's. Again, we wrote him cards and opened them on the day, just as Simon and I continued to give each other cards on Mother's and Father's Day. Ben might not have been in our house but he was in our lives. Every morning I spoke to his photo on the fireplace and told him about my plans for the day. More often than not, I ended with the same words.

'Mummy's going to find you very, very soon.'

It didn't seem to matter how many sightings we followed up, the result was still the same. Simon went on some trips; Mum and Dad tackled others. Stephen and Danny wanted to help but Stephen had won a place at college and, of course, Danny was still at school. He'd suffered more than a young teen should ever have to and, in hindsight, by trying to protect him we probably shut him out. So many things would have been done differently if we were thinking like clear-headed people. That wasn't us. It hadn't been us since 24 July 1991.

We were doing our best to make the search fund stretch as far as possible. Dad's car boot sales covered most of his flights and more often than not he would sleep on the nearest beach rather than bear the cost of a hotel room. It wasn't ideal but if it gave him another night to search for information as one lead after another hit a brick wall, he would do it. It was still preferable to going with a newspaper – I'm not one for washing your laundry in public. There isn't much worse than having to pose for photographs in the middle of the street after your heart has been skewered once again. We aren't celebrities.

I began to get more inventive in our fundraising. So many people responded to our publicity interviews asking what could they do – including real celebrities. One of them was the *Antiques Roadshow* star, Eric Knowles, who I met when I was invited to talk about the search on the BBC's *Pebble Mill* programme. As soon as the cameras stopped rolling, Eric asked me what he could do to help. When I wondered if he'd consider hosting a valuation day in Sheffield, he couldn't agree quickly enough. The local *Star* newspaper publicised the event and supplied Cutler's Hall for the day. By the time Eric arrived, the queue was already around the block. It was a marvellous day and Eric was on fine form, joking that it wasn't every day that Yorkshiremen would queue up – and pay – to meet a Lancastrian. We only charged a pound for every item he looked at, but it made enough to keep the Search For Ben account in the black for a few more months.

I'm not a natural public speaker and if I thought of the millions of people watching at home, I would never normally have the nerve to appear on television. When it comes to talking about Ben, though, I usually find the strength from somewhere. One day a producer from the *Calendar* programme rang me with a proposition that put that resolve to the test.

'We want to take you back to Kos.'

*

Watching the broadcast a few weeks later with Simon was worse than I actually remembered. The producer had wanted to capture our reactions as we revisited the scene of Ben's disappearance.

He got mine barely seconds after landing.

The *Calendar* boys must have flicked the cameras on as soon as they were allowed, because on screen you see me stepping out onto the walkway leading to the terminal exit – and then I just disappear.

One minute I'm walking purposefully alongside Mum and Dad. Then I start shaking and I look in pain. My legs are trembling and the camera zooms in on my face. I look terrified. My eyes are red and I'm panicking. And then nothing. It's like watching a horror film where a soul leaves the body. One minute I was looking at me – Kerry – and the next I was looking at a dead person. An empty vessel. And that's exactly how it felt.

I was possessed. That's the only way I can describe the sensation. My legs stopped working, my mind just switched off, I was aware of people around me but not what they were saying. I just somehow stopped *being*.

If *Calendar* hadn't captured it for the world to see, I'd think I dreamt the whole thing. The experience didn't last long and soon I was shuffling into the harsh midday sun. I'd been to Kefalonia, Corfu, Turkey and several islands in between without any problems except disappointment. Whatever I'd told myself, clearly Kos was no ordinary destination for me. It never could be. It was the place that stole my son.

For the purposes of the camera, we travelled back to the site of the old caravan then up the mountain road to the farmhouse. Michaelis hadn't done any more work on the property, although the villa being constructed two years ago was now complete.

Again I was struck by the eeriness of the silence up there: Kos was such a 'buzzy' island, the absence of regular traffic noise always stood out. I knew if I stayed there too long I'd convince myself I could hear Ben's cry. Mum and Dad looked uncomfortable as well, so we left as quickly as we'd come.

We couldn't visit Kos without paying a call to the police station. For once we had a reason to feel optimistic. Shortly before we'd left England, I'd explained my concerns about the police delays to Sheffield MP Bill Michie. He'd written to the Foreign Secretary, Douglas Hurd, and had received this response from his office: 'Mr Dakouras, the former Head of the Kos police, has been routinely transferred to Zakynthos.' I don't know if Dakouras's move was related to the complaints I'd raised about the handling of Ben's case, but the chance to begin again with a new face had to be a positive.

Unfortunately, Dakouras's replacement, Mr Kondilis, seemed cut from the same cloth. He was engaging, especially for the tele-vision cameras, although his message was as blunt as ever. 'We are looking,' he assured us. 'We don't give up.' To help his unstinting investigation, we handed over thousands of new 'Missing' posters with the updated image of Ben, and a message translated once again into Greek.

If you believed some of the press reports, baiting the Need-hams seemed to be a popular sport in Kos. I did believe them. Unlike Turkey, where everyone bent over backwards to help me – Chief Ayaz actually requested copies of the poster to disseminate in the resorts and to his staff – I could almost hear the whispers of the smear campaign that the whole population seemed to be conspiring in. I wasn't comfortable being there. There were no answers for me in Kos, only questions, doubts and accusations.

Douglas Hurd wasn't the only prominent politician to receive a letter. I tried to put as much pressure on everyone I could think of who might be in a position to help. Obviously that included the Prime Minister. I first wrote to John Major in February, to no avail. A follow-up letter in December produced an immediate response, including an apology for not seeing my earlier message. He said he'd discussed Ben's case with our ambassador and consul-general during a trip to Athens, and they were doing everything they could to speed up the communication between our countries' police forces. He was confident that everything that could be done was being done.

A few years earlier, I would have been dancing in the street to receive a personal letter from the Prime Minister. By the end of 1992, it was just another piece of correspondence to add to the pile alongside headed paper from Buckingham Palace and Kensington Gardens. Although both Her Majesty the Queen and Princess Diana, I was told, were following our plight with interest, there was nothing they could personally do.

Could or would? I don't like to bang the class drum, but when you open a newspaper and see the people the Queen just invites to tea, you have to question the priorities of her advisors.

I was doing all I could to stay positive. When one letter came back, I fired off another. Even if all I achieved was keeping Ben's name in the public eye, that had to mean something. I refused to let the government forget about him.

Bert was a regular visitor: on a weekly or monthly basis, dozens of new sightings were dismissed or investigated. There was no avenue we wouldn't explore. When Cork psychic, William Thackaberry, said he had traced Ben to Daytona, Florida, I insisted it was followed up by the US police.

Some people found my trust of the abilities of a medium amusing. All I knew was that after so many false alarms and disappointments, I could not afford to turn down any offer of help. In any case, I was beginning to experience my own visitations. Shortly after filming in Kos, I started having dreams about Ben. I'd always seen him on and off; now he was appearing every time I closed my eyes. Not as a nightmare. As a happy little boy who'd never gone missing, never known pain or separation from his parents. I always woke up with a smile on my face – until I realised it had all been my subconscious, and my stomach sank.

The dreams got stronger and more vivid. Then, one night, I woke up to hear Ben crying. Ben, my Ben. As I had done so many times before, I climbed out of bed and crossed the landing to his room. The only way he would be comforted was by my cuddles. Every time I pulled away, he cried again. When he asked me to stay, I just nodded and snuggled in the narrow bed alongside him. The next morning, a confused Simon found me still there. He tried to rationalise it, saying I must have been sleepwalking.

'No, I wasn't asleep. I remember every detail.'

The only thing I couldn't explain was where my Ben had vanished to.

A couple of nights later it happened again, earlier this time, in fact before I'd even nodded off. Once again I made the familiar journey to Ben's room, treading quietly over his soft, grey cord carpet. And again, Simon discovered me alone in our son's bed the following morning. For some reason he looked frightened, then angry. Nothing I said seemed to calm him. Every time I mentioned Ben he got more and more riled, yelling that I was imagining things, until eventually he stormed out.

What Simon saw as my descent into madness I took as a sign of hope. I had to. What other explanation was there for Ben coming back to me each night?

Then one night I was watching television downstairs alone when I remembered I hadn't put Ben to bed. I called out to where he was playing with his wooden soldiers on the carpet and told him it was time to go up. When he didn't move, I took his hand and led him up the stairs, got him changed into his pyjamas, washed his face and brushed his teeth and tucked him into bed. After I'd read him a story, I kissed his forehead and switched off the lamp. As I left the room I said, 'I love you,' and he said it back.

I went back downstairs and continued watching my programme.

How can I explain that now? Was I hallucinating? Was it a vision? Had I fallen asleep on the couch and started sleepwalking, as Simon said? Or was it something else? I remember with such clarity the whole sequence of events, even now. I genuinely believed I'd put Ben to bed that night.

In the cold light of the following day I took a harsher view. *What is happening to me?* I couldn't explain it any other way than that I was losing my mind. Every doubt I'd ever had about my abilities as a mother, or Ben's chances of coming home, flooded back. I wasn't worthy of him. I couldn't be; I was clearly insane. Maybe it was a good thing he was taken away. He'd been rescued from a lifetime with a madwoman.

I couldn't wait for Simon to go out. Then I poured myself a large glass of wine and composed a letter to my mother. 'I'm a failure.

Ben is better off without me. I can't even look after myself.' I knew that what I was about to do next would drive a stake through her heart, but what mattered more was putting an end to the torment. To the endless cycle of waking up and thinking Ben was in his bed and suffering his loss again and again and again.

I didn't want to die but I didn't want to live the life that I was trapped in. Ben was my reason for living but he was also killing me – slowly. Who could object to me speeding up the process?

Tears dropped onto the envelope as I sealed the edge and placed it, addressed, on the table. Then I poured another glass of wine and emptied a box of diazepam into my hand. I counted ten tablets. If each one had the power to keep me calm for an entire day, imagine what this many could do. All my problems would soon be over.

As the last pill was washed down with the final sip of pinot grigio, the only regret I had was not doing it in bed. Still, it wasn't too late. I pulled myself up and waded through the spinning room to the stairs. They went up, turned 180 degrees on a mini land-ing then carried on to the top. By the halfway point, I knew I'd gone far enough. It looked so comfortable I sat down, then leaned back, lay my head on my arm and closed my eyes. *I'm sorry…*

That should have been it. There was no reason for me to expect Simon's nephew – Shane – to come visiting soon after. Even less reason for him to have discovered the front door ajar. Yet that's what happened. I was vaguely aware of his voice as he called out Simon's name, then mine. Then there was a sudden thundering as he spied my foot sticking out from the mezzanine floor and sprinted up. No sixteen-year-old should have to see that.

I was lucky that Shane was older than his years. He dragged me up the remainder of the stairs and into the bathroom. I watched my heels bump over every stair as though they belonged to someone else. I didn't feel a thing, not even when he appeared with a glass of milk and forced me to drink it. Not even when he bent me over the bath and started shouting at me to throw up. I recognised the words but what could I do? He grabbed my wrist and pushed the milk to my face.

'For God's sake, Kerry, do it!'

Eventually I did, then collapsed in a heap. Shane covered me in a towel and ran to call for help.

I don't know if ten diazepam and a bottle of white wine are enough to kill you, but thanks to Shane I never found out. As far as I'm concerned he saved my life. I had migraines and stomach pains for a week after, and my doctor immediately slashed my supply of antidepressants. I'd let everyone down, she made that very clear. 'More than anything,' she said, 'you've let yourself down.'

Mum fluctuated between anger and upset. I needed to believe in myself, she said. And why didn't I go to her instead of being so stupid?

I knew I'd been irresponsible, but the same dark thoughts that led me to be so selfish prevented me hearing anyone's advice, however well intentioned. And then, after two weeks of turmoil, the penny dropped. Everyone was right. I had to believe I was a good mum.

Because that's what the tiny twelve-week-old baby in my tummy needed me to be.

CHAPTER SIXTEEN

HE'S DEAD

Leighanna Needham was famous from the moment she was born.

I don't remember much about 9 February 1994, except that my beautiful daughter arrived, unusually, bang on her due date at Northern General Hospital. And there to capture her first smile and burp was our friend from the *Daily Mirror*, Jim Oldfield, and a photographer.

It wasn't exactly a case of selling the rights like celebrities do in *Hello!* magazine because I think Jim was just trying to do us a favour. A few weeks before the birth, he'd asked if there was anything we needed, and of course I had a list as long as my arm. Every penny that came into our family was spent either on surviving or searching. Even our clothes came mostly from Dad's boot sales. That left the square root of nothing for virtually everything else.

'If we give you a £1,000 will that help you out?' Jim asked. I thought of the price of prams, pushchairs, cots and nappies and practically snapped his hand off. It was good of Jim, really, knowing that I would probably have let journalists in for nothing, just to keep the momentum of Ben's campaign going. In return, all I had to do was share my daughter's earliest moments with his readers. What mother doesn't want to show off her baby? These days, people post pictures on Facebook; I had the *Daily Mirror.*

I'd discovered I was pregnant while still recovering from my overdose. If I'd thought I was a bad parent before, the realisation that I could have damaged my unborn child was devastating. I remember begging my GP to be honest with me, to tell me if I could have hurt my baby. It only took a couple of days to arrange a scan, but I was on edge till the 'all clear' came back. I knew this was my second chance.

I couldn't deny the events of the past few weeks, however. I had tried to take my own life and, for the next few weeks, between Mum and Simon and my nurse, I wasn't left alone for a minute. They were all looking for any sign that I might try something so stupid again. They were all disappointed.

They didn't understand that a new baby was the reason I needed to stay alive. I was a mum who wasn't being allowed to live like one. I had all these maternal instincts and no outlet, no child to give them to. All those dreams and hallucinations of Ben crying out for me weren't just signs of me cracking up, I realised. They were a mother's love reaching out for a child, and my body telling me to hold on because a new person was coming who did need me. It wasn't Ben I was hearing late at night. It was Leighanna.

Looking back at the press reports from 1992 and 1993, Simon and I were asked repeatedly whether we would be trying for another child. As time went by, our answers changed from 'no' to 'yes'. When I did fall pregnant, however, it wasn't planned. Simon and I were going through a phase of not really getting on. Our long-term life together was looking shaky at best – something that probably added to my overdose attempt.

To his credit, as soon as I revealed to Simon that I was carrying his child, he couldn't have been more positive.

'This is just what we need, Kerry,' he said. 'This will bring us closer.'

'But what about Ben?'

'This baby has got massive shoes to fill, no doubt about it. Ben is still our little boy and we will find him. But this is a new chance for us. A new start.'

I hadn't been a nice person to be around for some time, I admit it, and Simon had borne the brunt of it. I very rarely spoke to him, preferring to bury myself in housework just to keep busy. Along the way, I had convinced myself he wanted to leave, ignoring the fact I was driving him away. But his reaction to the baby showed he really did care.

Happy as I was, you don't just flip out of a suicidal mood overnight. I shared my doubts with the psychiatric nurse.

'I can't look after myself, so how can I look after a baby?'

'You're a mother, Kerry. You'll find a way.'

About a month before Leighanna was born we moved house again, to another maisonette in the Foxhill area, just around the corner from Mum and Dad's new place. By the time my little 6lb 6oz bundle arrived, I genuinely thought the world had got that much better. I was part of a family again, I was a proper mum and I was desperate to take the second chance I'd been given. What could go wrong?

Despite all the protestations of love and a long life together, and the promise that he would never disappear like he had before

Ben's birth, Simon only stayed with us for a couple of weeks. The only difference this time was that he didn't walk out by choice.

He was arrested.

New mums are never far from a tear or two at the best of times. This wasn't the best of times.

We were still in Norfolk Park when the police knocked one day looking for Simon. They accused him of burgling someone's house when he was doing door-to-door selling.

'Well, Simon doesn't do that job any more,' I said. 'He hasn't for years. He works on building sites now, with his brother.'

That night I informed Simon the police were looking for him.

'It must be from years ago. Don't worry yourself. That's not going to help the baby.'

He was right. I did have a lot on my plate, with trying to co-ordinate searches, press interviews and getting ready to move house. Then, one day, as we were decorating the lounge in Foxhill, there was a knock at the door. It wasn't neighbours welcoming us to the street. It was the police. Without looking at me they read Simon his rights then marched him out. I had paint on my clothes and a crying baby in my arms. And they just took her father away.

Without Leighanna to look after, I would have gone straight to the medicine cabinet again. I already felt so fragile and this was a hammer blow. *Just when I thought things were turning around, it gets ruined again.* The pain of missing Ben was with me every day. Then there was Mum's trauma-related weight loss, Dad riddled with arthritis because of stress, their own marital problems caused by Dad's relentless obsession with the case, Ben the dog's disappearance, all our money worries and endless fruitless searches

– and now this. It was one thing after another, and I just prayed Leighanna could begin to tip the balance back in our favour.

Simon was put on remand in Leicester. The accusation against him was that while selling and fitting security locks on windows, he'd actually robbed an old couple. I pictured the old lady and thought of my grandma. I knew there was no going back for us if the charges were true.

Simon denied everything, apart from the fact that he had gone back selling door-to-door without telling me. He said someone else in his gang had done the stealing. While that was his story, I had to believe him. Every fortnight, his prison sent me a ticket and I pushed Leighanna onto the train for the journey to Leicester. It wasn't the sort of trip I had dreamed of taking my daughter on.

The remand centre didn't have jail bars exposed to the open air like in Kos, but if anything it was scarier being led through a windowless warren of corridors to see the father of my children.

Returning to an empty house was the worst part of all. Despite Mum being on call and my nurse never more than a day or two away, every hour I was left alone with my baby the doubts about my abilities as a mother grew louder in my head. The harder I tried to shake them off, the more awkward I was getting. If I filled a bath too cold or a bottle too warm that was a signal for tears. If I hadn't washed the outfit I wanted her to wear that day, cue more self-loathing.

On face value, I was showing classic signs of post-natal depression. Health visitors deal with this every day. What they didn't know, however, was how much of my depression had started a long time earlier and a long way away. It was there before Leighanna's birth, it was there after and it's still here today. The only difference is I'm aware of it now. I can recognise the signs and take appropriate measures before it escalates. Strong emotions, of course, are the biggest triggers. And when are emotions stronger than when you have a precious bundle of joy staring up from your arms?

Being alone also gave me a chance to think about Simon. When he announced, just before his appearance in the crown court, that he was going to change his plea to 'guilty' in order to implicate others, I wasn't surprised. Not at him being guilty, nor at him still trying to cover it up with a lie. When it came to the court date, I didn't show up to see Simon sentenced to five years.

The press had a field day. A lot of commentators said Simon had been harshly treated because he was a sort of celebrity and the judge had wanted to make an example of him. One year, five years, a hundred years – it didn't matter to me. There were people out there who wanted to give the whole family a kicking and took any chance they could get. They couldn't criticise us about Ben in public, so this was the next best thing. Everyone knew we lived in council houses and got by on disability allowances and charity – and now, thanks to Simon, we were thieves as well. It didn't make for easy reading. *Is the whole country thinking these things or just one or two journalists?* It made me question everyone I spoke to for a while.

What I couldn't know was that worse was to come.

Somehow I thrived as a single mum, although being in the public eye for the reason I was placed a huge responsibility on my shoulders. It wasn't good enough for me to be a normal mum: I had to be a brilliant one. Every time I stepped outside the house I felt strangers' eyes burning into me, assessing me, judging me. I swear

I heard people saying, 'I hope she looks after this one better than the last one,' but never clearly enough to challenge anyone on it. It didn't matter. Leighanna was my only concern. After one overheard remark, I remember looking at her snuggled up in her pushchair, and promising, 'Mummy's never going to leave you.' How many parents say that and have no idea it could even be a possibility?

I was true to my word – at first. When the chance to investigate sightings came up, I let my parents – often Dad on his own – handle them. Each time they went away I sat at home and chain-drank coffee; I had the concentration span of a pinball machine. I pictured every detail of the trip in my mind and could not relax till they returned. Hard as it was to endure the waiting, it would have been worse to actually travel. I couldn't let Leighanna see me go through the devastation I'd experienced in Turkey and Corfu. I needed to be strong. I was everything she had.

In the last few months before my overdose I'd thrown myself into housework to keep busy. Looking back, I know I had become obsessive about it. I also know it happened again when it was just me and Leighanna at home. I didn't have anyone to talk to at nights and, apart from shopping and going to the park, there was little going on during the day. I was back in the position I had found myself in when Simon abandoned me before. Although my family were at least close this time, all my friends were in Skegness, not Sheffield. Ploughing my energies into cleaning and mopping and tidying filled the void of a missing social life. It was as though I was afraid to be alone with my thoughts.

By the time Leighanna celebrated her first birthday in February 1995, Ben had been missing for over three and a half years. Towards the end of that year, she played a significant role in the search for her brother – role being the operative word. A TV company suggested doing a recreation of Ben's final moments, and there was only one possible candidate to play him.

If I hadn't already seen little Saliha in Turkey, I would have been more shocked at how much a girl can resemble a boy. Leighanna, at eighteen months, was the spit of Ben at the same age. So by the time she was twenty-one months – the age he was when he disappeared – she could easily pass for him on film.

I couldn't face going to Kos, not again, so Mum and Dad agreed to escort their granddaughter. I authorised the cutting of her hair to help her look like Ben as much as possible, and hunted out some clothes of his. I'd kept them in a box in his room, ready to unpack when he returned. When they had obviously become too small, I still couldn't bear to part with them.

I don't know how Mum and Dad got through revisiting the old haunts again. What they must have gone through watching Leighanna being directed to toddle down the lane while they pretended to eat a lunch – just like they'd done nearly four and a half years before – can only be the definition of hell. They both still blamed themselves for what happened to Ben. I think they wanted to take part in the programme as a kind of penance.

Of course, it wasn't all doom and gloom. Leighanna can be very theatrical at times but she doesn't like being bossed about, not now and not then. The TV crew tried everything to get her to walk where they wanted, while she was only interested in marching off in the opposite direction. The very things that had mesmerised Ben at the farmhouse – the flora, the animal noises, the distant goats and birds – took Leighanna's fancy as well. Showing a flash of ingenuity, one of the crew produced a plastic duck and, once their star had established how much she'd like to hold it, walked backwards, just out of camera, to entice the little girl forwards. The secrets of showbiz!

Viewing the finished film was almost as painful as if I'd gone out there myself. For those ten minutes of the recreation, I wasn't watching my daughter: I was watching Ben.

There was another reason I didn't travel with Leighanna to Kos.

By the time Leighanna was eighteen months old, I was bouncing off the walls. We saw relatives as often as we could, and my parents and brothers sometimes came to us. I remember one visit. After they'd gone, I closed the door and rested my head against the wood. I just needed a few moments before I went back into the lounge, back to the couple of small rooms where I'd spend the next thirty or fifty hours without speaking to another adult human being. I loved my daughter so much but I'd gone from being Ben Needham's mum to Leighanna Needham's, without a break in between. And all by the age of twenty-two. Somewhere in the process, Kerry Needham seemed to have been squeezed out of the picture altogether.

A few weeks later I was on the bus with Stephen. He told me a joke he'd heard at college and I burst out laughing. I noticed a woman across the aisle staring.

'Are you Ben Needham's mum?' she said eventually.

'Yes, I am.'

'How can you laugh when he's missing?'

I'd committed the crime of laughing at a joke. To this stranger I wasn't honouring my son. She didn't care that I saw him in Leighanna every day and that I spoke to his photograph as though he were really there. People see what they want to see, and I knew nobody was seeing *me*.

Getting a job seemed the obvious answer on so many grounds – it would take me off benefits, it would get me out of the house and it would allow Mum and Dad to spend more time with their granddaughter. But was I ready psychologically? It was because I had been working instead of looking after Ben that I was crucified by Greek public opinion. Worse, if I started now, there would inevitably be a section of society who saw it as me 'moving on' and criticise me for that.

My application for a weekend bar position in a club in Rotherham was submitted with more than a hint of apprehension. I knew that my reaction to their decision would decide me one way or the other. Less than a week later, I received a reply. I had the job – and I couldn't have been happier. I knew then it was the right decision for me.

My shifts were Thursday, Friday and Saturday night, roughly nine till two o'clock in the morning. Mum agreed to look after Leighanna, and I would either spend the day with them till my next shift or if it was Sunday, take Leighanna back to ours for the week. The club paid for taxis to get us home, so safety was never an issue.

I'd done a little bar work before and I'd seen my old friends Peter and Martin serve cocktails often enough, so there were no surprises for me workwise. The biggest impact was the other staff. For five or six hours a night, I actually spent time talking to people my own age – and that was before all the shouted half-conversations with the men and women queuing to be served. Even if my colleagues did know my story it wasn't an issue. To them,

I was just Kerry. Kerry the barmaid, Kerry the supervisor, Kerry the good laugh.

Kerry the mum was left outside the building.

At home I felt like I had the whole world on my shoulders, and looking at the rest of my team, I realised I was old before my time. They showed me what a twenty-three-year-old should look like. More importantly, they showed me how one could act.

I know now I was hiding from my real life. At the time I felt like I'd found it – I wanted to be free from the pain, the suffering, the depression, the responsibility I'd had weighing me down for a quarter of my life. So, when a girl called Joanna said everyone was going dancing after our shift, I was interested. There were clubs, she said, that didn't get busy till after ours shut. I'd never heard of anything so decadent, certainly never taken part. All that was about to change.

We'd only been at the club an hour and I started flagging. The others were still going like Duracell bunnies; obviously they weren't being deprived of sleep by a baby under two years old.

'That's not the reason we're still awake,' one of my girl friends said.

'How do you do it then?' I asked.

'We take these.'

She showed me a little pill, considerably smaller than an aspirin or diazepam.

'What is it?'

'Tell me you're joking.'

'I'm not. I've never seen that before.'

'Kerry – where have you been? It's ecstasy.'

And so my education continued. By the time I got home, I was already late for picking Leighanna up. Instead, I went to bed and faced the consequences later that evening. Mum said she had no problem with me having a night out, I just should have let her know.

How could I let my mother know the reason I hadn't picked up my daughter was because I'd been too wired on ecstasy?

My eyes were opened to the world and I was desperate to catch up with everything I felt I'd been missing out on. As well as the pill that kept you dancing till dawn, I was also introduced to amphetamines, again by someone convinced I was pulling their leg about never having tried them before. I'm sure some of them thought I'd been living in another era. I felt like they'd come from another planet. Their nocturnal lives were so exotic, so exciting, I couldn't wait for the end of the week so I could get to work and just let my hair down. It was wild, it was crazy and I loved being part of this new circle.

In one of the all-night clubs I was dragged along to all sorts of things went on, but it wasn't the drugs that make it stand out for me.

There were always two or three big blokes on the door to make sure there was no trouble. I was just filing my way in one night when one of the guys pulled me aside.

'Kerry Needham – is that you?'

I'd already had a couple of glasses of wine at the bar, and it must have shown as I stared up at the smiling, bald face looking back. Then the penny dropped.

'Mick? What are you doing here?'

It was Mick Baxendale, my old karate teacher from Skegness. His brother Steven owned the club, and Mick had moved down to manage it for him. I don't know if it was the wine or the fond memories, but when Mick asked me out later I said yes. It didn't matter that he was eighteen years older than me or that I hadn't seen him since I was at school. There was a connection between us and from that moment I was hooked. Although Mick later ended our relationship, even now I would describe him as the love of my life.

I really thought I'd found myself in that nocturnal existence. My new lifestyle didn't make me a better person but it did make me my own person. A person without a label.

The downside was that there was another person in my life, one who depended on me. Gradually, I began to see Leighanna less and less over a weekend. Then one day, I didn't pick her up on Sunday or even go back on Monday. I can't explain it. Mum turned up at Foxhill furious. I think I was still high. I honestly couldn't see why she wouldn't want to spend time with her grandchild. She couldn't see why I wouldn't want to spend time with my daughter.

Looking back, they were obviously worried about me. They'd seen the hurt I'd gone through with Ben, so they knew I was a good mother. What on earth could be happening to make me, as they saw it, abandon Leighanna? As much as they wanted to help out, they were willing me to rediscover my maternal instincts because that would mean I was back on track.

But also, I think they'd both admit now that they were actually a little scared to look after their granddaughter. I'd never blamed them for anything so maybe I was insensitive this time round. But clearly having such responsibility for Leighanna opened old scars. It made them doubt themselves. Could they be trusted? Were they worthy? In my eyes they were and always would be. But they were nervous. However you look at it, I'm not proud. I didn't respect their feelings. At that time, I didn't respect anything or anyone.

Over the next month I left Leighanna with Mum and Dad for longer and longer until, eventually, I didn't go back for her at all.

A couple of weeks later I came home, very much the worse for wear, and found my front door had been smashed in. I screamed and staggered into the house, praying the burglars weren't still there. The place was exactly as I'd left it, apart from in one room. The intruders seemed only to have been interested in Leighanna's clothes, her toys and her cot.

It didn't take too long for me to deduce that Mum and Dad had come for Leighanna's things. They'd given up on me.

People think depression is about feeling sad. It's not. It's about feeling nothing at all.

I don't know if it was a continuation of post-natal depression or still the guilt of Ben reverberating through me that drove me so far off the rails. I couldn't face being a bad parent for a minute longer. At that moment, I was glad Dad had taken Leighanna away. She deserved better than me. That's honestly what I thought.

I realise now that I was ill, I was unstable and, as I was about to learn, I was unthinking as well. For the latter, I was about to be seriously punished.

It's one thing to admit opinions with such candour to yourself but to elaborate them to a journalist is stupidity itself. If I hadn't been in such a destructive spiral of self-obsession I would have worked out what was going on. When I did, it was too late.

It began with Mum being interviewed on a sighting. Why, the journalist enquired, wasn't I there?

There were plenty of trips that Mum and Dad had made without me. We were a team. At one point, Mum was following a lead on one island, I was on another and Dad on a third. Mum could have replied with that. Instead, with her usual openness, she said, 'Kerry's had a breakdown under the strain of it all. She was physically incapable of coming.'

The *Sheffield Star* picked up on the story and asked for an interview. I clearly wasn't in the right frame of mind but I said yes. The usual mantra: this might be the piece of publicity that works. I regretted it the second I saw their front page headline: 'Kerry Gives Up Her Daughter'. Did I learn from it, though? No. When the *Express on Sunday* came calling, I again convinced myself that the positives outweighed any harm it could do. I began the conversation with my guard up but I quickly defaulted to my usual candid self and told them exactly how bad my life was. My son was missing, I was on antidepressants, Ben's father was in prison, I had no income and I was struggling to cope so much that Leighanna was currently staying with my mum and dad. I was even honest enough to say that there was a chance Ben had been taken by someone who could afford to give him a better life than I could.

The *Express*, of course, span that quote. They ran the huge headline: 'I Don't Want My Ben Back – Says Mother As She Shuns New Baby'. It was hurtful, and they twisted my words. I can't remember word for word but I never said that. It wasn't that I didn't want him back. It was that in my current state of mind I honestly questioned whether I deserved him.

That story did an awful lot of damage, some of which I still see when I encounter people who clearly remember it. I don't know how some of those newspaper people can sleep. Any family's situation can be distorted if you try hard enough. Peer closely enough, and you see the paper over everybody's cracks.

We were living under a microscope. Even Danny's school progress made the local press. I was reliant on the media for help in
finding Ben and so I never dared to turn anyone away, even when
I was medically incapable of proceeding.

Having a journalist turn against me was one thing. Hearing that
a Member of Parliament was repeating the *Express*'s claims as
though they were fact had me tearing out my hair. Kevin Johnson was just one of millions of people who would be affected
the following year by a Channel 4 *Cutting Edge* documentary
about Ben. As I've said, a tiny minority aside, I've always felt
overwhelming support from the British public: the unending
supply of photographs and goodwill messages that kept pouring in told me that Ben was never far from people's thoughts.
So it was no surprise to me when I heard that Kevin, a complete
stranger, had written to his local MP requesting more action
from officialdom. The request had been passed to my own MP,
David Blunkett. Between me, my parents and Simon's father,
Cliff, there wasn't an influential politician or holder of public
office that we hadn't implored via mail – I've got replies from
John Major, Tony Blair, Gordon Brown and David Cameron to
prove it. Even though we were the ones in the spotlight, receive-
ing letters from members of the public made MPs think about it
more. They appreciated it wasn't just the concern of one family,
it was the concern of the whole constituency and beyond. Ben
was the nation's child.

David Blunkett had, till that point, been very fair in his correspondence with us. I don't know what changed, but his reply to
Kevin was very unwelcome:

'Regrettably Ben's mother appears to have disengaged from what has happened and I understand her second child is now being cared for by the grandparents.'

That is an MP's letter to a stranger. It's one thing me being gossiped about on a bus or in the street, but from a man who, weeks later, was appointed Secretary of State for Education and Employment, as far as I was concerned it was unforgiveable.

Fortunately, the MP's response did not put Kevin off. He launched a petition calling for Parliament to recognise the British people's love for Ben and their desire to have the full weight of the country's resources dedicated to finding him. He presented the thousands of signatures to MP Margaret Hodge who promised to take it to directly to Robin Cook in the Foreign Office. I cry when I hear about people like Kevin – complete strangers – who just want to help.

I was too weak emotionally to respond to the *Star* and the *Express*'s revelations in any other way than try to kill the pain through my new hedonistic lifestyle. When that didn't work, I tried once again to kill the pain more permanently. *They can't attack me if I am dead, can they?* I remember the thought going through my mind and my trembling hands scrabbling at the lid of the diazepam bottle. This time I would have no Shane to save me. This time would be it.

I think I passed out before I'd even swallowed half the amount I intended to. I don't know how much time had elapsed, but I felt terrible when I opened my eyes. Spying the tablets lined up on the table sent a shiver through me. I remembered little about what I'd done and even less about why. It was Thursday. In a couple of hours I'd be at work. Why would I want to stop myself going there?

I don't know exactly how antidepressants work, but it's possible in taking half a dozen I had a rapid injection of calmness. All suicidal thoughts left me. Once again, I just wanted to party. On paper, however, it was just another response to the same problem. Suicide was one route out of pain. Drunken oblivion was another. They were all my attempts to try and hide from the suffering.

My local politician had written me off publicly, a national newspaper had held me up for criticism and my family couldn't bear to talk to me, yet none of these events was enough to make me sort myself out. I didn't honestly think anything ever would be until one day, when I received a surprise phone call from a shaky-voiced Simon in prison.

'What's the matter?'

'It's my dad, Kerry. He's dead.'

I couldn't explain it at the time but the passing of Cliff Ward, one of the sweetest, most generous men I have still ever known, sent a bolt right through me. Even as I hung up, tears streaming down my face, I knew my life was changing again. Cliff was really upfront, he worked tirelessly trying to get governments behind us, he was not afraid to show his emotions and he really cared about people. Basically, he was just the best example of a family man.

As I dried my eyes it felt like I was wiping away more than tears. After months of darkness, I was seeing cracks of light again. My head was clearing and I knew exactly what I had to do.

Half an hour later I took a deep breath and knocked on the front door of my mum's house. She opened it and just stared as

I stepped past her into the front room, where my daughter was sitting in her pyjamas laughing at a book. Leighanna looked up and said, 'Mummy!' like I'd been gone a day and not months.

Thank you, Cliff.

CHAPTER SEVENTEEN

I HAVE BEN
IN MY HANDS

Fuelled by the knowledge that I was over my problem and fully focused, and freed of their enforced parental duties, Mum and Dad began following up leads again. As destructive as the past year or two had been, without it I'm convinced I would still be in the dark place I was when we first returned to England. It was ultimately cathartic, although hell for everyone at the time. We've never spoken, as a family, about that episode of my life. It's possible Mum and Dad will learn things in this book that they didn't know. The only important thing at the time was that we all knew I was back for good.

The fifth anniversary of Ben's disappearance brought us all down, though. On paper it's just another day, no different really from the 23rd July 1996, or the 25th. In our hearts it was a milestone and, psychologically, a blow to be felt in the solar plexus.

Five years. My precious baby has been missing five years.

Were we any closer to finding him? Despite the tens of thousands of miles travelled and pounds spent, I had to say we weren't. We had new leads almost every day, and there was always hope that the next sighting would be 'the one'. Getting up every day and knowing you'd made absolutely zero difference for five whole years was a hurdle that until recently I would have been incapable of surmounting. With Mum and Dad's help, and the love of Leighanna and my brothers, I saw the positive. Everything we had done, however unsuccessful ultimately, had narrowed the search. It was happening painfully slowly, but it was a process of elimination.

Being a hands-on mum again gave my day-to-day life shape. My parents had Danny and, to a lesser extent, Stephen, to give them a reason to get up in the morning. As the boys grew older, even that was becoming less of a call. We really had to pull together to keep each other motivated and our heads above water. If one of us looked like sinking, the others were there, just like we had been there for each other in Kos five years earlier.

We didn't know it, but 1996 would be the year we came closest yet.

To commemorate the fifth anniversary of Ben's disappearance, Mum and Dad flew to Athens to conduct a press conference for the European media. There were two major pieces of news for the journalists to get their teeth into. First, we had another updated image of Ben to disseminate. I was grateful to the police boffins who'd created it, although it's surreal watching your child grow up through a computer's eyes. He will always be twenty-one-months old to me until the day I see him again with my own eyes.

Second, there was a reward. *TV Quick*'s offer of £3,000 was still on the table and the *Yorkshire Post* and *Sheffield Star* had added their own financial incentives. Yet an anonymous businessman had suddenly contacted us to say he wanted to donate considerably more. Dad handled everything, as usual, including arranging the meeting with our mysterious benefactor. After his wife or partner rang en route to confirm directions to the house, Dad put the phone down and said, 'I swear that was Princess Di!'

I'm not at liberty to say who it was – it wasn't the Princess of Wales – but they arrived in a gold-plated Rolls-Royce. It would have stood out anywhere. Parked next to Dad's battered old Transit, it looked like something from another planet.

When the couple departed, we were all left shaking our heads. '£500,000,' I said. '£500,000!'

Like so many people who have helped us over the years, this man just wanted to do what he could to speed up Ben's return. Where others could write letters, he could write cheques. The reward was never an official one sanctioned by the police or authorities, but unveiling this news in Athens, Mum and Dad felt like they were reading out the lottery results. A sharp intake of breath echoed around the conference hall, then the journalists broke out into a chorus of cicada-like questions, all spoken at once. Now we had their attention.

Unfortunately, when it came to news coverage and column inches in the newspapers, the conference was unexpectedly bumped down the list. One of Greece's most popular actresses, Aliki Vougiouklaki, had died the day before. She was, therefore, the lead item on the TV news and on front pages. Our reward was relegated, if covered at all.

Undeterred, Mum and Dad agreed to return later in the year to participate in another documentary – actually, in another two: one for English television and one for Greek audiences. The Greek programme began filming in October, shortly before Ben's seventh birthday. Apart from the July date, this was the time of year I dreaded most. Steeling myself, I managed to give an interview from home, as did everyone, before Mum and Dad flew off to take part in the studio section of the programme in Athens.

When they agreed, we had no idea how it would change our lives.

Shadows In The Mist is the Greek equivalent of *Surprise Surprise*, which arguably makes presenter Kostas Hardevellas the equivalent of the UK's Cilla Black or Holly Willoughby. Like *Surprise Surprise*, the programme uses its vast research budget to track down family members who've dropped out of touch with the rest of their kin – whether through divorce, estrangement or, occasionally, abduction – and then reunites them live on national television. It's not my idea of entertainment, but the joy those families experience cannot be denied. It was Hardevellas's dream when he spoke to us in Sheffield that he would be able to help our family too.

Perched nervously on the guest sofa in the Greek studio, Mum and Dad couldn't help thinking they'd made a mistake. The programme's heart was in the right place but it was all a bit too showbizzy for their tastes. Then our interviews were shown on a large screen and translated for the studio and home audiences, and my parents began to relax. Like he'd done so many other times, Kostas Hardevellas started his appeal to viewers for help. He showed the most recent computer update of Ben and, of course, he mentioned the reward. As far as Mum and Dad could tell, it was all going exactly as Hardevellas had predicted it would and, for the first time, they felt a genuine sense that the Greek people were going to deliver something more than shrugs. Their hunch turned out to be right, although nobody could have predicted the source.

The first clue came when Mum and Dad noticed Hardevellas's expression change and he became more animated, appearing to talk to someone in the production booth. Even with the language barrier, my parents knew something unexpected was going on. The presenter was now addressing the cameras with a massive smile on his face. He ended with a few words addressed, in English, to Mum and Dad.

'We have a caller on the line who says he has Ben.'

He has Ben? The words thundered through their heads as they looked at Hardevellas then at each other. But the host had turned back to the cameras and was talking in Greek. Mum and Dad could only listen in shock as a loud, clear, gruff voice boomed over the studio speaker. It was the caller – but what the hell was he saying? Whatever it was, the studio audience had gone completely silent.

If I'd been there I'd have throttled Hardevellas. I'm amazed Dad stayed seated for so long. He must have been in shock. A conversation about their grandson was taking place live on Greek television between a TV presenter and a man claiming to have Ben – and they couldn't follow a word of it.

Still grinning like the proverbial cat with the cream, Hardevellas said what my parents recognised as goodnight and they realised the broadcast was over. Now Dad could get some answers.

Kostas was bubbling. He knew he had a hit show on his hands. He also knew Mum and Dad were totally in the dark. He poured out everything. A viewer had seen the appeal for Ben, rung in and had stopped the show with six simple words: 'I have Ben in my hands.'

That's when the *Shadows In The Mist* studio audience went silent, just as I did when Mum relayed the information. There was only one potential problem. The caller's name was Andonis Bedzios – currently residing in Larissa Prison.

'You have to realise it is a very large reward,' Kostas said. 'The temptation to lie would be great for many people. A man like this...'

'Just because he's in prison doesn't make him a completely bad person,' Dad insisted later to me. I thought of Simon and agreed.

Mum and Dad were desperate to learn exactly what this criminal had said. All the blood drained from their faces when they did.

First, Bedzios had clarified that Ben couldn't be in his hands because of being incarcerated. Next he said the boy – 'Mikro Ben' as so many Greeks called him – was living in a gypsy camp in Veria, about sixty miles from Larissa. Then he told Hardevellas and the studio audience the following story.

Before being captured by the police a year earlier, Bedzios asked a gypsy leader, Christos Kerimi, to take his son Rabo into the camp and raise him in Bedzios's absence. Being separated from Rabo was too much to bear so, in a moment of madness, Bedzios broke out of the police van switching him between prisons and went on the run. From December 1991 to March 1992 he made his way as carefully as possible to Veria, where he hoped to be reunited with Rabo; at least until the police discovered him. He was surprised to see a younger, blond-haired boy playing with his son. He was even more surprised to learn the boy was the one 'stolen' from Kos the year before.

Bedzios's cousin, Grigoris, was a neighbour of Kerimi's. He had told Andonis, 'We need Rabo's birth certificate to register little Ben and have him baptised.' The plan was clearly to legitimise Ben's presence and to wipe his real life from the history books.

Andonis, for all his law-breaking past, was shocked by the mercenary nature of the proposition. When he questioned what Ben's real family must be going through, he was reminded that his own son's life could take an unfortunate turn if Kerimi were not to get his own way.

The meeting had taken place on 22 March 1992. I had one question: 'Why the hell has he waited till now to tell us?'

Kostas Hardevellas had asked the same question on his television programme, to which Andonis had replied, 'Kerimi had my son. I could not endanger him.'

Of course, if his story was true, that made sense. So what had changed? Why was he speaking out now, when he hadn't dared before? For that, Bedzios had replied, we were welcome to visit him and discover the truth for ourselves.

At the end of it, Mum and Dad were buzzing. This wasn't a sighting of a girl who might have looked like Ben in a year's time or a fleeting description of a child caught out of the corner of a holidaymaker's eye. This was a sworn statement that a mysterious boy was not only called Ben but that he had been snatched from Kos in 1991. I'm not saying I got the champagne out when they called me soon after, but it was the first time in five years we let ourselves entertain the notion of having something to celebrate.

'We need to see this guy,' Dad told Kostas. 'Now.'

Sensing a coup for his TV programme, Hardevellas agreed. Calls were made, deals were struck and the next day he, Mum and Dad and, of course, a TV crew, arrived in Larissa. Once again, another chapter of our lives was going to be played out on screen for everyone to see. I just prayed that this chapter had a happy ending.

I'd visited Leicester prison enough for one lifetime, but if the barbaric cells at Kos were anything to go by, a Greek jail was going to be a different proposition, and not in a good way. I did not envy Mum having to go inside. I certainly could not entertain the idea of taking Leighanna anywhere near it. For that reason alone, I stayed back home and waited for their call.

When it came, three things stood out for me. Number one, Bedzios had claimed he did not want to see a penny of the reward money. Number two, he had said Ben was living in a house in Patras, a large city in the west. And number three, he had a very personal reason for breaking his silence now: he claimed that Kerimi was mistreating Rabo and he said he wanted revenge. That was the clincher for me. As a parent, I recognised in Bedzios what it was like to feel powerless and yet prepared to do anything for your child. He told them he wanted us to rescue not only Ben but Rabo as well, and have Kerimi imprisoned in the process. If he was telling the truth, we would get our boy, his son would get a new home and his greatest enemy would be removed from the game. Everyone would be a winner.

Dad is usually a good judge of character. I trusted him on this one as well.

'Kerry, he looked your mother and me in the eye and swore on his son's life. I believe him.'

That wasn't the end of it. Bedzios said he'd kicked over the hornets' nest by calling into *Shadows In The Mist*. He told them that suddenly Kerimi was scared. There was talk of dumping 'Mikro Ben' outside the TV studios. He was too hot to keep now.

After so many years of dashed expectations, could this really be the moment? Disappointment when other sightings went wrong was like losing Ben all over again, so I had to have a very good reason to let my guard down. On this occasion I did. Four reasons in fact, because Bedzios wasn't the only person who was directing us to Veria.

We could never have guessed how influential Mum and Dad's appearance on *Shadows In The Mist* would be. We received word from the British Embassy that an anonymous caller had rung, claiming to have picked up Ben and Rabo in his taxi. Unfortunately the man refused to leave a name or make a statement. Then, in December, we were contacted by a private detective called Stratos Bakirtzis who had video footage of a boy he claimed was Ben. It took weeks to get through to us. My hand trembled as I inserted the VHS cassette into the video player. The scene was of the outside of a house. A man in his late fifties walked past, then a woman – and then a little blond boy.

Technology in 1996 was nothing like it is today. It didn't help that the film had been surreptitiously shot from inside a jacket, with the boy only captured in passing as the detective hunted for evidence of something else. Using pause and freeze frame I managed to inch through the tape to the clearest possible shot of the blond boy's face. Then I found the zoom button and focused in.

The seven-year-old face staring back at me was the spitting image of Simon.

The video contained another shock. The house where the boy was playing belonged, Bakirtzis said, to a certain sometime criminal family called the Kerimis.

It could not be a coincidence, could it?

Mum and Dad wanted to see Bedzios again, this time with an interpreter and not Greece's answer to Cilla Black. They also wanted to pursue this new claim with the police, but Ben's fund was empty. Luckily, a few weeks after Mum and Dad arrived back in England we were due to take part in a Channel 4 documentary called 'The Lost Boy', part of their *Cutting Edge* series. Suddenly, there were our tickets back to Greece.

Returning to Larissa, now it was Mum and Dad's turn for some covert recording. As they sat in the hire car outside the jail, tiny microphones, courtesy of Nick Godwin and his C4 production team, were secreted in their clothes. Whatever Bedzios said in there would be on tape for analysis later. Any discrepancies in his claims would be shot down, and we would know once and for all whether he could be trusted.

In the event, he didn't disappoint. Via the interpreter, Bedzios reiterated every claim he'd made on TV and in person to them before. When Mum and Dad left, they were convinced he was telling the truth. Now they had to convince the authorities in Veria to act. What they didn't know as they drove the sixty miles north, was that another 'coincidence' was about to make their job very difficult.

Somehow Bakirtzis's footage had ended up being broadcast on Greek TV. The detective denied any involvement, blaming one of his men. Whoever was responsible, the result was devastating for us because suddenly everyone in Veria was aware of the attention heading their way. Yes, the town had already been mentioned by Bedzios on TV but who really, outside our family, was taking the word of a convict seriously? This, by contrast, showed the authorities meant business. By the time Mum and Dad had arrived, there would be plenty of time for a guilty party to prepare – as they discovered when they entered the police station, and learnt that Kerimi had beaten them there.

Mum and Dad studied a photograph the gypsy had left for them. It was a boy with a shaved head, about eight years old.

'This is the blond boy from the film,' a policeman informed them. 'This is Rabo.'

As soon as Kerimi had become aware of the speculation about his family, he had brought the boy to Veria police station to be examined and photographed. This, the policeman explained, should be an end to the gossip about the family.

While Mum scrutinised the photo, Dad asked, 'Why has his hair been shaved?'

The policeman shrugged. 'Because of head lice.'

A suspicious person might think it had been shorn to hide the fact it wasn't as blond as the hair in the video – and Dad is a very suspicious person. The policeman, on the other hand, appeared not to be. When Dad demanded the police search Kerimi's house, he was shot down.

'This is Rabo.' The policeman tapped the picture. 'There is no other boy.'

None of it made sense. According to local information, Greek gypsies suffered endlessly at the hands of the police. Yet here was a golden opportunity to get a warrant and search the house, and they were turning it down. Another coincidence?

On paper, the police's story might seem very plausible apart from two factors. One, we had experience of trusting the Kos police force and look where that had got us. And two, even as they arrived in Veria, Mum and Dad heard a very different tale.

The man seemed to step out of nowhere. One minute Mum and Dad were walking along a deserted road, the next there was an agitated guy alongside them. Mum's immediate thought was of personal safety. The way the stranger was acting made her think he was a mugger, possibly on drugs. As he leant in nervously to speak, she nearly screamed. If she had, she would never have heard what he had to say.

'I'm the one who called the British Embassy,' he revealed. 'I know Kerimi has little Ben.'

The man was a taxi driver who regularly carried Kerimi's family. One day in January 1994, he'd noticed in his rear-view mirror that among the usual children was a blond boy.

'What's your name?' he'd called back.

Rabo had been the one to answer.

'This Ben – or Benzi.'

A second later, the woman in the cab with them had slapped Rabo around the face and told him not to say another word.

'It's no good hiding in the shadows,' Dad said. 'We need you to tell the police.'

The man looked over his shoulder every which way a dozen times before answering. 'I will tell the police. But not here. Not in Veria.'

Obviously, he was implying, not all of Kerimi's friends were gypsies.

I'm so glad Mum and Dad weren't alone out there. In particular, one of the *Cutting Edge* researchers, Melanie McFadyean, was brilliant. As the whole Kerimi mess looked like unravelling, she was the one who seemed to be able to see the ends of the string and begin to pull them together.

It was Melanie who accompanied Mum to see Rabo for herself. They found the boy at home with his 'parents': Kerimi and a gold-toothed younger woman. The adults were relaxed about Mum talking to Rabo and taking his picture, although they didn't want to be photographed themselves. Asked about the video the mother shrugged. 'I was in prison then. For stabbing a woman.' One flash of her golden smile told Mum exactly how little the crime played on the woman's mind. Even though absent, she maintained Rabo was the boy caught on film. She also said, still smiling, 'You can take him if you want. Have him.'

What sort of a woman, step-mother or not, can say that? If she wasn't joking, and Mum swears she was serious, then this just proves the regard that children are held in in some quarters. They're commodities, like sugar, oil, gold.

But the woman hadn't finished. As Mum gave Rabo some sweets and a little cuddle, she said, 'The boy you are looking for is in the gypsy camp.'

That was not how we expected a meeting with the Kerimi family to be. They were meant to be criminals, and now this woman was helping. Why would she volunteer this information if it wasn't true?

Mum realised why when they reached the camp in question. Rabo's mother had been lying. The expensive grin that was never far from her lips should have been clue enough, but the tip-off needed to be explored. An hour enjoying the hospitality of the camp's dwellers confirmed it. Kerimi was always trying to cause trouble for them. They wished they could help but it had been a bold lie. The question for Mum was whether it had been simply malicious – or a genuine attempt to direct attention away from the Kerimis themselves.

With Mum and Dad following other leads, Melanie took it upon herself to confront Christos once again. Accompanied by a local TV reporter sympathetic to the gypsy community, she found the sixty-year-old coming out of his house. At first Kerimi ignored them both while he coolly loaded large chunks of scrap metal from one flat-bed truck into another; he wasn't at all flustered by being interrogated by the woman from the television. If Ben was in the house behind him then nothing in Kerimi's face was showing it. But his true colours weren't far away. Something the reporter said obviously struck a nerve: his face turned red, he picked up a metal roof rack and as he threw it he screamed into the camera.

'I don't need to steal children. I am the gypsy king!'

The projectile landed near to where the reporter was standing and she took that as her cue to run.

Shaken but even more determined, Melanie and the reporter, accompanied this time by Mum and Dad, went instead to visit Christos's brother, Andreas. They all got close enough to his house to spy several women in possibly drug-induced states, plus a very animated disabled child pulling against the rope that bound him to a chair. There was no sign of Ben, or Rabo. But they did see Andreas.

Bad tempers obviously run in the Kerimi family. The Brits didn't need a translator to realise it wouldn't end well if they stayed on the gypsy's land. Andreas didn't have scrap to hurl so he grabbed something else from his car and marched angrily towards his visitors. Whatever he was holding was concealed under a cloth. Mum's mind immediately went to a scene from a gangster film where the hitman covered his gun with a bar towel. One look at Andreas's snarling face told her it didn't just happen in movies.

It should have been me facing off against that man. I am so upset that my mum has had to experience these things instead, but so proud of her and Dad as well.

Back in their car, the Greek reporter translated Andreas's final words: 'If you don't leave I will get my gun and shoot you.' It was decided that they should go back to the police station. The authorities would have to listen now.

They were wrong. Of course they were wrong. It was Kos all over again. Dad and Mum and Melanie reported everything that the Kerimis had said and done, and the policeman swatted it all away. If anything, he came close to accusing our side of harassing the gypsies. That, he said, was a crime.

'But what about the testimony from Andonis Bedzios?' Dad said. 'It can't all be coincidence.'

The officer inhaled theatrically and said, 'Bedzios is a mythomaniac. He lies. He makes up stories. Everyone knows this.' In fact, he went on, not only was our leading witness a fantasist, he was waging an underworld war against Kerimi and concocting accusations about Ben was just his latest weapon to damage Kerimis. In this version of events, of course, the Kerimis were entirely innocent.

Despite not swallowing anything the policeman said, his words laid our case pretty bare. We were choosing to believe one criminal over another.

We all had to take a step back. Were our decisions rational or were we just following the version of events we all so desperately wanted to be the truth?

I know what I believe, and it's that sometimes you can get the right result without showing the right workings out. That's what my maths teacher used to say. Stranded in Sheffield I couldn't, hand on heart, say that Andonis Bedzios was telling the truth but I could believe my mother when she said she and Melanie tracked down a woman who used to look after Bedzios's son. I've always believed that children don't lie about these things for no reason. So, while the woman stirred her cooking pot and Rabo helped, while telling her stories of his brother 'Ben', she had no doubt he was telling the truth. By the time Mum reached her, the woman said Rabo's brother was in another town with relatives. Rabo hadn't told her where. It was another dead end.

When I heard this I knew I could sit in Sheffield no longer. It was time for me to see Andonis Bedzios for myself.

CHAPTER EIGHTEEN

I WILL SMASH
YOU DOWN

Everything Mum had said about Larissa jail was true. It was grim, very grim. The prisoners looked terrifying and the guards even worse. The governor of the prisoner was also formidable looking. When he said he wanted to be present at my meeting with Bedzios, I was actually relieved.

As I listened to Bedzios's words, relayed through a lovely interpreter called Lampros Georgiocas, I stared into his eyes and I honestly saw a man looking back who believed he was doing the right thing. He was telling the truth, I know he was. The governor left him in no doubt what would happen if he wasn't.

'Bedzios, listen to me. If you are lying to these people about their boy, I will smash you! Understand me, Bedzios? I will smash you down!'

Bedzios looked at the towering figure looming over him and said, calmly and clearly, 'I speak the truth.'

Even before the translator had done his work, I knew he was right.

The problem with believing Bedzios was that it meant other people had to be lying. I hadn't been directly involved except on the end of a phone but I trusted my parents' instincts. When they suggested we go above the police force to pursue the prisoner's claims, I agreed.

Athens's Public Order minister listened intently to our story. At the end he promised a full investigation. In particular with regard to two of Bedzios's claims: that Ben was now living in Patras with a rich family; and that three German criminals had been involved with the original abduction.

While the minister's department acted, Dad took a ferry over to Kos to update Bafounis on our findings and to ask for a favour. The taxi driver who was too scared of possible corruption in the Veria police needed to be interviewed by another force. Dad asked if the Kos police could arrange this. Bafounis said yes.

Before he left Dad asked, as usual, if there had been any updates. Bafounis shook his head.

'What about the white car?' Dad asked.

Bafounis gave his trademark shrug. 'Not yet. We are still looking.'

As he made his way back to the port, Dad mused on how impressive Bafounis's English had got in the last few years. It was almost as if he'd understood every word back in 1991 and had just chosen not to communicate with us directly.

While dealings with Kos law enforcement tended to leave us with more questions than answers, two members of the Thessaloniki force in north-east Greece were about to make up for it. And they would be risking their lives to do so.

We were introduced to the officers by an improbably named woman called Mariana Zepante-Faithful. Mariana is an incredible person who set up the Illegal Adoption Society of Athens. She campaigned tirelessly, till her retirement, to reunite estranged families and to put an end to this pernicious trade in children. The fact that Mariana set up a foundation to combat illegal adoption tells me a lot. For all the dismissive shrugs we got on Kos at the mention of abduction, statistics in Greece bear it out. The country has one of the lowest birth rates of any country in the European Union. By the mid-1990s, the majority of baby trading involved children from the former Soviet countries abutting the northern border. It was big business, and for certain criminals has become as important to their trade as drugs trafficking or prostitution.

It was only a matter of time before Mariana's work brought her into our orbit. She'd found two policemen who swore that the original video shown to us by the detective, Bakirtzis, had actually been shot by Thessaloniki policemen during covert surveillance on Kerimi's house. How the detective had got hold of a copy was not known, but certain people within the squad saw an opportunity for leverage against the gypsy king. In other words, they knew full well that it was Ben in the film and they were blackmailing Kerimi on the strength of it. What they were getting in return was also not clear but, the officers said, it would be valuable. So much so, they were in fear of their lives just for bringing the information to Mariana.

With the policemen's help, we located a nice house in a well-to-do area just outside Patras where, they said, a rich family lived with their blond-haired son. A son, they both insisted, who had been sold to them by Kerimi. *A son called Ben*. We waited outside from early morning to late at night and watched the school bus come and go without anyone from the house boarding or getting off. The next day, the same story. If Ben had ever been there it was unlikely he was now. Someone, somehow, had known we were coming. The family had been tipped off.

Mariana wouldn't let that be the end of it. She went straight to the Public Order Ministry and demanded an investigation. There were raised voices and expressive hand gestures but dealing with officials, the police and basically banging on doors to get things done within their system had been Mariana's lifeblood for ages. We'd only dealt with Greek bureaucracy for a few years. She'd been doing it for decades.

A few days later, we were told the house and its family had been fully explored. The child was legally and legitimately the son of the rich parents.

'He is not Ben.'

We had to take their word, but they couldn't show me a picture.

Back in Veria, our fortunes took another turn for the worse. Our man in the shadows, the cabbie who had driven Ben and Rabo, had been interviewed by the police.

The Veria police.

Had Bafounis just ignored Dad's request or had someone intercepted the request? Or was it just plain human error? Either way, the man who swore to us that he had seen Ben left the police station having identified Rabo as the only child he had chauffeured. Whatever or whoever he was scared of had got to him. Nothing we said could change his mind. The only chink of light came when we actually spoke to the police afterwards. Mum asked if she could take a copy of the photograph of Rabo that the man had identified.

'We don't have one,' the officer said.

'Well, what did he look at then?'

'This.'

It was the picture of Ben artificially aged by the computers at South Yorkshire Police.

Eighteen months after Mum and Dad's appearance on *Shadows In The Mist* we were no closer to Ben than we had been before. Between a prisoner serving a life sentence for armed robbery, an in-fighting community of gypsies and two police forces, knowing who to believe was practically impossible. We still had some leads from Bedzios, but relying on the Public Order Ministry to produce results tested everyone's patience.

On our final trip to Larissa Prison, Bedzios had named three Germans who, he said, were involved in Ben's abduction. He claimed he had receipts showing they were paying him to keep silent. He seemed to be drip-feeding information as and when it suited him; he certainly hadn't mentioned this on the other occasions we'd spoken. Could we believe him? It was more a question of could we afford not to? Dad spoke to the police to put wheels in motion. Even as he left the station, he didn't hold out much hope.

Back in England, it was easy to imagine nothing had been done. Athens was meant to be liaising with Berlin via Interpol but it was taking for ever. I had the distraction of Leighanna to stop me climbing the walls but my parents didn't have that luxury and their stress showed itself in different ways. While Mum quietly withdrew, Dad grew more and more restless, chain-smoking and drinking coffee by the gallon. He couldn't stop talking about the possible outcomes and different scenarios. Mum admits she got sick of it. She said living with Dad was like having a drill pounding into her brain. My brothers also tried to avoid him and even I didn't always have the stomach for another round-the-houses telephone call full of 'What if...' and 'Why aren't they doing that?' But Dad was wired on caffeine and nicotine and guilt. If there was something else to talk about, he didn't know what it was.

A month after we returned from Greece, he realised the time for talking was over.

'I'm going back to Athens. I can't wait for them to get off their backsides.'

'Don't be stupid, we can't afford it,' Mum insisted. 'The fund's nearly empty.'

'There's enough for a flight.'

'What if another sighting happens in the meantime?'

'Well, I can't stay here and do nothing!'

Back in Athens, his first stop was to visit Bedzios. He wanted to know more about the Germans. Where were these receipts? What were the names and addresses? Bedzios would only give one name and the city of Munich. Then Dad went to the Ministry of Public Order to check up on progress. There wasn't any.

'How long does it take to get pictures of three men?' he asked.

'Soon. Soon.'

'I'll come back tomorrow, then.'

Without the money for a hotel, Dad found a secluded part of the beach and spent the night there. The following morning, he returned to the ministry and was met by the same story. For three weeks he travelled back and forth like that. Utterly frustrated, he decided to pay the British Embassy a visit. Their track record for helping our family so far had been pretty poor. That's how desperate Dad was.

BEN

The smart building on Ploutarchou Street looks similar to the home of the British government in London's Whitehall. For a moment, Dad let himself think that as a UK citizen he might get a decent reception. After his previous conversations with the consulate, he wasn't betting on it. When he was told that there was a new man in town, he couldn't have been more relieved.

Gordon Bernard was a dynamic man in his early forties and as different from his predecessor as you could imagine. Not only did he say that he would personally hound the minister for the pictures Dad had requested, he was also horrified by Dad's living arrangements.

'There's a guest apartment at my official residence,' he said. 'I insist you stay there.'

Even under Gordon's pressure, the Greek authorities seemed to have their fingers in their ears. So when Dad came across two men planning to drive to Germany, he decided to cut his losses and hitch a ride. He had nowhere to stay, no idea where to start looking and not a single word of German in his head. But that had never stopped him in Greece. Somehow he'd always got his point across.

Eventually he ended up in Munich and, armed only with a man's name, went straight to the British consulate. When an initial search proved unsuccessful Dad took it upon himself to work through local phone directories. It worked. With a name and now an address, the German police could do something. They tore the man's home inside out but found no trace of anything to link him to Bedzios's accusations.

Disenchanted, penniless and exhausted, Dad returned home.

The stress on everyone comes out at different times in different ways. My breakdowns have been very public. Whether Simon was driven to do what he did by the pressure, I don't know. Mum and Dad found themselves at odds with each other over almost every little thing. Her way of coping with the guilt she still felt all these years later about Ben's disappearance was to throw herself into domesticity. She found comfort in housework and took solace in friends. She wasn't running away, she was protecting herself.

Dad's approach was the opposite. Before his German trip, he'd already been a livewire. Now he was in a constant state of agitation. He was obsessed, he admits it. He dialled the same numbers every day to be told the same things time after time. He paced up and down the house, couldn't concentrate on his scrap-metal scavenging and bent the ear of anyone who came near. Mum begged him to calm down, to focus on himself, on his children and on her. He couldn't. Finally, after another blistering confrontation, Dad packed a suitcase and walked to the front door. He opened it, went to step out and stopped. He had nowhere to go.

We were all at our wits' end. The revelations from Andonis Bedzios had promised so much and delivered nothing but heartache and disappointment. Even though I believed him, where had it got us? We'd uncovered lies in Veria, in Thessaloniki, almost certainly in Athens and probably now in Munich. It was as though there was a conspiracy to keep us in the dark. If that was the case, then who was pulling the strings?

Dad just wanted to know why more wasn't being done. We all did. If we weren't ordinary working-class people then the authorities would have paid more attention, we were convinced of it. Instead, we had been ignored for six and a half years. I think certain people were just waiting for us to give up. They should have known that was never going to happen.

*

Not everyone was against us, even if often felt like it. Gordon Bernard rang one day to say he'd received a call from Bedzios.

'Kerry, this could be it. Bedzios says they're going to hand Ben over.'

I could picture Gordon's lovely kind, round face beaming as he broke the news.

'Is Bedzios serious?'

'He says deadly.'

The man who once claimed to have Ben in his hands was going to give him up.

Sometimes you're better off not knowing what's going on. This time I begged for information the second Gordon learned it.

The consul was summoned to Veria to meet Bedzios's lawyer, Fanny Zahoo. He could have sent an underling but Gordon went personally and made it as official as possible by travelling in his black limousine with the consular flags and diplomatic licence plates. He wanted to show the lawyer and anyone else that the full weight of the British government was behind him. It wasn't – not in my opinion – but no one else knew that.

The lawyer explained what she knew. There was going to be a handover of Ben. Whoever had him needed to be 100 per cent sure that he or she would not be arrested, so there would be a test to ensure Gordon was alone.

'What kind of test?' Gordon asked.

'You'll be given an address,' Zahoo explained. 'We will go together so I can ensure there is no police involvement.'

'Fine,' Gordon said. 'What's the address?'

'I don't know yet.'

'Well, who does?'

Right on cue, Zahoo's mobile phone rang. She answered and passed it to her guest.

'Gordon Bernard?' the caller said.

'Yes. Who is this?'

'I am Andonis Bedzios. I have an address for you.'

From that point on, it was like something out of a spy movie. Bedzios gave Gordon the address of a café and said, 'I will ring this number again in ten minutes. You should be outside waiting. Don't be late.'

Gordon went to argue but Bedzios cut him short.

'The clock's ticking.'

The black sedan screeched to a halt outside the café with seconds to spare. The phone rang exactly on ten minutes. How Bedzios was pulling the strings from a public phone in prison I don't know, but he seemed remarkably well informed. Someone was clearly helping him.

'You made it,' Bedzios said. 'Now...'

Gordon assumed he would be told where to find Ben. What he actually got was another address and another deadline.

He found the restaurant in good time. Then he was directed to a bar, then a kiosk in the street. Each time he threatened Bedzios not to mess around. Each time the prisoner told him to focus on the job in hand. Any foul-up, and Bedzios's own son could suffer.

Five times this happened. Five addresses, five high-speed dashes across the city. Five tense phone calls. By the sixth time Gordon was losing patience. He was hot, sweaty and out of breath. Clearly Bedzios had eyes on the ground, because he always knew where Gordon was. By now, he must have known there were no police anywhere near the operation and yet he was still playing this stupid game. Only one explanation made sense: Bedzios was stringing Gordon along. He had to be.

As if sensing the change in the consul's voice, Andonis had a different message this time.

'Listen very carefully, Mr Bernard. I have the final instruction.'

Gordon has told me how he could barely hear the voice on the phone for the sound of his heart pounding away. I know that feeling, what he was going through. This was it. This was the moment we had all been waiting for.

Gordon was given the name of a road, as usual. Instead of a building, however, he was told where to find a parked black Mercedes.

'The back door is unlocked. On the back seat is a red blanket. Underneath the blanket is your Ben.'

Gordon couldn't believe what he was hearing. Was this really it?

'What are you waiting for? Go, go, go!'

Six minutes later, Gordon leapt out of his car, engine still running. Fanny Zahoo was still unbuckling her seat belt while Gordon was yanking open the Mercedes' door. In one movement he tugged the red blanket out of the car and stared, open-mouthed.

The back seat was empty.

Gordon looked at the lawyer then back at the seat then up and down the street. The car hadn't been locked. Could Ben have wandered away?

He knew that hadn't happened. Someone had been monitoring them every second of the journey. It was impossible Ben would have been dumped here and abandoned. Not after so much elaborate planning. No, that hadn't happened. Which only left one alternative.

'He was lying right from the start.'

I've never heard Gordon angry but I bet Fanny Zahoo did. She told us that she was as every bit as furious as Gordon was.

'So what, then?' Gordon said, absolutely distraught. 'Where is Ben? What has Bedzios done with him?'

It was a slow and sombre journey back to the lawyer's office. After several attempts at calling Larissa prison, the phone rang. It was Bedzios. When Gordon had finished telling him what he thought of him, Bedzios put forward his defence.

'You are a victim, I am a victim,' he said. 'Ben was there, I swear. And then they got cold feet. They worried about Ben identifying them to the police and so they took him away. I have been stabbed in the back. We all have. I'm sorry.'

Bedzios was sorry, Zahoo was sorry and Gordon was sorry. But not like me.

I had not moved more than an inch from my phone since Gordon's call earlier that day. Anyone else who called I told to get off the line immediately. When it rang and I heard the distinctive hum and delay of an international exchange connecting me, I knew it was the call I'd been praying for.

Gordon began to speak. His normally rich voice was hollow. He was a powerful man with a position of strong authority but at that moment he sounded beaten.

'I'm sorry, Kerry. Ben wasn't there.'

To this day I still think Bedzios was telling the truth. I remember the way he looked me directly in the eyes when he spoke from his cell. Gordon, when he'd calmed down, also agreed that Bedzios sounded genuinely confused that someone had double-crossed him. The police, however, are convinced it was a con from start to finish. As far as Athens is concerned, Bedzios's testimony is tainted. If they thought he was a mythomaniac before, what they think of him now is unprintable. Why can't they see that there's nothing in it for him? His little boy, his own flesh and blood, was being looked after by the people he was accusing of having Ben. What sort of a warped mind would accuse those people with no proof?

As far as I'm concerned, Bedzios's story is still a live investigation, even if the police don't agree. He still gets in touch occasionally, although I refuse to see him until he promises me Ben.

But there is a twist in the tale. Two twists, actually. A few years later, the private detective Bakirtzis sued Christos Kerimi in court. I flew out with Dad to see it because I wanted to witness Kerimi under oath. I'm glad I did. When Bakirtzis got him onto the topic of Rabo, Kerimi admitted there were two boys in the camp. But, he claimed, he didn't know who the other boy was.

And he wasn't forced to say.

The lawyers just left it hanging. I wanted to shout out, 'It was Ben! It was my Ben!' but my mouth wouldn't work. I realised I was scared of Kerimi. If the gypsy king had my Ben, or even knew where he was, I did not want to rile him into doing something silly.

Soon after the court case, Bakirtzis died of natural causes. I was sadder to learn that Bedzios's little boy, Rabo, also did not survive. He was a bit backward when Mum and Dad first met him but he was nice, he had a good personality. When they next saw him he was in a wheelchair. He died before their next visit. I don't know how Bedzios discovered the news. I just know that when Rabo died, Kerimi's bargaining power over Bedzios died as well. If the gypsy did have my baby, what was stopping him from handing Ben back now?

CHAPTER NINETEEN

WHO COULD BE THIS?

The press campaigns that we ran in the beginning were targeted at holidaymakers and locals, asking them to be vigilant and keep an eye out for Ben. Later on, we expanded that message to reach young boys themselves. So I started saying in appeals, 'If you're a boy of Ben's age and you don't look like your family and you have a birthmark on your nape and above your right knee and you don't have a birth certificate, ask the question and if you don't like the answer, get in touch.'

It's a long shot but people who have been adopted in mysterious circumstances, like Mariana Faithful, often grow up with a sense of doubt; something in the back of their minds produces questions about their background. And I know that if Ben is anything like his sister, then he'll be the sort to ask those questions.

I've never known a child as inquisitive as Leighanna. Her earliest words had question marks at the end. She loved books, and before you turned a page she'd point to a picture and ask, 'Who could be this?'

Her thirst for knowledge didn't stop at books. I love having family photos around the place, so obviously Leighanna was one day jabbing her pudgy little fingers at those.

'Who could be this?'

I laughed. It wasn't the best picture of my dad but I was surprised Leighanna needed to ask.

'That's Granddad.'

Then she moved along the row.

'Who could be this?'

'That's Nana.'

'Who could be this?'

'That's your Uncle Danny.'

And then she'd reach the framed image of the smiling toddler clapping at the camera.

'Who could be this?'

I felt my stomach churn.

'That's your brother,' I said. 'That's Ben.'

I tried to make it as matter-of-fact for her as possible, but it tore my heart watching her take it in. What was going through her head? She knew her granddad, her nana, her uncles. She could put memories and experiences to their names and their pictures. What did this word 'brother' mean to her as a two-year-old?

As she got older and saw that my brothers were always around, the questions got harder.

'Where is my brother?'

Nobody teaches you how to explain to a youngster what a missing person is. How much do you reveal? Is it better to be open, or protect her by trying to cover it up? I took it step by step, talking about Ben when she asked and telling her, 'He doesn't live with us right now but he'll be home soon.' I didn't know and I still don't know now if I did the right thing. I needed her to understand that she had a brother because when he came home I wanted them to have a relationship. But I didn't want to scare her. I didn't want her to think that she could be taken from me as well.

My tears are never far away but seeing your daughter cry is the most upsetting feeling in the world. The more she grew up to understand about Ben, the harder it hit.

Maybe in trying to make her feel special and involved I was in danger of achieving the opposite. Boarding all those planes, having the media thrust in front of her, waiting in so many police stations across the world seemed like an adventure we shared. Maybe that all had a detrimental effect. But I just wanted her near me, and to be near her, and for there to be no secrets.

When Leighanna did her trawl of the family photo albums, there was one picture she didn't find. Simon's. After everything we'd been through, I couldn't stomach having his face watching me at home. But I would never be one of those mums who tries to influence a child against her father. I was the one with the problem with Simon, not Leighanna. One of the reasons I hated him so much was for being so selfish and getting locked up and not being around to see his daughter grow. A child deserves a father. My daughter didn't have that and I wished she did. That was why I was so grateful to Mum and Dad when they offered to take Leighanna to see Simon after he was transferred to Everthorpe Open Prison in Brough, Yorkshire.

In June 1997 the visits stopped – because Simon was released, three and a half years into his five-year sentence. I couldn't have been happier for Leighanna to have her father back in her life, although I admit I was shocked to discover he'd found a new partner while inside. There are various organisations that encourage people to write to prisoners, and Simon had struck up a pen-pal relationship with a woman, whom he later married. Naturally, the *Express on Sunday* ran a headline saying, 'Ben Parents Fight Over Little Sister'. We didn't fight. I was just concerned about Leighanna having to accept a stranger so soon after getting her dad back.

Unfortunately for Leighanna, that problem quickly disappeared as Simon moved to be with his new partner. There were a few visits, and then he stopped coming and the phone stopped ringing.

I was angry at the way Simon appeared to have cut off contact. We'd already lost one child – how could he walk away from another? I suppose he loved this woman enough to do anything, but it did make me sad for Leighanna.

Fortunately there was another man in her life. I'd met Pierce Mount one night when I'd been out with my friend, Joanna, at the Capital Club in Sheffield. We were dancing, minding our own business, when this tall, tanned, handsome guy came over, grabbed my wrist and checked the time on my watch. Stranger things have happened in clubs but I couldn't help watching him walk away. The cocky sod must have known I would be. He suddenly stopped walking, turned around then showed me his own watch.

Normally I stay away from any sort of arrogance like that, but I admit I was intrigued. The guy, Joanna said, was a professional boxer, trained by Brendan Ingle and a close friend of Prince Naseem. I wasn't surprised. It takes a certain confidence to get into the ring and this Pierce had it in spades. What he didn't have, though, was a girlfriend. According to his mates, having one wasn't his style: they liked to joke that he was too much in love with himself to be serious with anyone else. For most people that would have been a warning; I saw it as a challenge. It was like being back at school and hearing that Darren or Simon weren't the settling-down kind. I'd proved everyone wrong then, and I could do it again.

It worked. We got together and I discovered that behind the bravado and the vanity, Pierce actually had a heart of gold. When I saw how amazing he was with Leighanna, I knew we had a future. We didn't ask her to call him 'Daddy Pierce' but when she did, I knew it was the seal of approval I needed for him to move in and share our life and home.

That should have been the start of something brilliant but, as usual with me, there was a hiccough. Joanna was going out with Robert Baxendale and told me that my old love, Robert's brother, Mick, had split from his wife and was going through a tough patch. Naturally I contacted him as a friend. Within minutes of seeing each other, however, we both knew the friendship would turn again into something more. I anguished about finishing with Pierce but I knew it was unfair to string him along. On 10 October 1998, I told Pierce I was leaving him for Mick.

The following night, Mick was stabbed to death.

You never think you'll be involved with a murder case. Part of me thinks I handled it better because of what I'd been through with Ben. Another part thinks it affected me more. I'd already had someone precious snatched from me. Now it had happened again. It wasn't fair.

The details of the murder did not make pleasant reading. From police reports, it was a case of Mick defending the club from drug dealers. He was a black belt in karate and could snap a man in two. But he and the other doormen were no match for a group of scum with knives. Mick died that night in hospital.

The last thing on my mind was the bad timing of my confession to Pierce. When I did get around to thinking of myself, I assumed I'd lost two men. But Pierce said he would stand by me if I wanted him to. I had to admit I did, and for several years we were happy. Pierce threw himself into the Search For Ben campaign and organised boxing events and charity nights to raise money. We even appeared with Leighanna in an edition of *OK!* magazine. We really were a happy family.

Every family goes through its domestic upheavals but at the same time as I was trying to build some sort of a family life for Leighanna, I was fighting to keep momentum in the search for my son.

It was getting harder and harder to come up with angles to keep Ben's hunt in the press. A lot of journalists I would consider friends admitted that without a fresh sighting or lead, there wasn't anything they could do. One or two of them suggested I write a book about our family's ordeal. It wasn't something I was keen on at first, but as with every other decision I make, I asked myself, 'Would it help the case?'

We were recommended to an agent who was happy to take our project on. He lined us up with the wonderful Melanie McFadyean from Channel 4's *Cutting Edge* programme and she wrote a great proposal. Unfortunately, editors came back with the same response. They were very sad for us but as a book, the story didn't work because it had no ending, good or bad. It wasn't enough that by publishing it they could possibly speed up the ending and help us find Ben sooner.

As far as publicity was concerned, it was back to the drawing board and back, once again, to calling on the national and local media to channel our on-going progress. Then, one day, the *Sheffield Star* ran a headline that said: 'Cash And Kerry'. In it, they accused me of not giving an interview unless they paid a fee. I couldn't believe it. I'd never asked for a penny for myself, not now or at any time in the last seven years. Having the support of the press was the lifeblood of Ben's campaign. Why would I do anything to jeopardise that?

It turned out that the *Star* had not made up the story. Our agent had applied the normal rules of his business to our situation and decided our time should command a fee. That was quite normal for his usual clients but we weren't celebrities. We were desperate people grateful for every inch of copy we could get. With the book project stalled, we parted company amicably.

After a couple of negative headlines, I was relieved to see that public goodwill was still on our side. Kevin Johnson wasn't the only person provoked into action by 1997's *Cutting Edge* 'Lost Boy' documentary. Soon after its broadcast exposed my parents' tireless trek around mainland Athens and Veria in the face of police inertia, letters started appearing in newspapers calling for the country to boycott Greece as a tourist destination until that country's authorities took Ben's abduction seriously.

It's a powerful feeling knowing that complete strangers are rooting for you. We were contacted one day by a woman called Christine Bennett who said she wanted to raise money to help us afford to follow up potential sightings. She and her nephew, Daniel Barton, kicked it off by completing a sponsored cycle ride from Chester to Frodham. There were also pub collections, a magic show for children, an adult disco and a bring-and-buy sale.

People like Christine show all that's good in the world – and they pop up in the most unexpected places. I was stunned to receive a call from someone in the marketing department at the Iceland chain of supermarkets. Would we be interested in having Ben's details put on all their cartons of milk? I didn't need to be told that it was a common way of promoting missing persons in America. Even if they just put Ben's picture on one pint, that's better than nothing. The idea of hundreds of thousands of people being reminded of him every time they sat down to breakfast or a cup of tea was incredible.

I'm truly grateful for every individual act on Ben's behalf and every single report of a sighting, however slight it might seem. Having said that, some people have gone to tremendous lengths on my behalf, none more so than a lovely couple called John and Tish Cookson. In 1996 they were on holiday in Haraki, Rhodes, when they spotted a young fair-haired boy playing with a group of Greek kids. John was intrigued when the others referred to the boy as the 'Blond One'. When the Cooksons realised the boy spoke Greek, and so wasn't a tourist, alarm bells rang. With Tish keeping look-out and pretending to pose for pictures, John took several snaps of the boy.

As soon as the Cooksons returned from Rhodes, they got the pictures developed and sent them to us. Unfortunately, the images weren't sharp enough to be conclusive. On top of all the other pictures we were receiving at the time, we decided not to follow this one up personally.

Some people would have been put off by our reaction, but not John and Tish. When it came to booking their holiday the following year, they decided to go back to the same village. This time they made a point of tracking down the boy at his school and took pictures of him there, and again on the beach with friends.

Yet again, however, the results weren't clear enough to justify us or the police or a newspaper dipping into their pockets to investigate. If money were no object I'd have been over to Rhodes like a shot. Sadly, we could really only afford to pursue sightings that looked positive.

So it was, two years after their first contact with the Blond One, John and Tish went back for a third time to Rhodes. They'd bought a high-quality video camera for the occasion and refused to leave until they'd secured decent footage. That wasn't all they did.

John had read about DNA testing in paternity disputes. If police could prove a man was the father, they could also prove a child was his son. The only question was: how were they going to acquire it?

As it turned out, the boy made it very easy for them. When he saw John on the beach one day, the boy became fascinated by John's tattoos. It was perfectly natural for John to tousle the boy's head – and, in the process, he ended up with a beautiful single blond hair.

Now the media became interested. And as soon as I saw the video, so did I. I played that tape over and over and every time the boy looked more and more how I thought Ben would be. He had cute stuck-out ears, the same kind of nose and prominent eyebrows, the same skinny frame and even a double crown in his hair. I couldn't see any birthmarks, but what I could see was enough for my hopes to rise.

It would have been more cut-and-dry to compare the boy's DNA against Ben's, but in the absence of that, police scientists said they could make do with mine and Simon's. I had no idea how long it took to test such things but the wait was agony.

Some people didn't bother waiting. Our friend from the *Sun*, Martyn Sharpe, immediately flew out to Haraki and tracked the Blond One down to his family's taverna. With the prospect of identification via DNA, I was glad not to have to be there this time. I couldn't help remembering all the innocent people whose lives we'd turned upside down over the years in our hunt: the mothers and fathers convinced we'd come to take their child.

But Martyn had a job to do and, fuelled by his desire to get us the truth, he confronted the boy's parents, Nico and Panagiota Skyllarakis. While they couldn't show Martyn a birth certificate for the boy, they did produce a passport in the name of Savvas Skyllarakis, a medical history and dozens of photographs. They also quickly found several neighbours and friends to back up the fact that Savvas was their natural-born son. Several people remembered Panagiota giving birth, and many more recalled the day Savvas came home from hospital.

It looked like another dead end; a few days later, the DNA results confirmed it. Once again I'd allowed my hopes to be raised, and hurt another family in the process. But as the tears streamed down my face I knew, if I was honest, I would happily do it all over again.

Whatever it takes...

In 1999, our lives got that little bit worse with the news that Gordon Bernard was leaving his post as British consul in Greece, after his statutory four years. I was very sad to receive his hand-written letter. So many times he and his wife, Tina, had housed me or my family while we were in Athens. It was always his policy that we would work hard during the day then join his family for dinner and talk nothing of the case for an hour or two.

That was time for us all to relax, he insisted; to recharge our batteries and have a little bit of distance until the following morning's efforts.

Going to Greece now without Gordon's assistance was going to be harder in every way. At least we still had good friends like Mariana to call on. Her own pursuit of the truth about Ben was relentless. There wasn't a television station or politician she hadn't deluged with information and leads that they needed to be following.

Mariana had also arranged with the Kos police for us to pick up Ben's case files. I couldn't wait to get my hands on them, even though they were all in Greek. For eight years, I had been campaigning for the UK police to take over the investigation. Each time I was assured by the likes of John Major and Tony Blair and their staff that the Greek police and Interpol could be trusted to do a proper job. That wasn't an opinion shared by Mariana or me. With the files in our possession, and with Mariana offering to translate them, we could identify whether Chief Bafounis and his team had missed anything that South Yorkshire Police could actually follow up on.

It was as we were leaving – we were already in the corridor after saying goodbye – that I called out to Bafounis, 'Did you ever get to the bottom of the white car?'

He looked surprised, then smiled. Bafounis said he had a theory about who may have owned the car.

I was shocked. I hadn't heard this before but I was excited too. Finally, we had a lead, or so I thought.

But I should have realised at the time not to get my hopes up. Because nothing ever came of Bafounis' theory, nothing has ever been proven. The white car, like so much of Ben's case, would remain a mystery. It was another open-ended question.

CHAPTER TWENTY

GIVE US SOMETHING

The year 1999 was something of a landmark year for our family. Most importantly, of course, Ben turned ten. I marked the day as I always did with a card and a present and chat to him, wherever he is. Leighanna did the same.

This wasn't like the days of imagining he was with me and putting him to bed. It just didn't seem right to let his birthday pass without telling him I loved him. I'm not religious, as I've said, but part of me thinks if I say it loud enough, he'll hear me eventually.

Ten years is a milestone in anyone's life. For Ben, it marked four times as many years away from me as with me. That was a statistic I could have done with not working out. As a result, I needed to come to terms with a very unsavoury truth: wherever Ben was, he had probably forgotten I'd ever existed. Maybe that would change when he was found, and maybe it wouldn't. I had to face facts.

The boy I was investing so much energy searching for might not even want to come back with me.

I didn't dare tell anyone what I was thinking. I'd been burnt by the *Express* for my honesty once before. For my own peace of mind, however, I needed to accept it. If anything, it just made me more determined to find my son before he forgot me completely.

I wasn't the only one suffering, of course. Mum and Dad had always come across in the media pretty well, and it was only their own sense of guilt that persecuted them. Even so, when they had the opportunity to move back up to Lincolnshire, they grabbed it with both hands: after living in the goldfish bowl of Sheffield, where their every move was noted, anywhere seemed like a break.

Like so many of my parents' moves, it came about due to a conversation struck up by Dad. He and Mum had developed quite an eye for collectables and were students of the *Miller's* antiques guide. Their scavenger hunts often took them out to the tips and boot sales of Boston and beyond, and obviously they got friendly with the tip owners there. When a lease for a tip in Lincoln came up, Dad was advised to go for it. Not only would he get first choice of any collectables with resale value that came in, but he'd also be paid a wage. It took about two seconds for them to decide. And, having made a success of one tip, when a second came up for tender in Grantham they applied again – and won, with Mum this time at the helm.

With our parents' businesses booming, it was time for Stephen and Danny to branch out. Danny hadn't moved to Lincoln with them, opting instead to stay in my parents' old council property and finish his sixth-form education. Stephen, meanwhile, had been living with his partner, Angela, and two daughters, Sophie and Lisa. However, when they broke up he wanted to run away, but where to go?

Danny had the answer. He'd just finished his A-levels so between them, they bought an old ice-cream van, painted it blue and pink, called it 'Such'N'Such' then drove it to Benidorm to sell ice creams by day and party by night. When local police closed them down for lack of paperwork on the first day, they just shrugged it off and found jobs in bars. Danny in particular thrived. When he was asked to run the karaoke nights at the area's famous Black Chicken venue, he discovered he had a talent for singing. In fact, there wasn't a performer around who could cut an Elvis impression the way he did. Before long, Danny was earning decent money on the cabaret circuit doing full-on tributes to The King.

It's only later that we realised how much Stephen was still affected by his part in Ben's disappearance. Despite the whispering campaign on Kos, he was the only one of us actually accused by the police of harming Ben. The weight on his shoulders from worrying about whether we thought he was involved was an incredible burden to bear.

In the run-up to the tenth anniversary of Ben's disappearance, Stephen got the chance to put the record straight once and for all. We regret letting him now. Once again, it was a case of us being desperate to keep the publicity momentum rolling forwards for as long as possible, so when ITV offered a full documentary entitled 'Somebody Knows', we agreed – even if it meant Stephen going under hypnosis to see if his subconscious mind remembered anything his conscious memory had forgotten.

I only know what was shown in the broadcast. I wasn't at the hypnosis session and I haven't been given the full tapes. Stephen says he remembers everything he said while under the influence but, just in case, we had a solicitor on standby. I can't remember whose idea it was, but the session sounded like it was going to be more like a police interview than a chat with a journalist. In fact, Stephen later said, it was more terrifying.

The session began well. The hypnotist asked Stephen to describe the moment he left the farmhouse in Iraklis.

'I'm coming out of the farmhouse, Ben's playing, I'm walking to the road, I'm getting on my bike, Ben's still there, he looks up, I say, "Stay there, stay with Granddad," and I drive off.' Pretty much verbatim what he'd said ten years earlier.

Then the process seemed to get a bit weird. As Stephen's virtual self mounted his bike, he was asked if he wanted to pick Ben up.

'No.'

'Do you want to pick him up and put him on your bike and ride away with him?'

'No. He is just playing.'

As he pictured himself driving away from the farmhouse, Stephen was then asked to turn around and describe what he saw.

'I can't turn round,' he replied.

'Just try.'

'How can I turn around? I didn't turn round. How can I remember something I didn't do?'

Even in his dream-like state, Stephen was getting agitated. Tears filled his eyes – and mine later, as I struggled to watch the broadcast. He obviously felt uncomfortable with what he was being asked to say and at one point, the solicitor demanded the cameras be switched off. She said the TV crew were in danger of implanting false memories in Stephen. I'm not saying that is what was happening. In fact, in my opinion, it would have been impossible because Stephen's recollection of the truth was so strong. Even so, he said later that one of the psychologists had asked him, 'If you were to bury a child, where would you bury it?' If that isn't a leading question, then I don't know what is.

No one in the family had expected Stephen to suddenly confess to being involved in Ben's disappearance. That was never the point of the hypnosis as far as I was concerned. At best we'd hoped he'd remember seeing a face or a vehicle that had slipped his mind in the confusion. Just something to aid the investigation. But the only thing that came of Stephen's ordeal was even greater self-doubt about his own innocence and a return to the nightmares about being accused by the Kos police – nightmares he thought had ended years ago.

'What if I did do it, Kerry?' he asked me soon after. 'What if Ben was on the back of my bike. What if he did fall off? What if...'

'Stop right there. You're my brother, you're Ben's uncle and you did nothing wrong that day. Do you understand me?'

'What about the tears, though?' he said. 'I was crying on TV. I look guilty, don't I?'

'You look like a devastated uncle.'

He wouldn't be told and so I was glad when he went back to Spain. If anything could cheer him up, it would be time spent with his brother in the sunshine. Unfortunately, it wasn't the long-term tonic Stephen needed. Without a career in showbiz to look forward to like Danny, he returned to England, in the grip of depression, and moved in with Mum and Dad in Legsby.

Already broken and confused, Stephen became a virtual recluse, never venturing from his room unless the coast was clear. Every morning, Mum and Dad would find evidence that he'd been up and about, but he didn't want to see or speak to anyone. Not yet. Not till he'd worked through things on his own.

Ten years after Ben's disappearance the suffering continued, and not just for me.

*

On the plus side, when 'Somebody Knows' was broadcast there was another spike in sightings, although most turned out to be nothing. Our new police liaison, DS Malcolm Silk, visited with dozens of tourist pictures but as usual they were either too blurred or too vague. I love people for taking the time to contact us, but saying they saw a blond boy on a bus or in a shop and not giving an address makes it very frustrating sometimes.

Still, as I always say, we only need to be right once – and there was one sighting that caught my eye.

Once again I am indebted to an eagle-eyed holidaymaker, Ken Bywater, who witnessed a blond lad in Kefalonia arguing with a gypsy couple before boarding a ferry. Ken said he had no doubts it was Ben so he filmed the whole scene, even zooming in on the gypsies' truck's number plate. I was in pieces when I looked at the film. The ears, eyes, hair, the manner – they all bore a remarkable resemblance, not only to the latest computerised updated picture, but to how I felt in my heart that Ben would look today. I needed to know more. But I would have to wait.

As soon as Ken had arrived home from Kefalonia he'd delivered the tape to South Yorkshire Police. After verifying it with me, they'd passed it on via Interpol to the Greek authorities. Six months later, we still hadn't heard a thing. How long does it take to open a message from Interpol? How many seconds would it take to check a number plate? Yet again, it felt like the Greeks were doing as much as possible *not* to help find Ben.

I wasn't surprised it took so long to report – eventually – that the boy was not Ben. I had been bashing my head against a wall trying to get action for ten years. All I wanted was for South Yorkshire Police to be allowed to investigate Ben's case, but official after official, from the prime minister to my local MP, kept telling me the same thing: British officers are not allowed to investigate in another sovereign state without an invitation. Why not, when it's a British citizen that's missing? We're all meant to be part of the big European family. Why couldn't South Yorkshire officers, who know about the case, enquire about the sightings? Why did we have to pass everything via Interpol into the black hole of Greek bureaucracy? We needed detectives on the case, not paper pushers.

Once again I made my feelings clear in a letter to the prime minister. Previously, in 1997, Mr Blair had responded, as usual, that 'the embassy in Athens has made the Greek police fully aware of the importance that the British government attaches to finding Ben'. He added: 'If I felt there was more that could be done, I can assure you that I would take a personal interest in ensuring it was.' Four years later, it was the same blanket assurance that the Greek police were doing all they could.

Well, maybe that was right. Maybe they were doing all they could. So why not let British police do all they could and see if there was a difference?

I have to say, ten years down the line, I felt that certain people were beginning to wish I'd go away. I refused to let that happen, but keeping Ben's name in the media became harder and harder. As a result, sightings dried up from dozens a month to almost nothing from one year to the next. Of the few that made it through, Mariana flew to Sydney to pursue one report, while a family in Bulgaria were named as potential suspects later.

While the authorities and media seemed to be turning their backs on Ben, I'm proud to say that some decent people were prepared to do the opposite. A Welsh private investigator called Ian Crosby got in touch in 2003 and announced that, with my blessing, he'd like to take on Ben's search – free of charge. Obviously I was delighted for any help I could get. Among the many avenues Ian pursued was something so simple I couldn't believe no one had suggested it before: he set up a website called www.BenNeedhamInfo.com where visitors could read all about the case, see the latest computerised images of Ben and, most importantly, get in touch with us about any sightings. I knew very little about the internet at the time but I was blown away. The idea that anyone could tap into that page from anywhere in the world was incredible.

Ian understood the media's reluctance to tread the same ground so he also tried to enlist celebrities to publicise Ben's cause. Uri Geller was an early supporter and through him and former *Oliver!* actor Mark Lester, we received written support from Michael Jackson. If the King of Pop couldn't get Ben's name into the papers, nobody could.

Despite the hard work of a lot of people, there was a real despondency among the whole family at this time. Media appearances, police visits and sightings are incredibly stressful for all of us, but at least when you're busy you don't feel so useless. Every day I wasn't doing something to further Ben's search I felt like I was betraying him. But what could I do? Options were seriously few and far between.

The only positive to come from the media silence was the chance to focus on our own home lives, and God knows we needed to do that. Shortly after Leighanna, Pierce and I moved to a new house in Ecclesfield in 2001, Pierce and I split up. In all honesty, I probably let the relationship continue beyond its natural length because of how much Leighanna loved him. There was nothing he wouldn't do for my little girl, and that counts for a lot. Not enough, though, for me to lie to myself. I didn't love him any more.

Within no time I was enjoying having a house for just me and my eight-year-old daughter. Selfish as it sounds, I loved not sharing her with someone else. And when she was teased about Ben at school – because some kids can be like that – it felt natural that I was the one to put my arm around her. Pierce or her friends can say they know how she feels, but no one knows like me.

Speaking of Leighanna's friends, her best pal, Shannon, was the daughter of a guy called Pat. Pat and his brother, Ricky, owned a fencing business and in 2003 I joined as a receptionist. It wasn't demanding work but it paid the bills, with a little left over each month for the Ben Needham Search Fund. It also stopped me obsessing about the case for a few hours every day.

There was another perk to the job I hadn't foreseen. A fencer who worked there was a handsome fella called Craig Grist. We always had a laugh in the office or on the phone, so when he asked me out one night I assumed it was as mates, nothing more. Unexpectedly, the evening went well. So well, in fact, that on 19 June 2006 under the beautiful Cyprus sky, I became Mrs Kerry Grist.

The wedding took place in Cyprus for a very good reason: Mum and Dad and Danny had moved there the year before. By the end of 2004 they had been running, very successfully, three tips and recycling plants. Business was good. So good, in fact, that they decided to cash in their chips while they were still young enough to enjoy the benefits.

My parents' decision to sell up and relocate once again was hard for me to take, but I knew they had to do it. Their health and their relationship needed it. Even in Lincolnshire they had felt under scrutiny, like they had in Sheffield. I knew the feeling. If it weren't for Leighanna and my job, which I found surprisingly fulfilling now that my so-called 'receptionist' duties appeared to include making a lot of the decisions, I might even have joined them.

But there was also Craig to consider. Like others I'd gone out with since Simon, he had the difficulty of caring for someone knowing that she was a woman on a mission. Some, like Pierce, actually embraced wholeheartedly the 'Ben' campaign, but even he couldn't help feeling on the outside to some extent. I would never be entirely any man's while Ben was still missing. That part of my life had to come first. To his credit, Craig was very supportive. His real problem, sadly, was with Leighanna. The combination of her missing Pierce, being angry at not seeing Simon, and hitting teen-age meant that she wasn't always the model stepchild for Craig. He did his best, but there were countless days when the age-old refrain of, 'You can't tell me what to do – you're not my real dad' filled the house.

Shortly after my marriage, Pat left the business and a few years later, Ricky would decide to do the same. I've never been shy about taking an opportunity so I said to Craig, 'Why don't we buy it? I can run the business side of things and you can do the fencing.'

So we did. From receptionist to owner and managing director in six years. Not bad for a working-class girl.

Even with so much going on in my private life, I still never stopped badgering the media for attention. Every birthday, every anniversary, every single opportunity I could think of, I was on the phone to my contacts and pals at the papers or TV stations. They all said the same thing: they'd love to help, but they couldn't get it past their editors without something new.

Even my great friend Mark Witty, a producer and journalist for the *Calendar* programme, was left scratching his head. Mark has done more than most over the years to keep Ben's name in the public eye. Without his programmes, a lot of doors would not have opened for me, I'm convinced of that. But on this occasion, even Mark had to say, 'I need something, Kerry. Just give me something – *anything* – and I'll clear the schedules for you.'

But there was nothing. No police updates of note, no help from officialdom and no in-coming phone calls from the media whatsoever. Until, that is, Friday 4 May 2007.

It was six o'clock in the morning and whoever had rung the house phone that early was about to get a piece of my mind. Or so I thought. I didn't actually have a chance to say anything because as soon as I picked up the phone, I heard the voice of a friendly journalist.

'Kerry, have you got a comment about the little girl who was snatched in Portugal last night?'

CHAPTER TWENTY-ONE

I'M THE LAST
PERSON THEY WANT
TO HEAR FROM

Now they wanted to listen.

I looked down from my bedroom window at the mass of men and women filling my lawn and pathway and those of the two houses either side. After years of shouting into thin air, it seemed like every journalist with a car had found their way to my front door. And they all wanted to talk about the same thing: Madeleine McCann.

I never listen to the radio at work and I only ever play CDs in the car. Yet driving home the night before, I had caught the tiniest snippet of news as I changed discs. It had been something to do with a family in Portugal but I didn't know what, and I definitely didn't know how massive it would become. Not until the bombardment of interview requests began.

It wasn't an impressive sight watching grown adults squabbling amongst themselves, and jostling to be next in the queue to talk to me. Not when there was a little girl missing, two distraught parents and someone who knew firsthand exactly how it felt. I know they all had deadlines, but it wasn't the press's finest hour in my eyes.

I did twenty-seven interviews that day. In each one I learnt a little bit more about the news from Praia da Luz. My heart went out to Gerry and Kate. I knew exactly what they were going through. The tragedy was, there was nothing I could say or do that would make them feel better. If anything, the opposite was true. Twenty-seven times I was asked the same question:

'What's your message for Madeleine's parents?'

Twenty-seven times I replied, 'I'm the last person they want to hear from. Their child has been missing one day. My son has been gone sixteen years. They have to believe that Madeleine will be found today, tomorrow, soon. What they don't want is to have their worst-case scenario staring out at them from newspapers.'

Obviously no journalist was satisfied with that as an answer. 'You must have some advice for them, Kerry?'

I did. As far as I could tell, the Portuguese police were being as unsatisfactory as the Kos force had been with us. At best, I could advise the McCanns to keep an eye on the investigation, to not assume anything was being done unless they saw it with their own eyes, and to keep the police honest and on it and doing everything in their power. We'd made the mistake once of trusting the police to be pulling up trees in the hunt for my son. The truth was they didn't bother. Not for a long time. Not until it was too late.

The only thing I could say with any certainty was that no parent should have to endure the loss of a child.

By the end of that day I was exhausted. The questions had stirred up every emotion I'd gone through sixteen years ago. My pain – that I'd learned to live with over time – was as raw as ever. Of course, my heart was broken for the McCann family but, honestly, as I waited for Craig and Leighanna to come home, I could only think of Ben.

That didn't change over the next few days. Every stage the McCanns went through, I remembered experiencing myself. The shock, the denial, the disbelief, the rage, the fear. I could empathise with every second.

Well, almost. Some things were happening in Portugal that I could not relate to. I watched the news open-mouthed as official after official and dignitary after dignitary arrived in the Algarve to lend their support to the hunt for three-year-old Maddy. The British ambassador was on camera pledging aid, the Portuguese ambassador in London did the same, and was that the spokesman for Tony Blair saying that the prime minister was following the case personally? Not only that, the deputy PM, John Prescott, raised the subject in a House of Commons speech and the then Chancellor of the Exchequer, Gordon Brown, called the McCanns direct, all within days of Madeleine's disappearance. I could not have been happier that officials were taking the situation seriously. But I have to be honest; it opened an old wound for me. Where was my help? Where was my statement at Prime Minister's Questions? Where was my ambassadorial aid? In 1991, we couldn't even get the consul to become involved.

Maybe Ben's disappearance would have got this level of attention if it had happened now. Maybe it was just a case of bad timing, of technology catching up, of public reaction to cases of child abduction changing. Something told me not. The more I looked at what was happening to the McCann family, the more I felt they were being treated differently to us because they were different.

What were we back in 1991? Working-class people living in a caravan and a rented apartment in a foreign country, trying to make an honest living. We didn't have money and we didn't have connections. We stood shaking buckets at pop fans outside Wembley Stadium; the McCanns had a high profile 'Fighting Fund'. By October 2007, it already held more than £1 million in donations to finance independent investigations. Richard Branson, the multi-millionaire entrepreneur, then set up a separate fund to cover Kate and Gerry's legal fees. Several famous and wealthy people contributed, as well as members of the public.

The media and public response was phenomenal. JK Rowling supplied a 'Madeleine' poster to all bookshops selling her latest Harry Potter book. Maddy's father did a publicity tour of the United States. He and Kate later met President Bush at the White House and even had an audience with the Pope. Sixteen years earlier, us Needhams had rotted on our own in Kos until the money ran out, often only eating when a friendly journalist bought us a meal at the local taverna.

I don't begrudge Kate and Gerry one bit. I would have done the same and more if I'd had the opportunity or the connections. But I didn't, and it was very easy to believe that they were getting preferential treatment because they were richer than us and, to be frank, middle class. I honestly felt that, in the public's eyes, they were seen as the better people.

The thing is, I wouldn't change places with them for one second. I couldn't believe it when the Portuguese police came out and accused them of playing some part in Madeleine's disappearance. It's hard to know what to accept in the press sometimes, but it seemed clear that Kate and Gerry were being named as suspects.

The worst I had to put up with was the whispering on the island and the innuendo. I can't imagine how it must feel to have that accusation levelled at you officially, by the very people meant to be hunting for your child. My brother Stephen can identify with it – and I would say that carrying that weight has destroyed him. Simon had also had to endure press speculation for a while in the weeks after Ben went missing. Only he knows how it affected him afterwards. For the sake of Kate and Gerry's other children, I pray they recover.

The worst part about the parents being identified as suspects is them knowing that for every minute the police spend putting together a case against them, the trail of the real culprit is getting colder. *That* I can empathise with. British police follow multiple leads. I got the feeling the Portuguese preferred a one-at-a-time approach, like the Kos squad. It's like they work down a list, ticking avenues off one at a time. The idea of pursuing several at once seems alien to them. Kate and Gerry could put up with anything if it meant helping Madeleine be found. Knowing they were holding up the investigation by being accused must have crucified them.

Even worse than the police charges against them, in my opinion, the McCanns have also had to endure a public backlash. As the circumstances of Madeleine's disappearance became common knowledge, a lot of people questioned how the children could have been left alone while the parents dined in another part of the resort. Some people thought it was normal to do that, and to trust the hotel complex's night-time security set-up, on top of the parents nipping back regularly to check for sounds of crying. All I know is that that couple will have to live with that knowledge for the rest of their lives – long after Madeleine is found.

The twenty-four-hour news, the internet forums, Facebook and Myspace pages – these were all unthinkable in 1991. Coverage of Madeleine's disappearance saturated the news in the UK and beyond for weeks and months. Even today, she's not far from the media's thoughts. For all I know, Ben in 2007 would have earned the same attention. But there was something else I noticed during the search for Madeleine, something I had been told could never happen.

British police were in Portugal.

Let me say again: I believe that anything that speeds up the return of Madeleine McCann to her distraught family should be done. I do not and will never begrudge them anything. But where were the British officers searching for Ben? If not in 1991 then in 2007? He was still missing. I was still campaigning and fighting and begging the authorities to agree to send UK men and women over to Greece. Yet I was told it was impossible. I was told we needed to respect the local agencies and let them do their work. The Foreign Office, the Home Office and even Number 10 all said the same thing. But here were British police officers present in Praia da Luz. They weren't there to top up their tans, so what were they doing there that they couldn't do in Kos?

I was angry. Not that the McCanns had managed to achieve this, only that I had been denied. Wasn't my child worth the same international effort? Were my letters to the prime minister on incorrect paper or not in the right handwriting? Someone had to tell me why the search for my son seemed to be less important than the hunt for this poor young girl.

Sixteen years. Sixteen years I had been hammering on the door of Number 10 Downing Street, the Foreign Office and Buckingham Palace. Sixteen years of beseeching the British government to intervene in the international police operation to find Ben. We were wading through treacle in Greece. Their red tape was like rope around our limbs. Time over there, it seemed, meant nothing.

'Why are they ignoring *us*?' I was shouting at the television and I didn't care. Watching those boys in blue run around the Algarve was like having a politician whisper in my ear, 'You're not good enough.' It was as though they were saying I – *Ben* – didn't matter to them. Again, perhaps it was the media spotlight that prompted the sudden co-operation. Then again, perhaps not. It didn't matter. I'd been fighting for so long that one more battle would not break me. Clearly the excuses I had been given meant nothing. I needed to pull myself together and start fighting again. Harder this time, and empowered by the knowledge that I was right – and that they knew it.

Letters, phone calls, media interviews, public support. These were my weapons, my tools. If not for justice, then at least for equality. It was soul-destroying knowing that others had achieved what I so craved. But it had to remain my target, not my grudge.

The year 2007 passed into 2008, 2008 into 2009. Then in 2010, I heard that I was getting somewhere. The doors I'd knocked on a hundred times were beginning to creak. Finally, in 2011, they started to open.

I have to take some of the blame for it not happening earlier. Perhaps I was too aggressive in my demands. I'd asked – too bluntly maybe? – for English police to take over Ben's investigation. Maybe if I'd asked for less, suggested co-operation between the two national forces, that would have been more agreeable. After all, that is what I was assured had happened in Portugal.

It doesn't matter now. All I care about is that in 2011, South Yorkshire Police finally reached agreement with the force in Kos. After twenty years of begging, the British police were officially joining the hunt.

CHAPTER TWENTY-TWO

WE'LL NEED
HIS CONSENT

Ben's disappearance was going to be investigated as a 'cold case' – and South Yorkshire Police were *invited* to assist. That was the key word. They weren't going to take over or run things, at least not on paper. In reality, after ten minutes in the company of Chief Superintendent Matt Fenwick and his cold-case team of Ian Harding, Simon Carter and three others, I knew where the impetus would be coming from. Forget the hi-tech equipment and money at their disposal, these men and women had something I'd never experienced in two decades: they cared passionately about finding Ben.

Not everyone saw the sudden British involvement as a positive. When I participated in a Greek television programme, I was asked why it had taken so long for British officers to reach Greek soil. The implication was that I had been abandoned by my own government for twenty years.

I said, 'Because the British police needed permission to come here.'

The interviewer rolled her eyes. 'Well, who in Britain needed to give permission?'

'No one,' I said. 'It had to come from the Greek authorities.'

That was an awkward moment on live TV.

'Why haven't they given permission?' she asked, suddenly enraged on my behalf.

'I don't know! Ask them! This is what I've been begging your government to do for twenty years.'

The interviewer was gobsmacked. Like so many of her countrymen, she thought the delay had been our police not wanting to be involved. Once she knew the problem lay at a Greek door, she promised no stone would be left unturned in exposing this.

The international PR battle was slowly swinging my way. With Matt and his team on my side, I thought the days of fighting bureaucracy would be over as well. I was wrong.

In early 2011, Ian Harding asked me if Ben had had the Guthrie test when he was born.

'He might have done – what is it?'

'It's where doctors take a blood sample from a prick in the heel.'

'Yes,' I said. 'He definitely had that. I remember him screaming the place down.'

I could see that, despite his training, Ian was excited by the news.

'Do you remember the hospital?'

'Of course. The Pilgrim maternity ward in Boston. Why?'

'Because if they did the test, there's a chance they will still have the sample. And if they have the sample, that means they have Ben's DNA.'

It was only a small step but as far as I was concerned, it proved how seriously South Yorkshire Police were taking Ben's case. Unfortunately, Pilgrim Hospital seemed to have studied the same red tape manual as Interpol.

'Do you have Ben Needham's Guthrie sample still on file?' Ian's request was simple enough.

'Yes,' came the reply.

'Great, can we have it?'

'No problem. But as Mr Needham is over eighteen years old, we'll need his consent.'

'If I could get his consent I wouldn't need the sample!'

That drove Ian insane for months. Every time he thought he had got somewhere, there was another legal hoop to jump through, and of course it all took valuable time. I was used to waiting. South Yorkshire Police weren't. They had an investigation to get their teeth into.

It didn't matter what Ian and his colleagues said or did, the answer from Pilgrim's lawyers remained the same: no consent, no sample. It eventually took a High Court judge in London to rule on the issue. If, he decreed, Simon and I were to give our written consent, then Pilgrim could release Ben's DNA with legal impunity. Obviously we did that in a flash (although considering Simon's name isn't on Ben's birth certificate, I'm still not clear why his permission was needed).

It was an exhausting and expensive waste of everyone's time just to reach the starting line, but we got there. Finally, Matt Fenwick and his team could start their investigation.

Their first step was to get Ben's details logged on the British DNA database. Now every force in the land could access it, should they discover anything to compare it to. Most western countries also have a database but – stupidly, in my opinion – each one has to request and 'accept' every new entry. You'd think Ian would be able to press a button and have Ben's DNA show up on DNA lists all around the world. In fact, as I write, it's been accepted only by America, Australia, Turkey and Spain. Everywhere else it's being held up by the dreaded red tape. Greece, surprise surprise, is yet to have a database. But they're getting there.

South Yorkshire Police have been thorough and professional – all I ever asked for. Apart from requesting updated copies of all files from Greece, they also asked if we, as a family, would consider undergoing 'regression' therapy to see if we could recall details of the day Ben disappeared that might be hidden in our minds. Stephen, obviously, had reservations after his experience with a hypnotist before. But this was different and, watching me, Mum, Dad and Danny all undergo the same process calmed him.

With a clearer picture of the events of July 1991, Matt Fenwick was able to draw up a plan of progress. The first stage was to go through all original paperwork with a fine-toothed comb. Then he would make his move.

I'm so sad that it took another child being snatched for Ben's case to be brought back into the spotlight, but I'm grateful for the results. Without the global attention on Madeleine McCann, it's extremely likely I would not have been granted my wish of British police involvement in the search for Ben. The downside for me, personally, has been the constant questioning about Madeleine. I have nothing to do with her case. It's unfair to keep questioning me as though I'm an expert. I'm not an authority; I'm just another mum.

Having said that, my knowledge of the child-trafficking industry in southern Europe has given me one or two insights. For example, based on everything I've learned about illegal adoption in Greece, I find it unusual that the abductor took Madeleine and not her twin siblings. If you trade in children, it makes sense to steal them as young as possible. Those babies could, theoretically, be raised without ever questioning their past. Madeleine was nearly four years old. She would remember things. She would prove a more challenging target.

Which is why, to my mind, it points to a case of opportunism rather than planning. Leighanna used to wake up all the time when she was three and four. Sometimes she'd go to the bathroom then back to bed. Other times she'd come and find me to tuck her back in. I think Madeleine probably did the same. She wakes up – maybe she's had a nightmare, maybe she's hot or thirsty – and she tries to find her parents. She looks in the bathroom, she looks in their bedroom and she looks in the lounge. There's one door she hasn't tried so she turns the handle and finds herself outside the ground floor villa. She's half-asleep, she's three years old and she has no sense of direction and no fear. The only thing she's interested in is finding her family.

And that's when I think she must have been taken.

God knows what theories people have about Ben's disappearance. Unless it helps find him, I don't want to know. So when I was approached by an intermediary to meet Kate McCann, I was extremely reluctant. *Why would she want to meet me? I can't help her. If anything, looking at what I've gone through could make her feel worse.* Still, victims of other crimes have support groups. Perhaps it would help us emotionally to share our pain.

Then I received a letter from Kate suggesting a meeting so I said yes – providing it was a completely private encounter. I was happy to speak to her, mother-to-mother. For once, I did not want to be surrounded by cameras and Dictaphones and the full media circus.

Plans were made, a date was set. Then somebody spoilt it. My visit to London was suddenly part of a documentary. I heard every excuse going from the production team: it would help Ben, it would help Maddy, it would help Kate, it would help me. I'd had twenty years of saying 'Yes' to the media. This was the first time I said 'No'.

It wasn't until much later, in May 2012, that Kate and I finally got the opportunity to meet. Friday 24th was named 'International Missing Persons Day' and to mark the occasion, the charity Missing People was launching a Europe-wide 'hotline' number that could be called free-of-charge to give information about a missing person. As well as Ben and Madeleine, thousands of people go missing by running away from home for various reasons, and their loved ones don't know where they are. This free number – 116000 – can also be used to leave messages for them.

As parents of high-profile missing people, Kate and I were both invited to a reception at 10 Downing Street the night before we were due to meet. Our host was Home Secretary Theresa May, who could not have been more supportive about Ben's search. Kate was incredibly shy but we shared a few moments, unobserved by cameras and reporters.

While that conversation will remain private, I said I would be happy to talk about International Missing Person's Day the following morning on ITV's *Daybreak* breakfast programme. It would mean being collected from my London hotel at five in the morning, but the chance to spread the word about the hotline was too good to resist. The car arrived on schedule and I was spirited to the studios on the south bank of the River Thames. The make-up team assured me that no one would know it was so early by looking at me. At that moment, that was all I cared about!

I've done plenty of television programmes, many of them live. Even so, waiting in the wings to be summoned to the interview sofa by host Aled Jones was very nerve-racking. What I didn't know was it was about to get worse. Just as I heard the presenters wrapping up their previous piece, I was handed a copy of that morning's *Daily Mirror* and told, 'This is what Aled will be asking you about.'

The front-page headline was printed two inches high, but I could not take it in. Not at first. Slowly the fog cleared and the words, 'Is Lost Ben Buried Under Rubble?' screamed out. I needed to sit down – and not on a sofa in front of millions.

The story claimed that Dino Barkas had decided to announce now, twenty-one years later, that Ben had almost certainly been killed by accident during the building works at Iraklis. The body, the JCB digger driver said, was buried under rocks he himself had dumped that day.

In other words, he was saying Ben was dead.

CHAPTER TWENTY-THREE

I NEED TO KNOW

I felt so sorry for Missing People. It's incredibly difficult for an individual or a charity to get publicity. I know how hard it has been for me. They'd managed to secure a spot on the UK's leading morning television programme to promote their new international initiative, with me as the spokesperson, and now it was going to be hijacked. There was no doubt about that. With no preparation at all, I was going under the media scalpel.

I hope I gave a strong account of myself. The idea of Ben being injured and buried during the building works down the hill from Michaelis's farmhouse was one I'd heard before. As Aled Jones put the *Mirror*'s claims to me, picking his words with care, I gave the only answer I could.

'Ben is alive. He is not under that rubble.'

Obviously Aled pushed for an explanation, and I was happy to give one. Yes, building work had been taking place down the hill from Michaelis's farmhouse. Yes, Dino was transporting rubble from that site up around the fields behind Michaelis's property to dump at the top of the lane. But did he come onto land where Mum, Dad, Danny, Stephen, Michaelis – or Ben – were?

No.

What's more, the mound of earth pictured on the front page of the *Mirror* was already there when Ben disappeared. I remember that same night, Mum and Dad sat on it while we discussed what happened next.

By the time I left the South Bank I was a nervous wreck. On the train journey back to Sheffield, my phone didn't stop ringing. How did I feel about the mound being dug up? What was my reaction to the claim that Ben was dead? Would I try to stop police digging up the site? You name it, I was asked it. The journalists could smell blood.

I gave everyone the same answer.

'I have every confidence that Ben is still alive. More than that – I *know* he is. However, if the authorities wish to excavate the land identified by Dino Barkas, then I will not stand in their way. I do not believe Ben is buried there, so I am happy it will cross off another line of enquiry.'

I was still giving that answer four months later, when asked about rumours of an imminent excavation. One of my case workers from South Yorkshire Police, the brilliant Jane Morley, surmised that any search of the area was unlikely to happen soon because of the amount of preparation involved. International paperwork, as I well knew, took months to pass from one hand to another. So she was as surprised as I was to hear from Matt Fenwick himself that a date for the search of the farmhouse site had been set for two weeks later, in October 2012.

British officers were finally going to Kos.

After five years in Cyprus, Mum and Dad had then moved to a quiet village in the west of Turkey. Danny had remained behind to work on his career as an Elvis tribute act. The new house was only a boat ride from Kos but it seemed a million miles from anywhere.

I'd felt like a new person the second I'd arrived for my first visit. All the emotional baggage that weighed me down on the Greek islands and mainland, and even in England, just seemed to disappear. For the first time in years, I felt like I could relax; I experienced a sense of peace I had not enjoyed anywhere else, before or since.

So when my parents decided to return to England in 2010, I refused to let that sever my link with the place. That is how, in October 2012, when South Yorkshire Police were descending on Kos, I was instead on the other side of the Aegean Sea, on what was originally going to be a relaxing two-week holiday.

To be fair, Matt Fenwick could not have been more upfront with me. He and his boss, Detective Superintendent James Abdy, had first flown out to Kos twelve months earlier and I'd been updated every step of the way. One year later, in September 2012, Matt gave warning that a decision on the dig was imminent. The second he got the go-ahead to take a team to the island, he was on the phone to me. We decided that I should take as much holiday as possible then transfer over to Kos. I knew it wasn't going to be easy to enjoy myself with that hanging over me, but I said I'd give it a try.

I managed five days in my Turkish idyll. It really does reach out to me and I feel comfortable there. Nobody associates me in the region with a tragedy, like in so many other places. I can blend into the background and just be me. It's for that reason I haven't named the village here.

Mum and Dad and Danny had flown out with me, as much to hold my hand during what was coming next as for the holiday itself.

In preparation, I closed my Facebook account, my email and turned off my phone: as soon as the British media got wind of the police's movements, I would get no peace. The last thing I wanted was to have a pack of fifty reporters descend on my little haven in the sun. If they couldn't contact me, they couldn't ask me where I was.

The only call I decided in advance to take was from Lucy Thornton at the *Daily Mirror*. They'd broken the excavation story and had been running it prominently ever since. I didn't mind that the *Mirror* was, in my opinion, peddling an angle that was wrong, as they almost single-handedly kept Ben in the news from May to October. The least I could do was grant them an interview.

Lucy was happy enough talking by phone. The problem came when she said she'd need a picture to run alongside the story. Jokingly I replied, 'The only person I'll pose for is Andy.' Andy Stenning was the photographer who had been in floods of tears with me when we'd discovered little Panos in Kassiopi wasn't Ben. I wasn't even sure if Andy worked for the paper any more; I just knew he was a face I could trust.

'I'll see what I can do,' Lucy said. 'But we already have a guy in Kos. The editor might just want to use him.'

'Fine,' I said and that was that. The following morning, there was a knock at the door and standing there was Andy. It honestly felt like seeing an old friend. You don't know someone till you've shared their pain, and we had shared plenty. I knew then that I was not about to be stabbed in the back.

I wasn't needed in Kos, although Matt and I agreed it would probably be politically advisable for me to be present. Dad was more essential. He took the ferry out to the island on the Thursday to help target the police search: he could point out what was there before 24 July 1991, and what had appeared since. Originally, the police hoped that Michaelis would join them as well. Sadly, he passed away a fortnight before the search. He never did achieve his dream of renovating that farmhouse. To this day there has been no work on it since Ben's disappearance although, weirdly, a new cottage was built adjoining it. Whatever the reason, it died with Michaelis.

I planned to join Dad in Kos on the Friday. The night before, however, I knew I wouldn't be going anywhere in a hurry. I don't know if it was worry but my throat swelled up, and I couldn't speak or eat. I was sick all through the night and hollow the following day. My planned rendezvous with Lucy at the seaport in Bodrum was off. There was no way I could face the three buses – from the village to Ortaca, Ortaca to Mugla then Mugla to Bodrum – needed to get there. As she was in the country anyway, Lucy made her way inland to me instead. She took one look at the budget apartment I was staying in and said, 'You won't get better here.' An hour later, I was in a five-star hotel round the corner. By Saturday night, I was well enough to use the Jacuzzi in my room. Lucy even sent me down for a massage.

Her expense account's generosity didn't stop there. There was no way we were going near one bus, let alone three. A car took us directly to the port and then it was just a question of waiting for the ferry to depart. As I sat on the top deck, I realised I was shivering, even though the sun was pounding down. I didn't want to hear those giant engines start up. That would mean we were on our way and, I finally admitted to myself, I did not want to arrive.

Over the past few days I'd been as ill as I'd ever felt. The sickening feeling as the ship pulled into view of Kos was worse. This wasn't a normal visit. Twenty-one years ago I had cried as I left the island, convinced I was leaving my son behind. Now I was dreading arriving in case we found him.

I wasn't going there to catch up with Chief Bafounis or pick up some paperwork or follow up a sighting. It wasn't for pleasantries with the magistrate or prosecutor's office. It was because of the mission already underway on that mountain. The mission to dig up the remains of my darling Ben's body.

The harbour was soon in sight and with it the police station and the castle. I couldn't help flinching, cowering from the view in my mother's arms. I never enjoyed going back to the place where my life had ended. This time, even after the ship had docked, my hands needed to be prised from the rail. I was close to having to be carried off.

There were so many emotions. Fear, pain – but mainly rage. What got to me most was not the dread that Ben would be found. I knew with all my heart that he was not going to be discovered under any rubble. It was the certainty of the police's actions that I could not come to terms with. If the Greek police, who had to authorise the search, truly believed that Ben could be buried in the farmhouse grounds, then why had it taken more than two decades for them to go anywhere near it with a shovel? Why had it taken the British police a couple of months to do what another force hadn't bothered to do in twenty-one years?

I found myself rehearsing the speech I would give the first man in Greek uniform I saw.

'If you seriously believe Ben is buried there, then why the hell have you waited till now to look? You've put me through twenty-one years of crap. You've wasted my life. And why? Because you couldn't be bothered? Because you didn't want to waste the money? Because it was too hot to get all sweaty with a spade?

'I need to know!'

I think it was a relief for everyone that the only official greeting party was two members of the British police force.

I could not fault South Yorkshire Police's organisation. From transport, to our hotel rooms at the Kipriotis Panorama Hotel – ironically out near Ramira beach, where Mum and Dad parked their caravan the day they first arrived – there was a sense that they had everything covered. If they were half as effective at the dig site, we could all be confident that whatever conclusion they reached would be the right one.

And yes, I thought again, *If Matt Fenwick had been running Ben's case twenty-one years ago, my son would have been back the next day.*

My support officers, Jane Morley and Ian Marshall, had been waiting at the port when we arrived. Jane and Ian have lived through a lot of the ups and downs of recent years with me. They were exactly the cool heads I needed at that moment. Another cold-case officer, Ian Harding, was with them and, as soon as he could get away for the night, Matt joined us as well. If his logistical attention to detail had been impressive already, it was about to reach another level. As well as pulling the strings behind the eighty-man search team and numerous vans of equipment, he was also managing to keep the world's media in some sort of order. Matt had agreed to hold a press briefing every morning at ten thirty at the site. During that meeting, he promised to outline the day's goals. Then the press all had to leave until four o'clock, when he would reveal any findings. His plan was to be upfront with everyone from the start: that way there would be no speculation. On a site like the one being searched, there were bound to be dozens if not hundreds of animal bones buried. The last thing he wanted me or anyone to suffer was the product of a long-range camera lens and a headline screaming 'Is This Ben?'

Everything Matt had arranged seemed so perfect that when he asked if I'd make a speech at the press conference the following day, I naturally agreed. Only when he'd gone did the enormity of the request hit me. Jane and Ian helped me draft a few words thanking the police and media and the dozens of local volunteers who had given up paid work to help the officers clear the search site of trees and foliage. For years, I'd only heard my name whispered conspiratorially in Kos. But here were thirty farmers, schoolteachers, businessmen – people of all backgrounds – proving that not everyone on the island should be judged in the same light. Some of these people even worked nights, then came and helped us after just a couple of hours' sleep.

On Monday 22 October, at his morning briefing, Matt announced that I would be appearing at lunchtime outside the police station. At that very moment, I was doubting I'd be able to say a word. Every time I tried to say the speech, I got as far as talking about Ben and then I crumbled. Every single time. Normally with publicity requirements I manage to hold myself together just long enough to get through it. Then, as soon as the Dictaphone is turned off or the TV studio's recording light dims, that's when my defences tumble. If anything, I've been criticised on occasion for seeming too in control of my emotions.

That wasn't the problem on Monday morning. Even as we drove to Kos Town, I still couldn't see how I was going to get through it.

'Just do the best you can,' Jane said. 'As soon as it gets too much, hand it over to me and I'll finish.'

She even offered to read out the whole thing.

'Thanks, Jane, but I need to do this.'

I didn't want to attract too much unnecessary attention from holidaying beach-goers, so we set up the conference just to the side of the police station – as far away from the tourist-friendly dramatic arched main entrance as possible. Ian handed around copies of my speech to local reporters – it had been translated into Greek by a Greek officer who lived in England, and was yet more proof of Matt thinking of everything. Then Matt called for quiet, said my name, and beckoned me to the stage.

I could barely make out the words on my sheet of A4 because my hand was flapping so violently. It must have looked like I was doing semaphore. Even if I could decipher my scrawl, I was clutching the script so hard there was a danger I would rip it in two before reaching the end.

I didn't cry, but by the end it wasn't just my hands that were shaking. My legs felt like they didn't belong to me. I was seconds away from falling over when Jane's arm grabbed mine from one side and Matt took the other. Between them, they virtually carried me away from the press pack's prying eyes.

The next thing I remember is sitting in the little bar next door where Dad and I used to while away hour after hour waiting for news from Bafounis's men. Jane was telling me how proud she was of me. Mum was hugging me for all she was worth. In front of me was a shot of Bailey's liqueur. It took about ten minutes before I could hold it steadily enough to taste it. A second later, I was demanding another.

I needed it, because my next stop that day would take my stress levels to a whole new level.

Even in the luxury of a modern police car, the trip to Iraklis turned my stomach. As we turned off the road and headed up the lane to the site of the farmhouse, I realised that the whole area had been transformed. The land was swarming with men in hi-viz jackets, police uniforms and hard hats; there were even sniffer dogs waiting for their turn in the hunt. These creatures, specially trained to detect humans trapped in earthquake wreckage, had been driven out from England by van. For some reason, the idea of dogs enduring that sort of journey just for me was almost too much to bear.

I felt a hush descend on the place the moment I stepped out of the car. Hundreds of eyes suddenly swung my way. Machinery fell silent. The last thing I wanted to do was get in the way, but everyone seemed to want me to know they cared. I will never forget that moment. I took a deep breath, grateful I was cried-out for the day.

I was led around the area by an English police officer, who explained what every person was doing, what every piece of equipment was for. They had sonar devices, again normally used following earthquakes, as well as heavy plant machinery for clearing the foliage that had grown up over two decades. And I was confused by the presence of what looked like the expensive metal detectors that I'd seen growing up on the beaches at Chapel St Leonards. After all, we were looking for a child, not a bicycle.

'According to your mother's testimony under the regression, Ben was playing with a couple of Dinky cars the afternoon he went missing,' Matt explained. 'They've never been found. If the metal detectors pick up the cars, then the chances are good that Ben wouldn't be far away.'

Ben also had metal buckles on his shoes. I prayed they would not find either.

To each person at the site, I said the same thing. That I was grateful to them for giving up their time to take part in the search. Even those Sheffield police officers who were being paid to do their work had given up two weeks with their families. I hated being responsible for that.

Two Greek ladies – volunteers – cried when they saw me, which of course set me off again. The Greek-speaking British officer translated. The women were paramedics in their day-to-day lives, and they wanted to help me end the nightmare one way or the other. 'It's gone on too long,' one said. 'We wish your pain would end.'

So did I…

I stayed at the site with Mum and Dad for about thirty minutes. I wanted to remain longer but I could feel myself losing focus on what was being said. Being there, up on that hill, seeing the farmhouse and knowing what those dedicated men and women were doing there was eating into my soul. I told Matt I looked forward to his update later, then Jane and Ian whisked me back to the hotel, to my bed, to my tears.

We'd been through a lot over the last twenty-one years but I have to say that week in Kos in October 2012 was the most harrowing experience since Ben had gone missing. I'd got what I'd been clamouring for – a proper police investigation – and the whole world media knew it. So much time and money was being spent on my son's case and there I was, wishing it would fail.

People were working so hard on my behalf, I almost felt guilty for wanting Ben's body not to be found.

For all the luxury of the Kipriotis Panorama, it felt like being in a prison waiting for news each evening. On Monday night, it was Jane who brought the update: 'Nothing – don't worry. They're moving on to a different area tomorrow.' The following night I feared the worse when I was summoned to meet Matt at the police's hotel base. The second he saw me, he put out his hands in a calming gesture and said, 'Don't worry – nothing's been found.' He just wanted to explain that while they had discovered many bones that day, the expert they'd flown over from Britain confirmed each one as coming from an animal. 'I didn't want you to hear whispers and get the wrong impression.' Thorough, and considerate, to the last.

It was on the Wednesday that I heard the report I'd been dreading. The metal detectors had picked up something. A cursory dig had revealed pieces of two metal toys. Dinky cars, the very things Ben had been playing with, had been found.

Jane prepared me as best she could but it was Mum that Matt needed to see. She was the one who had been with Ben on 24 July 1991. She saw the toys he was playing with. It was her recollection that they needed.

The cars were in pieces. Bits of wheels and doors and body shell were packaged in separate evidence bags. The room went silent as Mum picked the first one up, examined it as best she could while blinking back her tears, then put it down. By the second bag she was uncontrollable. Everyone watching wondered the same thing: was she holding Ben's toys?

Collecting herself as best she could, Mum looked at Matt.

'I'm sorry,' she said. 'It's so painful remembering him playing that day. But,' she took a deep intake of air, 'these aren't Ben's.'

'Are you sure?'

'One hundred per cent.'

There was no reason why the cars had to have belonged to Ben. The search also revealed CDs, beer cans and various other detritus dropped by walkers, visitors to the new house and who-knew-who-else over the last twenty-odd years. For those few minutes while Mum was identifying them, however, I confess my heart was in my mouth.

On Thursday night Matt saw me personally. The dig had one more session to run but he would be leaving for England the following morning.

'We're just dotting the "i"s and crossing the "t"s now,' he said. 'I'm as certain as I can be that Ben is not buried anywhere on that hillside.'

I could have hugged him. Not just for the good news, but for the way he obviously cared about my feelings. Despite an unsuccessful mission in Kos which meant he and his team would now have a lot more work to do, he was genuinely pleased for my sake not to have found Ben.

'I apologise for the pain it's caused you, but it's an exercise we had to go through, and it's one we can now draw a line under,' he said. 'Our investigation can now look elsewhere, confident that this option has been dismissed.'

I couldn't wait to tell Mum and Dad, and pack my bags. We left that same night, hearts full of hope for the first time in years. It was official. We weren't looking for a body. We were looking for a missing person.

After twenty-one years of rumour and doubt, that was the best early Christmas present I could imagine.

EPILOGUE

A PHONE CALL AWAY

It's 2013, approaching twenty-two years since my son Ben disappeared. The investigation by the British police is proceeding slowly but methodically, helmed by officers who care about the result. One by one they are picking over the bones of the case left ignored for so many years, following each lead and answering every unresolved question we ever had. They will get to the truth; of that, I am absolutely sure.

For our own part, my family's hunt continues. A new website, HelpFindBen.co.uk, has been set up, and Ben also has his own Facebook page and Twitter account. Led by the indefatigable Scott Morrison – a wonderful man who just volunteered out of the blue one day to run our online side of things – we have begun several annual awareness events. On Valentine's Day 2012, Scott organised 'Tweet 4 Ben', in which hundreds of thousands of people all over the globe posted Ben's details for their followers to see and share. Among the many, many people who took the time to join in was Tom Cruise.

For the first time, I don't feel like my family is alone in fighting for justice for Ben. Each day without him is as horrible as ever, but there's no longer the sense of desperation caused by shouting unheard into the wind. We *are* being listened to. Ben's case *is* active. He *will* be found.

With Matt and his team on the case, we as a family have finally been able to take a step back for the first time, confident that we no longer have to carry the burden of searching alone. For Dad it couldn't have come a moment too soon. A few years ago, he suffered a heart attack caused, the doctors say, by the stress of twenty years of trying to keep his family afloat at the same time as helping me lead a worldwide manhunt. I don't think Dad's any easier to live with – he'll still bend anyone's ear on the subject of Ben, even if that person is Mum and she's heard it all a hundred times before. But at least he doesn't feel he has to be physically chasing every half-lead and whisper.

Mum has always been more introspective than Dad – and less hyperactive – but you can see the relief in her eyes that South Yorkshire Police has taken so much pressure off us. Of the pair of them, I think Mum most regrets coming back to live in England. But Dad's healthcare is here, so that's where she needs to be. Who's to say how long it will be before the wanderlust returns?

Like Dad, the toll on Stephen's health has been huge. I would say that he is the one who still suffers most from the events of July 1991. He still goes through the same things he did in the 1990s: the nightmares, the flashbacks and the guilt. Always the guilt for something he didn't do. I wish there was more we could do for him, but he knows we're there.

And then there's the person I'm most proud of in the whole world. My beautiful daughter, Leighanna. She's nineteen now, and building her own career. She has plans and ambitions, and I know she'll achieve them because she's already achieved the impossible, growing up so amazingly in such an unusual environment.

In a way, her suffering has been worse than any of ours because at least the rest of us got to spend nearly two precious years with Ben before he was taken. Mum, Dad, Stephen, Danny and I will always have those memories. They are what drives us every day.

Leighanna only has a void. She feels the pain we feel without anything to soften the blow. I couldn't be more proud of the way she copes. At school, she put up with all kinds of wicked insults – some of it just playground stuff, but hurtful anyway – and she handled it all better than I could have done. She can give as good as she gets, but she also knows when to turn the other cheek. I could probably learn a lesson or two from her!

But what's most impressive about Leighanna is that for years she grew up carrying a secret I only learnt a couple of years ago. We were enjoying a mother and daughter night on the sofa, having a laugh, reminiscing and catching up with each other's lives when she came out with it. Nine words that couldn't have hurt me more if she'd tried:

'I always thought you loved Ben more than me.'

That was a knife in the heart. At nineteen, Leighanna knows that was never the case. But, growing up, she admits to feeling second best, to living in her brother's shadow. Not all the time, admittedly – but as her mother, it destroys me to think she felt it even for *one* second.

I thought I was doing the right thing by keeping her involved; that's why she came on sightings when she was young. I didn't want her to feel on the outside of a club that Mum, Dad, Stephen, Danny and I belonged to. The search for Ben has been my job for more than twenty years. Of course I spend a lot of time talking about him, investigating leads, plotting the next step. I have to.

But I've always done it with Leighanna at my side, and she knows I'd do exactly the same if Ben were here and she weren't.

It's great credit to my daughter that she never blamed me for the way she felt. For her, it was just one of those things. But not for me. I've thought about it every day since and I've tried my damnedest to put it right. If I'm honest, there have been moments when I've had to remind myself that Leighanna is the one who needs me now. She's the one here, the one with the boyfriend troubles, the fashion crises, the crucial teenage-girl anxieties that need addressing immediately. Whatever I'm doing for Ben can wait a couple of minutes. His sister's feelings have to come first.

And, she knows that. Which is why it is only with her blessing that I can take the next step forward in my life. And, being the grounded, mature, wonderful person she is, she's given that blessing.

In September 2012, my brother Danny was approached by a Turkish businessman about forming an entertainment club in my favourite town over there, with his Elvis act being the main draw. I often think about following him out there. My marriage to Craig sadly ended in 2011, so I have no strings holding me back other than Leighanna. And, as she says, 'You'd only a phone call away.'

Turkey does feel like my spiritual home. Perhaps it was always waiting for me, or maybe it was just the right place at the right time. Maybe Kerry Needham at seventeen would have been bored there? Maybe ten years ago I'd have felt the village was holding me back? All I know is that after a lifetime of growing up, much of it in the public eye, it's exactly what I need now. I don't have to put on a front there. I can just be me. And that's something else that is new to me. Maybe one day, I will be able to find peace there but only time will tell.

Perhaps its proximity to Kos is one of the unseen pulls of the place? Perhaps, subconsciously, I plan to look to the west and prepare for the day Ben is found?

I also know the reality. That my baby might not remember me. That he probably won't want to give up his new life to come back to us permanently. He's a man now. Despite how I remember him, giggling or waddling, or dipping bread soldiers in runny eggs – he might even have a young family of his own. He might have his own responsibilities he can't let go.

It doesn't matter. The only thing that counts is that he is found and he knows he is loved and that he has always been loved and that we have never, ever given up our search. What happens from there is up to him.

Ten years ago, I could not have contemplated anything other than Ben running back into my arms. Now I accept it could be a slower process, possibly a hard one for both of us. But I do know that whatever it takes, I am ready. I've waited too long to get it wrong now. Whatever Ben wants, whatever Ben needs, I am there. And not *if* he is found.

When.

ACKNOWLEDGEMENTS

There are so many people who have made themselves invaluable to my search over the last twenty-two years. Many are mentioned in the book but some deserve special mention:

First, I have to thank all my family, who have shown me nothing but strength, support and love throughout my whole life. Also my friends who have been there through good times and bad.

From South Yorkshire Police: Jane Morley for her ongoing emotional and physical support; Ian Marshall, for his strength of character and sound advice; and Superintendent Matt Fenwick and his full team of cold case officers for their continued hard work and dedication.

The whole of the British media for giving me the opportunities to keep Ben in the public eye. In particular, Mark Witty, of ITV's *Calendar* programme, who so often on our behalf has gone beyond the call of duty as a producer and reporter; and Melanie McFadyean, exceptional writer for the *Guardian* and *Observer* and a true friend.

For their help with this book: my editor at Ebury Press, Charlotte Cole; my co-writer, Jeff Hudson; and David Riding at MBA Literary Agency.

Scott Morrison, for his dedication to the Help Find Ben website and social networking sites; Angela Smith, MP; Gordon Bernard and his family for his official and their personal support from the British Embassy, Athens; the public and authorities of Greece, for showing they had never forgotten about Ben.

ACKNOWLEDGEMENTS

And finally, every single person in Britain or abroad who has reported a potential sighting of Ben or submitted a photograph or just kept half an eye out for him while they were on holiday, thank you so much. With your continued help we will get there. We will find him.

HELP FIND BEN

Kerry and her family have worked tirelessly over the years to try and discover Ben's whereabouts. The Help Find Ben Needham Campaign is at the centre of everything they do. Every spare penny of their own money goes towards the campaign to cover costs for transport and accommodation while they follow up leads and organising events to raise awareness. Likewise, all of Kerry's royalties from the sale of this book will go toward the campaign to help cover these same costs.

For more information on the campaign and for the latest news and updates on the search for Ben visit www.helpfindben.co.uk